Scripts of Servitude

CRITICAL LANGUAGE AND LITERACY STUDIES

Series Editor: **Professor Alastair Pennycook** *(University of Technology, Sydney, Australia)* and **Professor Brian Morgan** *(Glendon College/York University, Toronto, Canada)* and **Professor Ryuko Kubota** *(University of British Columbia, Vancouver, Canada)*

Critical Language and Literacy Studies is an international series that encourages monographs directly addressing issues of power (its flows, inequities, distributions, trajectories) in a variety of language- and literacy-related realms. The aim with this series is twofold: (1) to cultivate scholarship that openly engages with social, political, and historical dimensions in language and literacy studies, and (2) to widen disciplinary horizons by encouraging new work on topics that have received little focus (see below for partial list of subject areas) and that use innovative theoretical frameworks.

Full details of all the books in this series and of all our other publications can be found on http://www.multilingual-matters.com, or by writing to Multilingual Matters, St Nicholas House, 31-34 High Street, Bristol BS1 2AW, UK.

Other books in the series

China and English: Globalisation and the Dilemmas of Identity
Joseph Lo Bianco, Jane Orton and Gao Yihong (eds)
Language and HIV/AIDS
Christina Higgins and Bonny Norton (eds)
Hybrid Identities and Adolescent Girls: Being 'Half' in Japan
Laurel D. Kamada
Decolonizing Literacy: Mexican Lives in the Era of Global Capitalism
Gregorio Hernandez-Zamora
Contending with Globalization in World Englishes
Mukul Saxena and Tope Omoniyi (eds)
ELT, Gender and International Development: Myths of Progress in a Neocolonial World
Roslyn Appleby
Examining Education, Media, and Dialogue under Occupation: The Case of Palestine and Israel
Ilham Nasser, Lawrence N. Berlin and Shelley Wong (eds)
The Struggle for Legitimacy: Indigenized Englishes in Settler Schools
Andrea Sterzuk
Style, Identity and Literacy: English in Singapore
Christopher Stroud and Lionel Wee
Language and Mobility: Unexpected Places
Alastair Pennycook
Talk, Text and Technology: Literacy and Social Practice in a Remote Indigenous Community
Inge Kral
Language Learning, Gender and Desire: Japanese Women on the Move
Kimie Takahashi
English and Development: Policy, Pedagogy and Globalization
Elizabeth J. Erling and Philip Seargeant (eds)
Ethnography, Superdiversity and Linguistic Landscapes: Chronicles of Complexity
Jan Blommaert
Power and Meaning Making in an EAP Classroom: Engaging with the Everyday
Christian W. Chun
Local Languaging, Literacy and Multilingualism in a West African Society
Kasper Juffermans
English Teaching and Evangelical Mission: The Case of Lighthouse School
Bill Johnston
Race and Ethnicity in English Language Teaching
Christopher Joseph Jenks
Language, Education and Neoliberalism: Critical Studies in Sociolinguistics
Mi-Cha Flubacher and Alfonso Del Percio (eds)

CRITICAL LANGUAGE AND LITERACY STUDIES: 24

Scripts of Servitude

Language, Labor Migration and Transnational Domestic Work

Beatriz P. Lorente

MULTILINGUAL MATTERS
Bristol • Blue Ridge Summit

For my father, Felino Lorente (1940–1998) who showed me just how rewarding asking questions could be

DOI 10.21832/LORENT8996
Library of Congress Cataloging in Publication Data
A catalog record for this book is available from the Library of Congress.
Names: Lorente, Beatriz P. author.
Title: Language, Labor Migration and Transnational Domestic Work/Beatriz P. Lorente.
Description: Bristol, UK; Blue Ridge Summit, PA: Multilingual Matters, 2017. | Series: Critical Language and Literacy Studies: 24 | Includes bibliographical references and index.
Identifiers: LCCN 2017023808| ISBN 9781783098996 (hbk: alk. paper) | ISBN 9781783098989 (pbk: alk. paper) | ISBN 9781783099023 (kindle)
Subjects: LCSH: Foreign workers, Filipino–Singapore. | Women foreign workers–Singapore–Language. | Women household employees–Singapore. | English language–Social aspects–Singapore. | Language and languages–Economic aspects–Philippines.
Classification: LCC HD6305.F55 L67 2017 | DDC 331.4/864089992105957–dc23 LC record available at https://lccn.loc.gov/2017023808

British Library Cataloguing in Publication Data
A catalogue entry for this book is available from the British Library.

ISBN-13: 978-1-78309-899-6 (hbk)
ISBN-13: 978-1-78309-898-9 (pbk)

Multilingual Matters
UK: St Nicholas House, 31-34 High Street, Bristol BS1 2AW, UK.
USA: NBN, Blue Ridge Summit, PA, USA.

Website: www.multilingual-matters.com
Twitter: Multi_Ling_Mat
Facebook: https://www.facebook.com/multilingualmatters
Blog: www.channelviewpublications.wordpress.com

Copyright © 2018 Beatriz P. Lorente.

All rights reserved. No part of this work may be reproduced in any form or by any means without permission in writing from the publisher.

The policy of Multilingual Matters/Channel View Publications is to use papers that are natural, renewable and recyclable products, made from wood grown in sustainable forests. In the manufacturing process of our books, and to further support our policy, preference is given to printers that have FSC and PEFC Chain of Custody certification. The FSC and/or PEFC logos will appear on those books where full certification has been granted to the printer concerned.

Typeset by Deanta Global Publishing Services Limited.

Contents

Acknowledgments		ix
Series Editors' Preface		xi
1	Language and Transnational Domestic Workers	1
	Scripts as Templates for Language Practices	6
	Scripts as Enactable and Convertible Templates	9
	Nodes in the Migration Infrastructure	11
	Centering institutions	11
	Subjects	12
	Transnational Domestic Work	13
	Transnational Domestic Workers in Singapore	16
	A profile of Filipino domestic workers in Singapore	19
	Method	21
	Overview of Chapters	24
2	The Making of 'Workers of the World': Language and the Labor Brokerage State	27
	The Philippines as a Labor Brokerage State	29
	History of labor migration from the Philippines	30
	Patterns of labor migration from the Philippines	35
	Language in the Philippine Labor Migration Enterprise	40
	'Our labor force speaks your language'	40
	The history of English in the Philippines	42
	The making of English-speaking overseas Filipino workers	45
	The making of skilled workers of the world	49
	Summary	52

3	Assembling the 'Supermaid': Language and Communication Skills for 'Vulnerable Occupations'	53
	Protecting the Filipino Domestic Worker	55
	The Supermaid: Rebranding Filipina Domestic Workers	56
	Scripting the Supermaid	60
	Workplace communication skills	60
	The language and culture-specific training	63
	Summary	65
4	Marketing Domestic Workers: Maid Agencies in Singapore	66
	Transnational Maid Agencies as Mediating Institutions	67
	Maid agencies in Singapore	69
	Positioning Products	73
	Representations of Filipino domestic workers in Singapore	73
	The relative values of English linguistic capital	77
	Styling the Domestic Worker	80
	Performing the script of servitude	82
	Displaying servitude	89
	Summary	94
5	The English-Speaking Other Looks Back	96
	The Idea of 'Good English'	97
	Good English is *'puro Ingles'*	98
	Singlish is not 'good English'	99
	'You have to use your own accent'	103
	A Hierarchy of Desirable Employers	104
	Singaporean Chinese employers	105
	'White' expat employers	113
	A Hierarchy of Domestic Workers	116
	More than just a maid	117

	The value of 'daldal'	120
	'When we speak to Indonesians, our English is baroque'	121
	Summary	124
6	Translating Selves: The Trajectories of Transnational Filipino Domestic Workers	126
	English in the Philippines	126
	English in Singapore	128
	'I have lost my English'	129
	'You're the one who adjusts, not them, right?'	132
	Revising the Script	135
	'Yung madam/Madonna ko'	135
	A register for offstage identities	140
	'Pa-English-English' in the Philippines	142
	'Lord, help me to English my tongue'	145
	Summary	146
7	Conclusion	148
	Language and Labor Migration	148
	Language and Transnational Domestic Work	149
	Developing Alternative Scripts	151
	Preferred Futures	152
Appendices		154
References		160
Index		170

Acknowledgments

I am indebted to the migrant women who participated in this study, who shared their time and stories with me and patiently, thoughtfully and humorously answered my questions. Their experiences and their stories, their strength and their laughter are the foundation of this book. I am indebted as well to the Filipino Overseas Workers Skills Training Program of the Bayanihan Centre in Singapore where I based most of my fieldwork. I am especially grateful to Encarnacion Montales who welcomed me to the Centre and to Lily Sabsalon who helped me make sense of what I observed and heard, and whose friendship kept me grounded in the everyday realities, hardships and triumphs of transnational domestic work. Lily passed away in the Philippines in April 2017 while this book was in production. She is much missed.

Some parts of this book are based on materials that have been published. My thanks to the John Benjamins Publishing Company for permission to use the chapter, Lorente, B.P. (2013) The grip of English and Philippine language policy. In L. Wee, R.B.H. Goh and L. Lim (eds) *The Politics of English: South Asia, Southeast Asia and the Asia Pacific*. Amsterdam: John Benjamins Publishing Company, pp. 187–204. This is now part of Chapter 2. Another part of Chapter 2 is from Lorente, B.P. (2012) The making of "workers of the world": language and the labor brokerage state. In A. Duchêne and M. Heller (eds) *Language in Late Capitalism: Pride and Profit*. New York: Routledge, pp. 183–206. Part of Chapter 4 is from Lorente, B.P. (2010). Packaging English-speaking production: maid agencies in Singapore. In H. Kelly-Holmes and G. Mautner (eds) *Language and the Market*. Basingstoke: Palgrave Macmillan, pp. 44–55. Every reasonable effort has been taken to contact copyright holders. Any errors will be rectified in future editions.

I owe a debt of self (*utang na loob*) to Alastair Pennycook whose interest in this project, year in and year out, as I conducted the study, presented papers, submitted the dissertation and wrote the book, inspired me to keep going. I am very grateful to Jan Blommaert whose ideas and encouragement have very much shaped this book. I am also very grateful to Alexandre Duchêne whose critical and incisive comments pushed me to craft a more nuanced final manuscript, and whose enthusiastic support for this project was invaluable. Thank you to Ruanni Tupas whose friendship and intellectual generosity through the years have been vital to this project. I also owe thanks to Anne Pakir who, as my dissertation adviser, gave me the support and the freedom I needed to think differently, and to Chng Huang Hoon and Lionel Wee who read and incisively commented on the dissertation. Last but not least, a big thank you to the wonderful team at Multilingual Matters: Anna Roderick, Kim Eggleton, Laura Longworth, Florence McClelland and Sarah Williams.

The research for this book has been presented at a good number of conferences. Thank you to the many audiences who listened, commented on and asked questions about my work. Thank you very much to the community of scholars I have the privilege of knowing and learning from, especially: Noorashikin Abdul Rahman, Alfonso del Percio, Mi-Cha Flubacher, Monica Heller, Kasper Juffermans, Bonnie McElhinny, Stefanie Meier, Sebastian Muth, Gene Segarra Naverra, Shanthini Pillai, Anuradha Ramanujan, Angela Reyes, Aileen Salonga and Cécile Vigouroux.

Finally, I am grateful to my mother, Amelia Lorente and my sister, Lora Frances Lorente-Lorenzo for their loving confidence in me. I am especially grateful to my husband, Bruno Trezzini, who supported this project from its very start, and whose critical and extensive feedback on earlier drafts of this manuscript were the crucial turning points in refining my ideas and my writing. Thank you for everything.

Series Editors' Preface

This is a significant book and an important addition to our series for a number of reasons. As the title suggests, it locates the language of servitude critically within a much larger picture of mobile domestic work. It thus situates the language, work and mobility of these women in relation to the global market, shedding light on the intersectionality of gender, class, ethnicity, migration and language. This work brings important insights into the commodification and regulation of language within the neoliberal world order, the gendered nature of particular forms of work, the implications for employment, abuse and discrimination, and the mobility of many current workers in insecure and underpaid jobs. Such concerns matter deeply at this particular historical juncture with the rise of new forms of populist, xenophobic nationalism and isolationism in wealthy nations confronting mobile populations of refugees and an emergent class of itinerant, impoverished and insecure laborers. It is often this precarious and peripatetic workforce (on construction sites, in private homes, in health care facilities) who support the growing extravagances of the wealthy, as capital is concentrated in the hands of the very rich while huge economic disparities are ideologically normalized, and the very idea of welfare and the public good is increasingly on the retreat.

Anyone who has spent time in a city such as Hong Kong will know that its Filipina domestic workers are an 'issue', as they flood the city streets on Sundays to meet and socialize (having little other time or place to get together), in what might be seen as an alternative precursor to the Occupy movements that sought to reclaim public space (Martín Rojo, 2016; Chun, 2014). On these Sundays, there is also much of the busy work of globalization from below (Mathews, 2012), as *Balikbayan boxes* (to ship goods home from overseas Filipinos) are filled with items sourced from the lower end of Hong Kong malls to be sent back to family and friends in the Philippines. While these boxes may be filled and despatched from the pavements of Hong Kong, the *Balikbayan box* system has also become institutionalized, like other sections of local industries in Singapore's cheaper malls with their Thai, Nepalese and Philippine foods, beauty salons and currency transfer offices (Low, 2009). There is often a certain poignancy to the labels on these boxes in the disparity between the 'From' label (the employers' address in an expensive location in expatriate Hong Kong, where the domestic worker has only a small room behind the kitchen) and the 'To' address (a suburb, say, of Dumaguete City, where the remittances sent back have allowed the family to build a larger house). Remittances matter for families and the economy, with the Philippines ranked 3rd in the world (after India and China) in the total amount of remittances sent home (Global Remittance Guide, 2017). As with other Pacific island nations, such as Tonga, these relations of migration, remittances and mobility have important implications for other flows of language, religion and popular culture (Pennycook, 2015).

The newspapers in cities such as Hong Kong also provide regular reports of abused workers, beatings and unpaid wages. Back in colonial times (just 25 years ago, let us not forget), the role and status of these women was played out amid colonial discourses of servants, language and the public space (Pennycook, 1998). In response to a letter by Elsa Katarungan (*South China Morning Post*, April 23, 1993), which criticized the Ramos administration in the Philippines and ended 'We will continue to work like slaves all over the world because this administration is just as inept and corrupt as all the others before it', Sheila Grange (*SCMP*, April 26, 1993) took umbrage to this view of slavery: 'Does Ms Katarungan think that only the Filipino race are hard workers? Focusing primarily on Hong Kong for the present, what about the expatriate manager who often leaves the house at 7:30 in the morning, returning often as late as 8 or 9 at night with a ton of paperwork to get through before the morning. What about the times he leaves on a business trip when officially his working day is over, or he travels to a destination on a Sunday?'

In December 1993, a heated debate started over whether a notice in a lift in a block of flats was discriminatory. The notice, positioned next to a sign saying 'No dogs allowed' (echoing the infamous signs of colonial Hong Kong and Shanghai that reportedly said 'No dogs or Chinese' – shattered in a famous Bruce Lee *Kung Fu* moment), announced (in Tagalog and Chinese) that maids should use the service rather than the main lifts. Responding to the outcry over this sign, Robert Thio (*SCMP*, December 3) defended its use, arguing that 'I have observed that many Filipino maids speak loudly among themselves in the lifts of buildings and on public buses.' This, he argued, 'is a nuisance and generates resentment among other people.' He went on to argue that maids needed to be educated about how to behave in public. Not surprisingly, this letter produced a number of angry responses, though there were others who could not see a problem here: 'In the name of commonsense and reason, what is wrong with requiring service staff – domestic servants – to use a service lift?' (R.T.B. Barrie, December 16, 1994); 'There are exclusive clubs in this city where maids are designated certain areas and quite clear notices are put up to this effect. Will the indignant do-gooders next suggest that the maids now be allowed to sip Gins and Tonic in the Members' Bar? In Hong Kong, they are employed as maids and so, what is all this indignation about asking servants – yes, that's what they are and that does not make their contribution any less valuable in their own right – from being asked to use the service lift?' (Mina Kaye, *SCMP*, December 14, 1993). These were the common discourses around maids in Hong Kong in the 1990s, who had to confront not only difficult working conditions but also discourses about talking in the public space and their position as servants within a colonial political economy.

This book takes us into the present lives of these domestic workers. Things have moved on in various ways (though discursive shift can be slow) and these domestic workers now have more support and better regulation than they did 25 years ago, though this also entails, as Lorente makes clear, an inscription into a neoliberal order of supermaids and scripts of servitude. This book thus follows on very nicely from the most recent in this series, Mi-Cha Flubacher and Alfonso Del Percio's edited (2017) *Language, Education and Neoliberalism: Critical Studies in Sociolingustics* which highlights specific realizations and articulations of neoliberal language practices and their normalizing effects on identity formation across a range of settings. There we saw how language becomes commodified, objectified, standardized and quantified in the service of various neoliberal educational agendas. We also saw how diversity was appropriated in the marketing of language services, or what Flores (2017) calls the *Coke-ification* of bilingual education for Latinx students in the US. Once English ability starts to add value to the market price of a domestic worker, and once domestic workers become part of a national export industry, the role of English in education becomes more important. For the Philippines, like other countries such as Pakistan, Bangladesh and India, with relatively low economic development but relatively strong access to English, the language becomes one of commercial opportunity, so that businesses such as call centres on the one hand open up jobs for local college-educated employees, but on the other hand distort the local economy and education system and perpetuate forms of global inequality (Friginal, 2009), and unequal Englishes (Tupas & Salonga, 2016).

Language, as with all books in this series, is crucial, and fortunately Lorente is not so much interested in bland descriptions of Singapore or Philippine English but in the ways language and capital are intertwined: how the export of domestic and other workers affects language and education policy back in the Philippines, how these domestic workers now market themselves to prospective employers, and how they deal with the local language politics of places such as Singapore. It is a pity that so much work has focused on putative varieties of English from a world Englishes perspective, when what we really need to address are the questions of *unequal Englishes* (Tupas & Rubdy, 2015; Tupas & Salonga, 2016). As Kubota (2015: 33) points out, while pluralist approaches to English have opened up an understanding of postcolonial diversity, there has also been a tendency to 'romanticize the multiplicity of local language use without sufficiently interrogating inequalities and injustices involving race, gender, class and so on.' All varieties of English are in complex relations of power with other varieties and intertwined with questions of access and discrimination along lines of class, gender and race.

As Martin (2014) observes, the sociolinguistics of English in the Philippines is far more complex than merely placing it in the 'outer circle' as if that explained the many Englishes used there. There are circles within circles in the Philippines, amid questions of access, education, style, disparity and difference (Tupas, 2010). The issue, therefore, is not centrally about how Philippine English differs from American English but how English resources are spread and used, and become available or inaccessible to people of different classes and ethnicities across these islands. 'Can all English users regardless of their racial, gender, socioeconomic, and other background equally transgress linguistic boundaries and engage in hybrid and fluid linguistic practices?' (Kubota, 2015: 33). Any claim to a variety of English, while at one level a defiance of inner circle norms, is also always a political claim in relation to other varieties, and a claim amid competing social, economic and political values, a question of *unequal Englishes*, 'the unequal ways and situations in which Englishes are arranged, configured, and contested' (Tupas & Rubdy, 2015: 3).

It is the interlocking relations of language, gender, domestic work and migration that this book engages with. This links to work on how a new *precariat* class (Standing, 2014) – a precariously employed and mobile proletariat that lacks security in relation to the labor market, training, income and representation – has emerged over the last decades. While this notion has come in for a reasonable amount of criticism – as Munck (2013) points out, the idea of precarious global workers has a long history, and the idea of the precariat overlooks the point that work has always been precarious for most of the majority world (having a 'decent job' is not something that many can aspire to) – it nonetheless gives us a way of understanding the difficulties and insecurities of undertaking work under such conditions. Filipino workers can be found on boats and construction sites among many other workplaces, but it is in domestic and health care that many women work. Crucial within these wider class formations, therefore, are the gendered nature of this work and the ways this fits into patterns of domestic labor and transnational migration (Chang, 2000; Ehrenreich & Hochschild, 2004; Parreñas, 2001). And equally important is how this gets played out in relation to language, not only in terms of the capital of English and other languages but also the everyday operations of linguistic diversity in relation to forms of labor (Duchêne *et al.*, 2013; Gonçalvez & Schluter, 2017; Piller & Lising, 2014).

What makes Lorente's book particularly important is the close relationship she developed with the women in this book. This is in part a result of the kind of linguistic ethnography that we have favoured in this series since this allows researchers to dig deeper into the communities they are exploring. This is also, however, an aspect of the author's positionality in relation to these women. Indeed, as with many people from the Philippines, her own family is intertwined with these histories. This means that not only do we see how domestic workers are made, produced and scripted, how their scripts of servitude are anchored in marketing processes that are part of the discourses that construct desirable workers, and how English as capital operates in relation to their lives, but we also see the hopes, desires and trajectories of these women as they come to appropriate English and forge decent lives for themselves. Like another important book in this series (Takahashi, 2013), this allows us to appreciate not only the lived experiences of women who have already moved to study and work elsewhere, but also that these are part of much wider trajectories, as these women move on to other places, work and lives. We see how these women cope, how they struggle, how they make sense of their lives, how they develop strategies of resistance and everyday antiracism (Aquino, 2018), how their negotiated status in relation to styles of English is also about the quotidian ways in which they cope with routine racialized domination (see also Jenks, 2017, in this series). This book thus links many of the concerns that we have tried to make central to this series, connecting a critical understanding of language and power to wider concerns of discrimination and inequality, as well as resistance and resilience.

Alastair Pennycook
Brian Morgan
Ryuko Kubota

References

Aquino, K. (2018) *Racism and Resistance among the Filipino Diaspora: Everyday Anti-racism in Australia*. London: Routledge.
Chang, G. (2000) *Disposable Domestics: Immigrant Women Workers in the Global Economy*. Cambridge, MA: South End Press.
Chun, C.W. (2014) Reflexivity and critical language education in Occupy L.A. In J.B. Clark and F. Dervin (eds) *Reflexivity in Language and Intercultural Education: Rethinking Multilingualism and Interculturality* (pp. 172–192). London: Routledge.
Duchêne, A., Moyer, M. and Roberts, C. (2013) Introduction: Recasting institutions and work in multilingual and transnational spaces. In A. Duchêne, M. Moyer and C. Roberts (eds) *Language, Migration and Social Inequalities: A Critical Sociolinguistic Perspective on Instiutions and Work* (pp. 1–24). Bristol: Multilingual Matters.
Ehrenreich, B. and Hochschild, A.R. (2004) *Global Woman: Nannies, Maids, and Sex Workers in the New Economy*. New York: Metropolitan Books.
Flores, N. (2017) From language-as-resource to language-as-struggle: Resisting the Coke-ification of bilingual education. In M.-C. Flubacher and A. Del Percio (eds) *Language, Education and Neoliberalism: Critical Studies in Sociolingustics*. Bristol: Multilingual Matters.
Flubacher, M.-C. and Del Percio, A. (eds) (2017) *Language, Education and Neoliberalism: Critical Studies in Sociolingustics*. Bristol: Multilingual Matters.
Friginal, E. (2009) Threats to the sustainability of the outsourced call center industry in the Philippines: Implications for language policy. *Language Policy* 8, 51–68.
Global Remittance Guide (2017) http://www.migrationpolicy.org/programs/data-hub/global-remittances-guide
Gonçalvez, K. and Schluter, A. (2017) "Please do not leave any notes for the cleaning lady, as many do not speak English fluently": Policy, power, and language brokering in a multilingual workplace. *Language Policy* 16 (3) 242–265.
Jenks, C.J. (2017) *Race and Ethnicity in English Language Teaching: Korea in Focus*. Bristol: Multilingual Matters.
Kubota, R. (2015) Inequalities of Englishes, English speakers, and languages: A critical perspective on pluralist approaches to English. In R. Tupas (ed.) *Unequal Englishes: The Politics of Englishes Today* (pp. 21–42). London: Palgrave Macmillan.
Low, K.E.Y. (2009) *Scents and Scent-sibilities: Smell and Everyday Life Experiences*. Newcastle: Cambridge Scholars Publishing.
Martin, I. (2014) Philippine English revisited. *World Englishes* 33 (1), 50–59.
Martín Rojo, L. (2016) Occupy: The spatial dynamics of discourse in global protest movements. In L. Martín Rojo (ed.) *Occupy: The Spatial Dynamics of Discourse in Global Protest Movements* (pp. 1–22). Amsterdam: John Benjamins.
Mathews G. (2012) Neoliberalism and globalization from below in Chungking mansions, Hong Kong. In G. Mathews, G.L. Ribeiro and C.A. Vega (eds) *Globalization from Below: The World's Other Economy* (pp. 69–85) London: Routledge.
Munck, R. (2013) The Precariat: A view from the South. *Third World Quarterly* 34 (5), 747–762.
Parreñas, R.S. (2001) *Servants of Globalization. Women, Migration, and Domestic Work*. Stanford, CA: Stanford University Press.
Pennycook, A. (1998) *English and the Discourses of Colonialism*. London: Routledge.

Pennycook, A. (2015) Early literacies and linguistic mobilities. In C. Stroud and M. Prinsloo (eds) *Language, Literacy and Diversity: Moving Words* (pp. 187–205). New York, Routledge.

Piller, I. and Lising, L. (2014) Language, employment and settlement: Temporary meat workers in Australia. *Multilingua* 33 (1–2), 35–59

Takahashi, K. (2013) *Language Learning, Gender and Desire: Japanese Women on the Move*. Bristol: Multilingual Matters.

Tupas, R. (2010) Which norms in everyday practice and why? In A. Kirkpatrick (ed.) *The Routledge Handbook of World Englishes* (pp. 567–79). London: Routledge.

Tupas, R. and Rubdy, R. (2015) Introduction: From World Englishes to Unequal Englishes. In R. Tupas (ed.) *Unequal Englishes: The Politics of Englishes Today* (pp. 1–21). London: Palgrave Macmillan.

Tupas, R. and Salonga, A. (2016) Unequal Englishes in the Philippines. *Journal of Sociolinguistics* 20 (3), 367–381.

1 Language and Transnational Domestic Workers

Myrna, a Filipino domestic worker (FDW),[1] had been working in Singapore for 11 years when I interviewed her. She had left the Philippines in 1993 because she needed a job that could support her three children; her pay as a factory worker at a plastics factory in Manila was not enough and she had separated from her husband who was unemployed and unfaithful. Myrna applied to work in Singapore through an employment agency in Manila whose advertisement for Singapore-bound domestic workers (DWs) she had heard over the radio. When the 'Singaporean owner' of the maid agency was in the country for interviews, she went for one:

> **Myrna**: They want to know whether you know English. [BL: How did you know that they want to know whether you know English?] Because their questions are in English! Then they touch your hands, they say it's so that they know whether you know hard work. Of course, I know hard work, I'm at a factory!
> *They want to know whether you know English* [BL: *Pa'no mo alam na gusto nilang malaman kung marunong kang mag-Ingles?*] *Kasi yung mga tanong nila sa Ingles eh! Tapos hinihipo nila yung kamay mo, para daw malaman nila kung marunong ka sa hard work. Siyempre, marunong ako sa hard work, nasa factory ako eh!*[2]

After the interview, Myrna was videotaped so that prospective employers in Singapore who went to the maid agency could see and listen to her. She was supplied with a 'maid's uniform' and was required to put her hair up in a ponytail and wear no make-up or jewelry. She was told to say a few things about herself in English, using a chart that was a guide for her while she spoke:

> **Myrna**: I said my name, my age, what were my jobs, why I want to go to Singapore. It was easy because there was a guide in front of you, there was a chart so all you have to do is fill in the blanks. That's why employers think all Filipina maids know English.

[BL: How did you feel when you were videotaped?] I was nervous because I was not used to it. Then they made us sing because they said those who take care of children should know how to sing a lullaby. They said 'even if it's just Bahay Kubo'[3] so one (of the applicants) did sing Bahay Kubo (laughs). [BL: What did you sing?] I can't remember but it was an English song. We have a lot of English songs back home right? So I sang...just a few lines because it was not necessary to complete it as long as you show that you can sing (laughs). And then we were even in uniform (laughs). It is funny, isn't it?

Sinabi ko yung name ko, yung age ko, anong mga naging trabaho ko, why I want to go to Singapore. Madali naman kasi may guide na sa harap mo, may chart so ang ginagawa mo lang e mag fill in the blanks. Kaya akala ng mga employers marunong mag-Ingles ang lahat ng Pinay na maid. Ninenerbiyos ako kasi hindi ako sanay. Tapos pinakanta pa kami kasi daw pag mag-alaga ng bata dapat marunong kang kumanta ng lullaby. Sabi nila 'kahit Bahay Kubo lang' so yung isa, kumanta nga ng Bahay Kubo (laughs). [BL: Anong kinanta mo?] Di ko na maalala pero English na song. Di ba marami namang English na songs sa atin? So kumanta ako ...konti lang na lines kasi di naman kelangan na kumpleto basta lang mapakita mo na marunong kang kumanta (laughs). Tapos naka uniform pa kami (laughs). Nakakatawa ano?

Myrna's story is a window to how language is embedded in the production of one of the largest and widest flows of contemporary female migration, that of women from the Philippines who work as DWs in countries in Asia, the Middle East, Western Europe and North America (Tyner, 2004). As of 2010, Filipino women were working as DWs in at least 72 countries, with significant numbers in Saudi Arabia, the United Arab Emirates, Hong Kong and Singapore, and a handful in countries as disparate as Angola and Switzerland (Philippine Overseas Employment Administration, 2010).[4] Structured by the international division and the persistent gendered distribution of reproductive labor (Glenn, 1992; Parreñas, 2000, 2001), the migration of Filipino women like Myrna is at the nexus of long-existing as well as emerging inequalities between regions in the global economy; between labor-sending and labor-receiving countries; and between class, race and gender. This globalization of care has resulted in the emergence of care chains and DWs as part of a transnational service class (Mirchandani, 2004).

To begin to understand how language is central to the production of Filipino women into 'servants of globalization' (Parreñas, 2001), it is necessary to ask what counts as language in this particular context (Blommaert, 2010: 12) and how language counts. While Myrna described her interview and videotaped recording as having been done in 'English', an understanding of English as a fixed and unified system or as an enumerable and countable entity is inadequate for explaining what is important here (Makoni & Pennycook, 2007).

What counts in this instance are what Blommaert (2010: 23) calls the 'bits and pieces' of language and, just as importantly, Myrna's role in producing them through the question and answer format of the interview where Myrna gave the answers; the chart with the standardized script which Myrna had to read to present herself in the videotape and that she had to personalize by filling in the blanks; and the few lines of the 'English' song that Myrna chose to sing to prove that she could take care of children. It matters that these 'bits and pieces' are recognized as being in 'English'. As a shared code between Singaporeans and Filipinos and as the language that is considered to be the global lingua franca, Myrna's delivery of her answers in English signals her potential mobility to Singapore and a premium that she should get for speaking it, even as her scripted use of it fixes her place as a foreign DW in Singapore. These 'bits and pieces' of linguistic resources are configured with other semiotic ones – the maid's uniform, the lack of make-up and jewelry and the ponytailed hair – to produce Myrna as a particular person: a migrant FDW for the Singapore market. What counts in this context then is Myrna's performance of what I call a *script of servitude*, a template that indexes the DW and that is crucial to and embedded in large-scale and everyday processes that produce her as a specific mobile, laboring body.

These large-scale and everyday processes of production are transnational. Myrna's performance has been assembled transnationally by the employment agency in Manila that recruited her and the maid agency in Singapore that interviewed and selected her for placement in the country; both agencies stand to profit from it, as does Myrna and her family. Language literally counts because it makes a difference that a Filipino woman is using 'English' in this context. English-speaking FDWs 'reign as a kind of labor aristocracy in the regional and global domestic service industry' (Ong, 2006: 201). In 2004, the year I interviewed Myrna, the starting salary of FDWs in Singapore was S$350 as compared to S$280 for Indonesian DWs and S$220 for Sri Lankans, and the supposed English proficiency of FDWs was consistently cited as a rationale for their higher salaries (Lorente & Tupas, 2002). What Myrna does seems sufficient to reinforce the belief among employers in Singapore that 'all Filipina maids know English', and her specific bits of language are enough for the agency to package her for the

Singapore market. The interviews and the scripted videotaped recording are standard practices among transnational maid agencies in Asia. Myrna was not the only woman who was interviewed and videotaped for prospective employers elsewhere in Asia that day.

Myrna's performance also socializes her into her role as a paid reproductive worker, i.e. domestic worker. As a domestic worker, Myrna herself indexes the higher status of her employer. It is, as Anderson (2000: 2) has argued, her personhood, rather than her labor power which the employer is attempting to buy.

While the video may give the appearance that Myrna is a 'mimic maid', Myrna's story makes it clear that she had to temporarily perform a role when she did the interview. The discomfort and anxiety she expresses shows the cost of extracting this performance from her. The performance involves a rearrangement of her self: the way she dresses, the way she looks and the way she uses English; it is not something she is used to. At the same time, she is acutely aware that the videotaped recording is a 'presentation of self' (Goffman, 1959) and of what the temporary linguistic and semiotic display is for. In her laughter, she distances her present self – the Myrna who is speaking to me and telling me the story 11 years later – from the Myrna who had to perform a script. Myrna is hardly passive.

This book is about language, 'a practice as well as a resource that can have both symbolic value and exchange value in a market economy' (Duchêne *et al.*, 2013: 5), and how it is embedded in the 'migration infrastructure – the systematically interlinked technologies, institutions and actors that facilitate and condition (the) mobility' (Xiang & Lindquist, 2014: 124) of transnational FDWs like Myrna. This book shows how the transnational mobility of labor is, in part, dependent on the selection, assembly and successful performance of particular assemblages of linguistic resources that index migrants as labor and not as people. Transnational domestic work is the product of the international division of reproductive labor in which migrant women from developing countries perform the reproductive labor of class-privileged women in developed ones, even as they may pass on their own reproductive labor to other women who are too poor to migrate (Parreñas, 2001). As such, it is a powerful site where one can examine the specific realizations of the inequalities of globalization and the particular ways in which these inequalities intersect with and are produced by language (Blommaert, 2005, 2010).

To begin to understand how language is a central element in transnational labor migration, in general and in transnational domestic work in particular, this book takes as a starting point the *scripts* produced for and by transnational DWs at various nodes in the infrastructure of migration. As templates for language practices that are (re)assembled and circulated at different though intrinsically interrelated scales, scripts are sites where the subject-positions of transnational DWs like Myrna are constituted and contested. This book traces the structural, historical and everyday processes that shape the scripts and the consequences of their performance. In accounting for how scripts can constitute subject-positions, I draw from the notions of register and capital. *Register* (Agha, 2000, 2006) emphasizes the enactability of scripts. As registers, scripts link speech repertoires to images of a person, to relationships between speakers and interlocutors, and to the conduct of social practices. This enactability is made possible by continuous historical processes that link ways of speaking to ways of being. The notion of *capital* drawn from Bourdieu's (1986, 1991) perspective on the economics of linguistic exchange highlights how scripts are a means of assembling linguistic practices and speakers as resources, and framing their legitimacy in terms of their convertibility in multiple markets shaped by relations of power (Park & Wee, 2012). In this way, scripts are linked to ideological (Seargeant, 2009; Woolard & Schieffelin, 1994) and material processes of distinction, stratification and commodification. They can serve as nodal points from which one can explore the tensions that are produced when language is deployed as entity, commodity and capital (Park & Wee, 2012) in the practices that sustain the ongoing and often unequal linkages between social actors across national borders (Vertovec, 2009).

My use of scripts of servitude (instead of scripts of domestic work) is deliberate. While 'servitude' is a vexed term, I use it in the same way as Ray (2009: 4), that is, 'to capture the persistence of forms of dependency and submission in relations of what is today, for the most part, paid domestic work'. Domestic work is 'one of the oldest and most important occupations for millions of women around the world' (International Labour Organization, 2010: 1). It is estimated that globally, between 52.6 and 100 million women and men perform domestic work in and for households; 83% are women and girls, making it the biggest employer of women today. The two regions with the largest number of DWs are Asia and Latin America, and in the Caribbean and the Middle East, they make up more than a quarter of female wage workers (International Labour Organization, 2011). Domestic work is rooted in a global history of slavery, colonialism and servitude (Haskins, 2012; Haskins & Lowrie, 2015; International Labour Organization, 2010) and its persistence is '…a striking example(s) of the long term power of underlying structures and the weight of persistent social forms' (Higman, 2015: 33). As such, in echoing the figure of the 'servant', I hope to highlight historical continuities and how DWs '[...] slip in the analytical space between body as personhood and body as property' (Anderson, 2000: 3). This continuity and durability of scripts and the contradictions that they may covertly normalize underlie some of the themes I focus on in this book.

This book's empirical anchor is the case of transnational FDWs in Singapore whose mobility is enabled by the development of a regime of government-regulated circular migration in Asia (Lindquist *et al.*, 2012) that is also emerging in other parts of the world (cf. Piller & Lising, 2014). This regime of government-regulated circulated migration is one where migrant workers make multiple and temporary moves between home and foreign places of work. Such regimes reflect the desire of states to mobilize labor, not people (Wickramasekara, 2011). Current regimes are based on the differentiation of workers according to their 'human capital' and the corresponding constraints on their mobility, e.g. restrictions on length of stay, choice of employer and occupation (Castles & Ozkul, 2014). This is the case for transnational DWs in Asia. There are no paths to citizenship for transnational DWs. As legal labor migrants, transnational DWs are in their 'host' countries on strictly temporary terms and they have to return home (or get a renewal) once their contracts are due. These flows are encouraged, facilitated and enforced by states and 'are all part of an overarching mode of governance that emerged in Asia in the 1990s. This mode of governance seeks to regulate mobility through mobility. The states regulate mobility not by blocking but by facilitating movements' (Xiang, 2013b: 2–3). This has consequential but understudied effects on how language in globalization and, more specifically, in migration is understood.

Analytically, the study considers the case's specific context and how its different parts are configured. As case studies help researchers connect the actions of individual people to large-scale social structures and processes and vice versa (Neuman, 2000), this study considers how social actors in the arena of transnational domestic work produce scripts. These social actors are the Philippine state, transnational maid agencies and FDWs in Singapore.

Scripts as Templates for Language Practices

Scripts are prominent in the literature on interactive service work (Leidner, 1993) that involves 'social interactions in spaces where the service provider and the service purchaser are *co-present*' (McDowell, 2009: 8), and in call centers (Cameron, 2000a, 2000b; Hall, 1995), the iconic workplace of the new economy, where social interactions between customers and customer service providers are mediated by technology. Both fields are a feature of the tertiarization of the economy where the key motor of development is the provision and sale of services and symbolic goods (Heller & Duchêne, 2012). In both fields, scripts entail emotion work (Hochschild, 2012) of which 'interactive inequality, [the] asymmetry in the amount of attention, care, respect, recognition and deference individuals receive' (Otis, 2012: 8), is a central feature. To accomplish emotion work, interactive service work draws from various modalities (speech, gestures, facial expressions, etc.) and call center work relies on speech and its features. In both fields, scripts are a means of regulating and managing work and workers with the aim of increasing efficiency while also ensuring that practices embody a single corporate brand.

The dominant script in language work in the new economy is that of 'linguistic Taylorism' (Heller & Duchêne, 2012). The script of linguistic Taylorism is the main strategy used for dealing with tensions between standardization and variability. The strategy is

> [...] to provide workers with standardized scripts which mimic socially conventionalized interactions (Cameron 2001), or to use those scripts for the provision of automated services, removing the human element altogether. This strategy requires making a series of script form choices regarding which linguistic elements to include, from conversational sequencing and the pragmatics of utterances to specification of relevant linguistic dimensions (prosody, phonology, lexicon, syntax, morphology, phonology). To the extent to which variability is understood to be important to attend to, taylorism requires the *multiplication of standard scripts*. It also requires *standardizing speakers* (thus, for example, in most Canadian call centers, a code appears on the screen of designated bilingual workers indicating whether service is to be provided in French or English – both is not an option, either for caller or respondent. (Heller & Duchêne, 2012: 12–13, emphasis mine)

In the script of linguistic Taylorism, the extent to which speakers are scripted and just how specific a script may be depends on '... the degree to which the overall production process has been designed and engineered to maximize profitable transactions by minimizing the amount of time any one transaction can take... The referential/instrumental certainly lends itself to streamlining, and work in valued languages seems more likely to be scripted, particularly for provision of service and information' (Urciuoli & LaDousa, 2013: 184).

It must be added that underlying scripts of linguistic Taylorism is the goal of standardizing the disposition of workers so that they internalize and embody the scripts, however general or specific they may be, without needing supervision. In this way, the scripts of linguistic Taylorism could also be considered a form of governmentality, a technology intended to elicit certain capacities and attitudes toward oneself and others that are deemed to be beneficial for the individual and the collective (Foucault, 1991, 1997).

Linguistic Taylorism produces disjunctures; taken to an extreme, it could 'entirely decouple language from identity, and open the door to a radical reinvention of legitimizing discourses for social organization' (Heller & Duchêne, 2012: 12–13). Linguistic Taylorism and its links to the expansion of capital in a neoliberal global order are crucial for understanding the multiplication of scripts: the way in which they have proliferated as practices across markets in late capitalism, and the way in which they are rationalized and legitimized in economic terms. The scripts of linguistic Taylorism are concrete linguistic resources that connect language to profit.

Given the multiplication of scripts, it is important to keep asking how they are produced, why they are produced, for whom they are produced, who produces them and with what consequences. Thus far, studies of such scripts have productively focused on the scripts produced by non-state actors, that is, by corporate entities, most memorably in the form of call centers (Cameron, 2000b; Salonga, 2010). But the script of linguistic taylorism can be and has been adapted by state actors like the Philippines, which is a labor brokerage state (Rodriguez, 2010). This highlights the 'uneasy distinctions between state and market' (Lindquist *et al.*, 2012) and provides us with a way of thinking about how 'inauthentic' language (e.g. English) can become linked to a commodified authenticity (e.g. overseas Filipino worker [OFW]) while still sustaining the discourse of pride that '[...] helps to build the modern-nation state's signature structure of feeling' (Heller & Duchêne, 2012: 5). It also provides us with a way of understanding the complex realizations of language and identity in non-Western countries where the project of decolonization, usually associated with the development of 'authentic' national languages, has been subsumed or subverted by globalization, even before the former process was complete (Canagarajah, 2005: 419). When examined as a practice of a nation state, one might consider that, as instruments, the scripts of linguistic Taylorism are, in a sense, decoupling the elements of the 'homology of nation, state and language' (Gal, 2006: 15) that has been a powerful language ideology and relinking them in different, though no less powerful ways.

The previous discussion highlights how a consideration of the *relocalization* of scripts, in terms of how they are produced, why they are produced, for whom they are produced, who produces them and with what consequences, can lead to an understanding of the *multiplicity* of scripts:

the way in which their '[...] repetition [is] an act of difference' (Pennycook, 2010: 36). Scripts are repeated at different scales which makes 'the spatial reach of [the] actions' (Xiang, 2013a: 284) of the social actors who produce and use them qualitatively different. Relocalizations of scripts at the scale of corporate identity will not be the same as relocalizations of scripts at the scale of consumer service representatives; the effect of relocalizations at the scale of states will differ from the effects at the scale of the FDWs and their employers. Furthermore, if one considers scripts to be regimes of government, then the notion that scripts are multifarious and that their performances are relocalizations may enable us to describe how '(r)egimes of government do not determine forms of subjectivity. They elicit, promote, facilitate, foster, and attribute various capacities, qualities and statuses to particular agents. They are successful to the extent that these agents come to experience themselves through such capacities, qualities and statuses' (Dean, 2010: 44).

To account for how scripts are embedded in social processes that produce transnational DWs like Myrna, I now turn to two aspects of scripts: their enactability as registers and their convertibility as capital.

Scripts as Enactable and Convertible Templates

Scripts are enactable because they are registers. Registers are 'linguistic repertoires stereotypically associated with particular social practices or persons who engage in such practices' (Agha, 2006: vii). This definition is different from definitions of register in applied linguistics where register is understood as context-specific language that can be drawn on as and when the situation or 'context' arises. Agha's definition of register is important for understanding scripts for two reasons. First, his characterization of registers as linguistic repertoires significantly broadens what can be considered part of a register, and by extension, what could then be part of a script. Second, his association of registers to '*enactable* pragmatic effects, including images of the person speaking (woman, upper-class person), the relationship of speaker to interlocutor (formality, politeness), the conduct of social practices (religious, literary or scientific activity)' (Agha, 2006: 23), highlights the indexical nature of registers, and provides us with a way of understanding how scripts get linked to 'personhoods'.

As a linguistic repertoire, a register then could consist of 'a complex of specific semiotic resources, some of which belong to a conventionally defined "language", while others belong to another "language"' (Blommaert, 2010: 102). According to Blommaert, these specific semiotic resources could include accents, language varieties, genres, modalities (e.g. writing), etc., and truncated versions thereof. Arguably, linguistic repertoires would also include linguistic practices, the 'bundles of (language) activities that are organized into coherent ways of doing things' (Pennycook, 2010: 25) and that are 'deeply intertwined with other social practices' (Pennycook, 2010: 26). As such, linguistic repertoires could also include definable activities such as making a joke, confronting an employer, cajoling a child, etc.

Registers link ways of speaking or, more broadly, 'languaging' to ways of being, which in turn can 'do' things in the world. This is because register has the property of indexicality, it 'points to' a set of social relations, identities, values and situations (Gal, 2006) and it invokes social meanings and carries information about its speaker's identity and social position (Urciuoli, 1996). An indexicality can also be creative and performative, such as when 'it sets up new relations, or makes relations explicit and overt, or sets up terms of interaction' (Urciuoli, 1996: 7).

Scripts emerge out of processes of enregisterment, the 'sociohistorical processes [...] by which the forms and values of a register become differentiable from the rest of the language' (Agha, 2006: 37). As templates, then, scripts are 'social regularit(ies)' (Agha, 2006: 26) recognizable through the 'metapragmatic evaluations of language' (Agha, 2006: 26) that social actors make and they provide us with a way of linking the actions of social actors at different scales.

Scripts are convertible because their enactments have value that can be exchanged for other forms of capital – symbolic capital (legitimacy), economic capital (wealth, property, income), social capital (social networks) or cultural capital (taste, education, manners) – that can be exchanged in different markets (Bourdieu, 1986). Like linguistic capital, scripts are unevenly distributed and their distribution (i.e. who performs which script) is a function of the retranslation of social differences (Jenkins, 2002). Mary Louise Pratt (1991) refers to these encounters as 'contact zones', situated encounters between 'agents endowed with socially structured resources and competencies' (Thompson, 1991: 2).

What determines the value of scripts can be gleaned from Bourdieu's (1991: 66, emphasis original) position that 'utterances are not only [...] signs to be understood and deciphered, they are also *signs of wealth*, intended to be evaluated and appreciated, and *signs of authority*, intended to be believed and obeyed'. This points to how the value of linguistic resources and for that matter, of templates of language practices, is not determined by supply and demand. Instead, '...varieties and practices that are indexically linked to powerful speakers come to be valued more highly than others not only because those speakers have greater institutional control but also because the symbolic power accorded to them is transferred to their utterances' (Park & Wee, 2012: 28). How such 'powerful speakers' are assembled in the context of regulated labor migration in general and transnational domestic work in particular is explored in this book.

Nodes in the Migration Infrastructure

This section outlines the different nodes in the migration infrastructure where scripts are produced. The scripts of centering institutions and individual subjects are intrinsically related and they constitute a complex web of practices that produces both the mobility and the marginality of transnational FDWs.

Centering institutions

Centering institutions are 'real or imagined actors perceived to emanate authoritative attributions to which one should orient in order to make sense' (Blommaert, 2005: 251). They 'occur at all levels of social life, ranging from the family over small peer groups, more or less stable communities [...] the state and transnational communities, all the way through to the world system' (Blommaert, 2005: 75).

The authority of centering institutions is premised on their 'production' of 'orders of indexicality' (Blommaert, 2005, 2010). This (re)production of orders of indexicality involves the mapping of linguistic forms into linguistic functions and consequently, into hierarchies of values and meanings. Centering institutions also engage in 'reallocation processes' where 'the indexical links between signs and modes of communication, and social value scales allowing, for example, identity construction, status attribution and so forth [...] are severed and new ones are projected onto the signs and practices' (Blommaert, 2005: 619). Such reallocation processes are especially salient in the current era of globalization that is characterized by mobility. The orders of indexicality which centering institutions (re) produce also mean that these institutions are settings of subject-making. As such, centering institutions are sites where homogenous and uniform identities may be constructed and discursively imposed, via these institutions' authoritative attributions.

Two institutions in the migration infrastructure feature prominently in this study: the state and transnational labor brokers. Blommaert (2005: 219–220) has highlighted three main functions of the state as a centering institution. These are

(1) The state is a switchboard between various scales. In particular, it is the actor that organizes a dynamic between the (transnational) world system and (national) 'locality' [...].
(2) [...] the state organizes a particular space in which it can establish a regime of language perceived as 'national' and with particular forms of stratification in value attribution to linguistic varieties and forms of usage [...].
(3) The state has the capacity to provide an infrastructure for the reproduction of a particular regime of language: an education system, media and culture industries [...].

Another centering institution that should be taken note of is what is called a 'mediating institution' (Blommaert, 2003). Mediating institutions are active agents of relocalization processes. They are distinct from states, in that they may operate transnationally or at the substate level. Mediating institutions such as the music industry, international English training programs, airlines, tourism and service industries and, in this case, transnational labor brokers serve as the intermediate nodal points between global flows and local contexts. At the same time, they emanate orders of indexicality that are embedded in and draw from 'larger' institutions. These institutions at the intermediate level play a particularly pivotal role in globalization by 'assigning specific new functions to sociolinguistic items (either "global" items or "local" ones) and accomplishing specific targeted (globalized) goals with them' (Blommaert, 2003: 610). In doing so, they potentially exert their centering function by 'disseminating systems of rules, conventions and practices that condition the creation, circulation, and use of resources, information, knowledge and belief' (Tyner, 2004: 15), even as they may be embedded across larger centering institutions such as the state.

In the case of transnational FDWs, I will focus on the Philippine state and transnational labor brokers (i.e. maid agencies), the scripts they produce in subject-making processes and how these scripts are part of the space-specific distribution and valorization of linguistic resources.

Subjects

The focus on subjects and how they make sense of the scripts that may be assigned to them or how they produce their own '...moves beneath the structural and institutional bases of social processes to deconstruct their minute effects on the subject. It does so to identify the subject-positions constituted within social processes' (Parreñas, 2001: 31). At this scale, what is explored is how 'personal feelings, attitudes and predispositions' contribute to a continuing selfhood that is 'embedded in [people's] daily routines and experiences' (Carter & Sealey, 2000). A consideration of subjectivity is important because it can serve as a window to how macrosocial forces are linked with the mundane practices of the everyday (Park & Wee, 2012). This consideration of subjectivity has to be rooted in a conception of agency (Giddens, 1986) that takes into account the intervention of individuals in highly rigid regulatory frames (Butler, 1990) such as those indexed by scripts. Locating individuals in objective conditions is necessary so as not to discount the social, political and economic dimensions of power formations that are realized in seemingly mundane and everyday situations. The fact that individuals occupy relatively enduring structural positions does not mean that their lives are completely determined by them and that every social action which an individual engages in is merely a reflection and reproduction of the social system in which it takes place. The agency that is referred to here is not unconditional free will; it refers to 'situated practices' (Giddens, 1986: 56) – it is action or intervention located within multiple interlocking structuring frames.

To focus on the subject, this book examines the situated practices of the transnational FDWs themselves, how they negotiate the scripts of servitude that are assigned to them and how, in this process, they produce their own scripts, (re)evaluating, (re-)indexicalizing and (re-)valuing templates of their own linguistic practices and that of others. As workers who embody the boundary-making processes and boundary-breaking flows of globalization, FDWs weave subject-positions 'out of multiple affiliations and positionings that link their cross-cutting belongingness with complex attachments and multiple allegiances to issues, peoples, places, and traditions beyond the boundaries of their resident nation-states' (Vertovec, 2001: 580).

Transnational Domestic Work

Domestic work is defined as 'any type of work performed in and for a household' (International Labour Organization, 2011: 2) and a DW is 'any person engaged in domestic work within an employment relationship' (International Labour Organization, 2011: 2). By and large, domestic work, which can include child and elderly care, cleaning, cooking and other tasks connected to taking care of the family, is lowly paid, devalued and considered to be unskilled work, work that women can 'naturally' do. The devaluing of domestic work in society comes from a history of classed, gendered and racialized divisions between the public/private sphere, between the roles of women and men in the household, between women themselves (related to modernity) and in distinctions between women who are paid to do the dirty work ('DWs', 'maids', 'servants') and women who, unpaid, manage the dirty work of the household ('mothers', 'wives').

The definitions do not capture how domestic work is more than just physical, mental or emotional work as such; it is reproductive work, the physical, mental and emotional labor that 'creates not simply labor units, but people' (Anderson, 2000: 13). Reproductive work is a commodity purchased by class-privileged employers (Parreñas, 2001) and so, as I argued earlier, paid DWs themselves are social indexes that point to the higher status of their employers. As Anderson (2006: 227) argues, 'Paid DWs reproduce people and social relations, not just in what they do (polishing silver, ironing clothes) but also in the very doing of it (the foil to the household manager). In this respect, the paid DW is herself, in her very essence, a means of production'.

There is a well-established link between domestic work and female international labor migration. This is attributed to the growing demand for care work in developed countries. This globalization of care has resulted in the emergence of care chains and DWs as part of a transnational service class (Mirchandani, 2004).

It must be qualified, though, that this demand for care work is not triggered by the same factors. In countries like Singapore and Taiwan, and cities like Hong Kong, transnational DWs take the place of women who work as a result of large-scale changes in those societies. The overwhelming presence of transnational DWs in the Middle East is not so much about women joining the workforce as it is about DWs serving as status symbols (Fernandez & de Regt, 2014).

While scholarly work on transnational DWs is comprehensive (cf. Constable, 1997, 2002; Ehrenreich & Hochschild, 2002; Fernandez & de Regt, 2014; Huang *et al.*, 2005; Lan, 2006; Lutz, 2002; Parreñas, 2001), there is a significant dearth of studies that focus on language (with the exception of Lan, 2003).

Piller and Pavlenko (2009: 17) note in their review of sociological studies on migrant DWs that the literature makes it clear that '…women who join the "care drain" are most unlikely to speak the language of the host country or they may have only limited proficiency in it'. They are right to point out that the non-existent or limited proficiency of transnational DWs in the languages of their destination countries may work for employers as a way to keep up the pretext of distance in the household and as a way to rationalize the inferior status of the DW. Indeed, there are many international news stories of migrant DWs being abused by their employers and being unable to seek help because of their limited or lack of proficiency in a majority language in their destination country. In Singapore, for example, the FDWs I knew sometimes spoke about the abuse that their

Indonesian counterparts faced and how they were not able to 'fight back' because they could not speak or read English (see Chapter 5). As I discuss in Chapter 4, levels of 'proficiency' in English play an important role in how DWs in Singapore are stereotyped and segmented into different 'product types' to suit the market.

A few other studies also consider how language proficiency, and in particular English proficiency, becomes part of racial stereotypes of DWs in countries like Canada, Taiwan and Singapore (Cheng, 2006; England & Stiell, 1997; Huang & Yeoh, 1998; Pratt, 1997). These stereotypes that, among others, segment DWs into different 'worker-types', e.g. a nanny, a housekeeper or a caregiver for the elderly, are a selection factor for employers (Oishi, 2005). It must be noted here that these racial stereotypes that, in part, draw on language proficiency, shift depending on the country that the DW is in. Thus, a FDW in Canada said 'They think you're as stupid as your English is' (England & Stiell, 1997) but a FDW in Taiwan said 'They have more money, but I speak better English' (Lan, 2003). It must also be noted that while stereotypes of DWs may draw on their supposed language proficiency, no objective yardsticks have actually been used for measuring that proficiency (Huang & Yeoh, 1998). These are points I return to in Chapter 4.

Another strand of studies has considered how the desire to learn a language, particularly English, shapes the flows of au pairs into countries like the UK (Burikova & Miller, 2010; Cox, 2015), while also serving to rationalize and support flows of migrant women, especially from non-EU countries, into countries like Norway, Denmark, Sweden and Switzerland (Cox, 2015). In these countries, au pairs are constructed as being on linguistic and cultural exchanges, and one of the requirements for employers is that they pay for their au pair to attend language classes. This rationalization of migrant au pairs that is premised on language desire is worthy of further study.

Studies of transnational DWs that do mention language as a characteristic of a DW frequently cite the 'English' skills of FDWs. There is little mention of what other transnational DWs, e.g. Sri Lankans and Indonesians, speak or they are constructed as not speaking English. The English skills of FDWs are linked to the higher wages and the higher status that FDWs have in the field of transnational domestic work in Asia (including the Middle East) (Constable, 1997; Lan, 2006; Ong, 2006; Parreñas, 2001; Paul, 2011).

The ubiquity of English-speaking FDWs can be read in two ways. First, it could be that a transnational DW who speaks English is 'unexpected' (Pennycook, 2012), which raises questions about who is typically associated with English 'proficiency' and what the expectations are of (transnational) DWs. Second, it could also be that this is 'expected', that the English-speaking FDW who is 'labor aristocracy' is a durable construct. This is not to say that FDWs cannot actually speak English, it is to say that 'English' and 'Filipino DW' seem to be indexes that co-occur with each other. In the field of transnational domestic work, it seems that to use one is to call into being the other. The personhood of an English-speaking FDW is evident not just in the scholarly literature but also in popular fiction where if there is a character who is a nanny or a housekeeper, there is a good chance that she is Filipina and that she speaks English. For example, in the most recent Bridget Jones novel (Fielding, 2013), the housekeeper of Bridget Jones' new boyfriend is Martha, the 'small, smiling Filipino lady... bustling in the kitchen area'. In *My Hollywood*, one of the main characters is Lola, 'the small, dark, well-joined' (Simpson, 2010: 10) Filipino nanny of a family in Los Angeles.

Transnational Domestic Workers in Singapore

Among the countries where migrant women in general, and migrant Filipino women in particular, have come to occupy a niche as DWs is Singapore where, as of June 2014, in a population of 5.47 million, there were 218,300 foreign DWs (Ministry of Manpower, 2014). They form a significant part of the 980,000 work permit (WP) holders in the city state. Approximately one in five households has a DW (TWC2 report and computed from Population Trends 2014, Department of Statistics) (Transient Workers Count Too, 2011). The majority of foreign DWs come from Indonesia and the Philippines.[5] It is estimated that 70,000 Filipino women and 125,000 Indonesian women are working as DWs in Singapore (Tan, 2015); a marked increase in women coming from Myanmar has been noted. DWs also come from India and Sri Lanka, as well as Pakistan, Bangladesh, Thailand and Nepal.

The history of foreign DWs in Singapore needs to be understood within the context of the culture of waged domestic help in the country and the state's bifurcated migration policy which differentiates between different classes of immigrants. Rahman *et al.* (2005: 234) point out that the ubiquity of foreign DWs in Singaporean households can be attributed not just to the high female labor force participation rate but also to an 'ingrained patriarchal division of labour in Singaporean households', where housework and the care of children and the elderly are considered to be the responsibility of women. In this regard, Singapore has a history of waged domestic help from the *mui tsai* and *amahs* of the colonial period to the 'servant girls' and older women from the rural areas of Singapore and Malaysia at the onset of industrialization to the foreign maids today (see Rahman *et al.* [2005] for a brief history of waged domestic help in Singapore).

The entry of 'foreign maids' (as foreign DWs are popularly known) into Singapore was facilitated by the introduction of the Foreign Maid Scheme in 1978, which was meant to support and encourage the continued participation of local women in the formal economic sphere in order to ameliorate the urgent labor shortage in Singapore (Wong, 1996). Under this scheme, FDWs are considered to be low-skilled 'foreign workers' and the state consistently maintains a tight policy of keeping their immigration in check and ensuring their transient and temporary status as migrant contract workers (Rahman *et al.*, 2005: 238). Among the ways in which DWs are regulated in Singapore are the imposition of: (a) two-year WPs, the renewal of which are largely dependent on the discretion of employers (DWs can only stay for seven days after the WP has been cancelled); (b) a marriage restriction policy where, as WP holders, foreign DWs have to seek the permission of the Controller of Immigration before marrying a Singaporean or a Singapore permanent resident; (c) a monthly levy on employers (as of February 2015, S$265 or S$120 concessionary rate); (d) compulsory biannual medical check-ups for DWs to screen for pregnancy and infectious diseases such as HIV and tuberculosis – DWs found to be pregnant are subject to repatriation without exception; and (e) a S$5000 compulsory security bond, all or part of which may be forfeited if the DW goes missing or if the employer does not pay the DW's salary on time.

Foreign DWs are subject to the control and regulation of Singapore's migration regime, which differentiates between 'foreign talent' and 'foreign workers'. Foreign talent hold employment passes and are allowed to apply for dependant's passes and/or long-term social visit passes for their immediate family. They can also eventually apply (and are often encouraged by the state) to be permanent residents or citizens of Singapore. To qualify for an employment pass, foreigners must earn at least S$3300 a month, and they must have recognized qualifications. Foreign workers usually have dirty, dangerous, difficult (3D) jobs, hold WPs and are subject to a 'use and discard' policy that ensures that they remain a transient workforce in the state (see Rahman *et al.*, 2005; Wong, 1996; Yeoh & Huang, 1998a, 1998b, 1999; Yeoh *et al.*, 1999).

In the years between 2005 and 2013, changes have been made to the regulation of foreign DWs with the Singapore state seemingly playing a more active role in regulating and ensuring the welfare and well-being of foreign DWs in Singapore. As can be seen in Table 1.1, these have included setting a minimum age (which was 18 before 2005), making medical and personal accident insurance compulsory for employers, requiring safety awareness workshops and orientations for new employers and, after almost a decade of lobbying by civil society organizations, formalizing a weekly day off. It must be noted, though, that despite these changes, the most fundamental and important ones have not been made. DWs and foreign DWs are excluded from the Employment Act, which would, for example, mandate maximum working hours and working conditions.

Table 1.1 Summary of changes in the requirements for foreign DWs in Singapore, 2005–2013

Year	Changes or additions to requirements for foreign DWs
2005	Minimum age of 23 years, maximum of 50 years at time of application
At least 8 years of formal education, with a recognized certificate
New DWs must pass a qualifying test, which is in English
Employers orientation program (for first-time employers of foreign DWs)
Safety awareness seminar for new DWs
Additional requirements for employers who changed FDWs more than four times a year
Maid levy: S$295, concessionary rate: S$200
2007	Maid levy: S$265, concessionary rate: S$170
2008	Compulsory medical insurance of S$5,000 for WP holders, including foreign DWs
2010	Compulsory medical insurance coverage of S$15,000 for WP holders, including foreign DWs
Compulsory personal accident insurance with minimum assured of S$40,000
Changes to the conditions for forfeiture of security bond: employers are no longer liable if the DW gets pregnant or breaches other WP conditions that relate to her own behavior. Half of the deposit could be forfeited if the DW goes missing but the employer has made a reasonable effort to locate her. The deposit could also be forfeited if the employer does not pay the DW's salary on time.
2012	One-day settling-in program replaces the qualifying test and includes a safety awareness seminar
2013	Mandatory weekly day off but FDW may be compensated if she works on the day off or a replacement day off may be negotiated
Maid levy: S$265, S$120 concessionary rate[a]

[a] The concessionary rates are paid by families with children, and by individuals who take care of disabled or elderly family members. The new concessionary rates in 2013 differentiated between Singaporeans and non-Singaporeans.

A profile of Filipino domestic workers in Singapore

The biographical data of the migrant Filipino women who participated in this study are summarized in Appendix 2 and their educational background, prior work experience and reasons for coming to Singapore are summarized in Appendix 3. In both tables, the participants are arranged in the order in which I interviewed them. I interviewed Adora and Beth together in March 2003, and I interviewed Precy over the phone in October 2004. As can be seen in Table 1.1, 15 of the participants were single, two were married with children, one was separated with children and one was a single parent. At the time of the interview, the participants' ages ranged from 26 to 39 years, with their average age being 31 years. The participants had spent an average of nine years in Singapore. Among the participants, there were relative newcomers like Cathy who was just about to complete her first two-year contract, and 'old-timers' like Edna and Precy who had worked in Singapore for 15 years. The participants also came from a range of regional backgrounds, as can be seen in their provinces and 'mother tongues'. Ten of the interviewees were from Luzon, seven from the Visayas and two from Mindanao. The general biographical profile of the participants is very similar to the statistical profile of the cohort of 208 FDWs from which they were drawn (see the previous section on class cards). However, the profile of the group of participants in terms of the nationality of their employers does not reflect the trend of the cohort where most of the students were employed by Singaporeans. At the time of the interviews, 11 of the participants were employed by 'expats', six by 'Chinese' (i.e. Singaporean Chinese), one by Filipinos and one was a 'part-timer'.[6] Yet, it must be noted that 17 out of the 19 participants had worked for 'Chinese' employers before working for 'expats'.

The educational backgrounds and previous work experiences of the participants reflect the structural linkages between the feminization of wage labor and globalization (Sassen, 1988). In terms of educational background, 11 of the participants had post-secondary education: five were college graduates with degrees in midwifery, tourism, elementary education and industrial technology; six had some years of college or post-secondary vocational education. Seven of the participants were high-school graduates and one had two years of high-school education. Almost all of the participants had been engaged in low-waged labor prior to working in Singapore. Three of the participants were DWs in the Philippines before coming to Singapore, reflecting a trend in the Philippines and in other developing countries where women from rural areas migrate to cities to find employment as DWs. Six women worked in factories; three were service crew members at fast-food chains in Metro Manila; three worked as paid 'volunteers' at day-care centers. The movement from domestic and factory work in the Philippines to domestic work abroad, in particular, shows how 'globalization simultaneously demands the low-wage labor of women from traditionally Third World countries in export-processing zones of developing countries and in secondary tiers of manufacturing and service sectors in advanced capitalist countries' (Parreñas, 2001: 25).

The work experiences and the reasons the participants had for coming to Singapore also point to the immense income disparities between developing and developed countries wherein DWs in Singapore can easily earn more than public school teachers in the Philippines. Beth, who was the only one who had worked at an 'office job' before coming to Singapore, told me that her salary in the Philippines was barely enough to cover her room, board and transportation costs; she saved much more money as a DW in Singapore. For four of the participants (Edna, Glo, Jocel and Loida), domestic work in another country (Singapore or Kuwait) was practically their only work experience. All of them had relatively high levels of post-secondary education, but they all told me that they had not been able to find jobs in the Philippines.

While the participants were definitely at the receiving end of formidable structural forces, this does not preclude their agency as individuals navigating and negotiating the process of labor migration. All of the FDWs I interviewed engaged in overseas labor migration as a deliberate strategy to contribute economically to their families back in the Philippines. A majority of the participants explicitly told me they left so they could help send siblings, children and other family members to school. All of the participants had contributed, in one way or another, the necessary economic capital for family members to earn a university degree. Cathy's eldest son was a first-year nursing student at the time I interviewed her. Peng had sent all of her eight siblings through secondary education and different levels of post-secondary schooling. Glo had sent one of the children of each of her five siblings to university.

Though less common, another reason why the interviewees had migrated was so they could earn their own keep, travel and be 'independent'. Beth, who was helping her mother pay off bad loans, wanted to earn her own money before marrying her boyfriend back in the Philippines. Loida saw her migration to Singapore as a stepping stone to her dream of working and living in the United States. Glo told me that she had looked at migration (she initially worked in the Middle East) as an 'adventure', especially since she did not have any plans after she finished her degree and since it looked like she would not earn enough even if she took the board exam for midwives. Perhaps the most striking example of this was Connie. The only girl and the second youngest of seven siblings, Connie left home at 16 to earn her own keep because her parents had divided their land among her married brothers and their families, and there was nothing left for her. Her father offered to pay for a two-year junior secretarial course. 'Stubborn' and 'wanting to prove' herself, she found a job as a DW for a Manila-based family. At 18, she applied to work overseas as a DW and was turned down because of her age. She tried again at 19 and was denied. She was finally allowed to apply (because of her 'persistence') at 20. At 32, she had bought her own property in Isabela and built a house for her parents. She also owned a small piggery and poultry farm, which her brothers helped to run.

This acknowledgement of the agency of the FDWs in their decision to migrate, however, needs to be tempered with an understanding of the painful dislocations they undergo in becoming transnational DWs. The FDWs often described their choice to migrate and work as DWs as 'sacrifices'. Cathy and Gina missed their children. Cathy especially missed her youngest son who was two years old at the time I interviewed her, and she worried that he might not remember her when she went back home. Gina told me how she mothered her children from afar, SMS-ing her reminders for them to do their homework and help their father with the housework. Myrna had become estranged from her three children in the 11 years that she had worked in Singapore to support them and she rarely spoke to them except about money matters. Jocel and Peng spoke wistfully about finishing their college education. While all of the FDWs I interviewed told me that they were not ashamed of the honest living they earned from being DWs, they also told me how they wished they did not have to scrub toilets for a living.

Method

In this ethnographically informed study, I draw from different types of data, including newspaper articles and opinion pieces about the language situation in the Philippines and foreign DWs in Singapore; websites and advertisements of Singapore-based maid agencies; official documents circulated by Philippine government agencies; interviews with FDWs; sociolinguistic questionnaires; class cards and language journals collected from the students I taught under the Filipino Overseas Workers in Singapore (FOWS) skills training program from 2001 to 2006; ethnographic information recorded and gleaned from Sundays at the

Bayanihan Center; visits to Lucky Plaza, a shopping mall along Orchard Road (the main shopping road of Singapore) where Filipinos and FDWs congregate to buy Philippine-made products, eat Philippine food, send remittances back to the Philippines, etc.; and conversations with FDWs from my English classes, from other classes at the center and in my own neighborhood. These various data types are described in greater detail below. Using these different types of data enabled me to connect macro to micro, and to trace developments historically.

Since 2007, I have been regularly updating and adding to these secondary data sources as well as learning about new developments by systematically conducting searches on the internet and by visiting the Philippine Overseas Employment Administration (POEA) and the Overseas Workers Welfare Administration (OWWA) in Manila on trips to the Philippines in May 2008 and December 2009. I kept in touch with some of the women I interviewed via mobile phone and eventually, starting in 2008, via Facebook. Facebook proved to be the more dependable medium for keeping in touch.

My 'field site' was the FOWS skills training program where I volunteered as an English teacher from 2001 to 2006. Before the FOWS skills training program was relocated to the Bayanihan Center on Pasir Panjang Road in 2002, it was housed in the halfway home for 'runaway' FDWs along Holland Road. That a volunteer organization would be housed in the embassy is significant and says something about the historically close ties between OWWA and volunteer organizations. It was there that I started volunteering. FOWS offers a range of courses including cooking, baking, dressmaking, tailoring, computer literacy (i.e. the Microsoft-sponsored program), accounting, karate, judo, modern dance, voice lessons, nursing aide and English. Students who enrolled in the nursing aide program were also required to enroll in the English class.

For my analysis of centering institutions, I collected official documents and information from, on the side of the Philippines, the Bangko Sentral ng Pilipinas (BSP), the Department of Labor and Employment (DOLE), the National Statistics Office (NSO), the Overseas Workers Welfare Administration (OWWA), the Philippine Overseas Employment Administration (POEA) and the Technical Education and Skills Development Authority (TESDA). In Singapore, I collected information mainly from the Ministry of Manpower (MOM) with some input from the Philippine embassy in Singapore. Most of this information was available online. I also collected articles and opinion pieces from newspapers in the Philippines and Singapore that talked about OFWs, foreign DWs and the language situation in the Philippines. To describe how transnational maid agencies in Singapore construct foreign DWs in general, and FDWs in particular, I examined internet websites and visited the premises of a number of maid agencies. I double-checked my observations with FDWs who had undergone interviews with maid agencies and/or were working for the maid agencies as recruiters.

To flesh out the subject perspective of this study, I mainly use a set of open-ended and in-depth interviews I conducted with 19 FDWs between May 2003 and October 2004. These 19 FDWs were part of the cohort of 208 students I taught from 2001 to 2005. The 19 interview participants were among my students who had indicated that they would be willing to be interviewed for my study. I was only partly successful in ensuring that they came from different backgrounds, in terms of their age, educational attainment, length of time in Singapore and, especially, the nationalities of their employers. Also, since I knew my students sufficiently well by the time I started doing the interviews, I aimed to get a range of biographies or life stories that would best reflect the different trajectories of migrant Filipino women. My interviews with the participants lasted from one to three hours; the participants spoke rather freely about their personal histories and their experiences as migrant women in general, and as foreign DWs in Singapore in particular. I draw from these stories and voices in how I frame and contextualize my discussions. The participants who I interviewed were in Singapore before the Reform Package in 2005.

In this regard, the participants knew and identified me primarily as their English teacher and as a highly educated (*'may pinag-aralan'*) and 'professional' Filipina who by spending Sundays volunteering at the Center and teaching without pay was also kind (*'mabait'*) and not pretentious (*'hindi mayabang'*). Even when I conducted the interviews after they were no longer my students, having me as the audience of their 'performance' must have affected how they shaped their answers and narratives during the in-depth interviews. Outside the classroom, we found commonalities (I was also a migrant, also a Filipino woman) and topics where they were the experts (they had lived in Singapore longer than I had). Some of my participants told me that they had proudly told their employers that their volunteer English teacher at the center was a Filipina studying for a PhD in English in Singapore. They said that this was to prove to their employers that there were Filipinas who were not maids and that they did have volunteer teachers at the center who were qualified (*'hindi lang kung sinu-sino'*).

Overview of Chapters

The book is organized to highlight the ways in which scripts are produced by and intersect with the different nodes of the migration infrastructure that mobilizes FDWs. As such, the chapters focus on different institutions and/or social actors in the migration infrastructure: the Philippine state, transnational maid agencies and the DWs themselves. While these actors operate on different scales where the reach of their actions are qualitatively different from each other, their practices are intrinsically interrelated. This is visible in the scripts they produce and/or experience.

The first three chapters focus on institutional actors, namely the Philippine state and transnational maid agencies in Singapore. Chapter 2 traces how language and labor migration came to be intertwined in the Philippines. As such, it establishes the grounds for why and how scripts emerged as a brokering practice of the Philippine state. The chapter traces the history and infrastructure of labor migration from the Philippines and examines how language is a central resource that the Philippine state uses to assemble readily deployable, competitive, made-to-order and flexible Filipino 'workers of the world'. The shifts in how the Philippines scripts its workers, namely the shift from an emphasis solely on the English proficiency of migrant workers to an emphasis on 'foreign languages' (especially the languages of the destination countries of OFWs), 'workplace communication skills' and the supposedly innate language adaptability of Filipinos coupled with the rise of training institutions that provide such skills, represent a multiplication of scripts and are indicative of how the Philippine state instrumentalizes language as a strategy for coping with increased competition and adjusting to both the diversity and unpredictability of the labor markets that it targets. Chapter 3 focuses on how the Philippine state 'protects' and controls the FDWs (i.e. 'household service workers') who are the focus of the book. The state does this via institutional processes that enregister migrant FDWs in a script of servitude. FDWs represent one of the largest and widest flows of contemporary female migration and they form the majority of OFWs who are deployed by the Philippines. They are also the migrant workers who embody a national anxiety over the nation's status in the global scene. This chapter historically traces how, as 'vulnerable workers', FDWs came to be the most scripted and most extensively 'branded' OFW. This scripting highlights not just the multiplication of scripts but also their multiplicity, as this skilling of the FDW has allowed the state to legitimize its discourse of protecting the worker, while displacing the responsibility of such protection to the FDWs themselves. Chapter 4 examines the role of transnational maid agencies in Singapore and the mechanisms they employ to differentiate and style transnational DWs in general and FDWs in particular. This chapter shows how the maid agencies' creation of nationality-based stereotypes of DWs reflects their embeddedness in the linguistic and semiotic economies of receiving states and their flexibility in producing 'new' niches for 'new' types of workers. Transnational maid agencies in Singapore produce their own niched order of indexicality by styling the linguistic behavior of migrant Filipino women according to a script of servitude that is expected to be embodied by them. In particular, in this chapter, the processes by which maid agencies script the prospective DW's performance in videotaped interviews, and coach and require them to display linguistic deference in, for example, pre-employment training sessions, will be discussed.

In Chapters 5 and 6, my analysis focuses on the FDWs in Singapore themselves and on uncovering how they experience the scripts that may be imposed on them as well as how they reconstitute and produce scripts of their own. Chapter 5 begins with how FDWs define 'good English', a quality that is central to the linguistic template ascribed to OFWs and FDWs by the Philippine state, as well as by transnational maid agencies. The chapter then explores how the FDWs' construction of 'good English' is intertwined with their hierarchies of desirable employers and hierarchies of foreign DWs in Singapore. Just as particular templates, linguistic and otherwise, are attributed to FDWs by the Philippine state and by transnational maid agencies, FDWs too attribute particular sets of linguistic and non-linguistic practices to different employers and the other DWs they encounter in Singapore. In positioning different employers, Indonesian DWs and themselves, FDWs reproduce and reinforce nationality-based and racial stereotypes. At the same time, FDWs differentially draw from the values of 'good English' to temporarily subvert their relationships with their employers and/or to carve out spaces where their identities are not dominated by servitude. As such, the script of 'good English' that the FDWs deploy seems to reify existing linguistic and racial hierarchies, even as it seems crucial for reframing relations of power, especially between FDWs and their employers. Chapter 6 is about the spatial and temporal trajectories of FDWs and how they deploy various relationships with English in various moments in time and space as the distribution and value of their semiotic resources in their linguistic repertoires change. The chapter traces how FDWs talk about their use and attitudes toward English in relation to: (1) the Philippines before they migrated; (2) Singapore where they work as foreign FDWs; (3) the Philippines where they temporarily return for holidays, visits or stays in between contracts or employers and finally; (4) Canada where some of them project preferred futures as caregivers under the country's Live-in Caregiver Program. In tracing these trajectories, this chapter builds a picture not just of how FDWs experience the scripts that they encounter, but also of how they appropriate and sometimes subvert such scripts. Thus, in the process, they seem to learn and build a repertoire of mobile practices that enable them to be 'resourceful speakers' (Pennycook, 2012). Finally, Chapter 7 summarizes the main points of the book and its contributions to the sociolinguistic study of labor migration and transnational domestic work. Chapter 7 also revisits the continuing stories of the migrant Filipino women who participated in the study.

Notes

(1) All of the participants' names have been changed. In Singapore, 'FDW' is used as an acronym for foreign DWs. In this study, though, I have chosen to use FDW to refer to a transnational *Filipino* DW; this use is specific to this study.
(2) All the translations from Filipino or Ilocano to English are mine. 'BL' refers to the author, '...' indicates a pause in speech and '[...]' indicates ellipsis.
(3) 'Bahay Kubo', which literally means 'Nipa hut', is a popular Filipino folk song that names the different local vegetables that grow in the garden around the Nipa hut.
(4) Detailed statistics on the deployment of overseas Filipino workers (OFWs) per skill per country and per sex are only available up to 2010.
(5) There is no official breakdown of the total number of FDWs per nationality. Newspaper reports are based on embassy estimates.
(6) The categories of 'expat', 'Chinese' and 'part-timer' were the FDWs' own categories. By 'expats', they refer to foreigners (usually 'Westerners') working in Singapore. A 'part-timer' is an FDW who cleans homes on an hourly basis and who (except on paper) is not working full-time for one employer.

2 The Making of 'Workers of the World': Language and the Labor Brokerage State

On July 31, 2007, the Technical Education and Skills Development Authority (TESDA), the government agency in charge of managing and supervising technical education and skills development in the Philippines, launched the Language Skills Institute (LSI). The LSI was tasked to offer courses in English, Spanish, Mandarin, Korean, Nihonggo, Italian, Russian and 'other languages as may be needed' (Technical Education and Skills Development Authority, 2007). A national LSI would be located in Manila and there would be at least one regional LSI in each of the 15 regions of the country. To make the language courses accessible to most Filipinos, scholarships under the President Gloria Macapagal Arroyo (PGMA) Training for Work Scholarship Project would be offered so that those who were interested could become 'world class' for 'free'. Speaking at the launch, the then director general of TESDA, Augusto Boboy Syjuco, gave the reason for setting up such an institute:

> In a globalizing labor market, the usual knowledge, skills and attitude that our workers possess are no longer sufficient. *We need to provide interventions to allow them to gain workplace communication skills not only in English but also in other languages, especially those spoken in the usual destinations of our Overseas Filipino Workers (OFWs)*. With the right knowledge, skills, attitude, language skills and culture orientation, our OFW should henceforth be called Pinoy Workers of the World (Pinoy WOW). (Syjuco, 2007, emphasis mine)

That a national government would engage in 'skills discourses' (Urciuoli, 2008) and that it would establish and fund a language institute where its citizens could learn the necessary 'workplace communication skills' in the languages of the countries they are likely to migrate to for work (i.e. the 'usual destinations of our Overseas Filipino Workers') is not surprising, given that the Philippines is considered to be a labor brokerage state, that is, it is a state which – through institutional and discursive practices – 'mobilizes its citizens and sends them abroad to work for employers throughout the world while generating a "profit" from the remittances that migrants send back to their families and loved ones' (Rodriguez, 2010: x). The Philippine state's emphasis on language and communication skills for the mobility of its citizens is a marked contrast to the emphasis on language for the integration of prospective and new citizens in migrant-receiving countries (Extra et al., 2009; Hogan-Brun et al., 2009; Menard-Warwick, 2009; Piller, 2001; Slade & Mollering, 2010).

Syjuco's reference to a 'globalizing labor market', where 'workplace communication skills not only in English' and knowledge of the languages of the destination countries are necessary in order to ensure the continued competitiveness of migrant Filipino workers, broadly reflects how, in the new economy, language has become a key resource in distinguishing as well as adding value to products as new markets are sought and niche markets are developed (Duchêne & Heller, 2012a; Heller, 2010; Heller & Duchêne, 2012). As a labor brokerage state, the Philippines' success in accumulating profit relies on it being able to continue to assemble, standardize and script the Filipino as a sought-after commoditized figure who embodies the 'perfect worker' (Terry, 2014) who can 'fit' anywhere in the world, as someone who is short term, contractual, incredibly mobile, 'resilient', 'loyal', 'equipped with extensive educational training' and with a 'natural ability to adapt to different work cultures' (Philippine Overseas Employment Administration, 2006b). As can be gleaned from the rationale for the launch of the LSI, as well as from the preceding descriptions of Filipino workers, language is an important part of this assemblage.

This chapter is about the ways in which language is instrumentalized by a labor brokerage state in its labor enterprise of producing and circulating a particular 'figure of personhood' (Agha, 2007, 2011; Park, 2014): a Filipino 'worker of the world' who can be marketed globally, and yet is flexible enough to meet the needs of local labor markets. What is being commodified here is not labor nor language *per se* but workers and how they are represented calls attention not just to how the Philippines, as a labor brokerage state, is commodifying its labor force, but also to how the state legitimizes its activities. As Tyner (2004) has thoughtfully pointed out:

> To view the Philippine state as simply bowing to the spatial logic of capitalism potentially obfuscates the contradictory and contested activities of the state. Although capital accumulation, such as the desire for remittances, is a primary catalyst for state intervention, the state must also cope with the equally important political repercussions of

social relations and the fundamental problem of sustaining legitimacy in the eyes of its citizenry. The balance of these often contradictory interventions significantly influences state legitimacy and informs the discourses of migrant labor. (Tyner, 2004: 2)

The processes by which the Philippine state produces 'workers of the world' are processes of subject-making, of transforming prospective migrants not just into ideal workers but also into ideal migrant subjects, even before they leave the country (Rodriguez & Schwenken, 2013).

The Philippines as a Labor Brokerage State

The Philippines is the world's largest 'exporter' of government-sponsored temporary contract workers in terms of both magnitude and geographic scope (Tyner, 2004). State-sponsored temporary labor migration from the Philippines began in the 1970s as an attempt to resolve deteriorating social and economic conditions in the country brought about, largely, by the restructuring of the Philippine economy toward commercial agriculture and export-oriented industrialization (EOI) under the auspices of Ferdinand Marcos' 'New Society', a program that was launched at the same time that Marcos declared martial law on September 21, 1972, and that emphasized individual and national discipline and the sacrifice of personal liberties for economic development (Tyner, 2004). Around 36,000 Filipinos left the country as temporary migrants in 1975. By 2013, there were 10.23 million overseas Filipinos. Forty-eight percent or 4.86 million are permanent migrants whose stays do not depend on employment, and they include legal permanent residents, including those naturalized in their host country; the majority of these emigrants (3.13 million) are in the United States. Forty-one percent or 4.2 million are temporary migrants, most of whom are overseas Filipino workers (OFWs) whose stays overseas depend on their work contracts, which may range from six months to two years; they are expected to return to the Philippines at the end of their work contracts (Commission on Filipinos Overseas, 2014). There is an OFW in almost every country and territory in the world. The 2013 Stock Estimate of Overseas Filipinos released by the Commission on Filipinos Overseas listed OFWs in 221 countries and territories: there was one OFW on the island of St Helena and there were 948,038 OFWs in Saudi Arabia. Seventy-five percent of OFWs are in five countries: Saudi Arabia, the United Arab Emirates (UAE), Singapore, Hong Kong and Qatar (International Organization for Migration, 2013: 65). Most OFWs find employment in the service and production sectors with the topmost occupation being domestic work (International Organization for Migration, 2013: 66). The number of deployed OFWs continues to rise regardless of whether the government strongly supports the 'facilitation' of jobs overseas, as was the case under the administration of Gloria Macapagal Arroyo who was president from 2001 to 2010, or whether the government supports local job creation and the increased protection of OFWs, as was the case under Benigno Aquino III who was president until 2016.

The Philippines is highly dependent on remittances. The country has been the fourth largest recipient of migrants' remittances after India, China and Mexico (International Organization for Migration, 2013: 114). However, of these four countries, it is the one that has been considered to be the most dependent on them (Economist, 2006). Remittances from overseas Filipinos are the country's premier foreign exchange earner, dwarfing foreign direct investments and exports. Remittances consistently account for approximately 8.5% of gross domestic product in the Philippines (International Organization for Migration, 2013). Remittances from overseas Filipinos seem to hit new record highs every year. In 2012, remittances amounted to US$21.391 billion; in 2013, remittances were US$22.98 billion; and in 2014, remittances were US$24.34 billion (Bangko Sentral ng Pilipinas, 2015). The leading regions where remittances come from are the United States, where most Filipinos who are permanent migrants are based, and the Middle East, where a significant proportion of OFWs work (Bangko Sentral ng Pilipinas, 2015). It has been estimated that remittances support half of the country's population, keeping the economy afloat and generating consumption-led economic growth despite high unemployment, slow poverty reduction and relatively stagnant investment (Department of Labor and Employment [DOLE], 2005; Fujita-Rony, 2003; International Organization for Migration, 2013).

OFWs are not just crucial to the economic growth of the Philippines, they are also central figures as sources of national pride. OFWs are hailed as the *bagong bayani* or the 'new heroes' of the Philippines. Their sacrifices, in leaving their families and their homes, in taking on difficult work overseas, etc., are valorized and celebrated (cf. Guevarra, 2010). This discourse of national pride is fundamental to how the Philippine state sustains the legitimacy of its labor migration project in the eyes of its citizenry.

History of labor migration from the Philippines

While labor migration from the Philippines could be said to have *officially* begun in the 1970s, it is important to note that the Philippines was hardly a newcomer to global labor circuits. The history of labor migration from the Philippines shows how present-day patterns of labor mobility have been shaped by historical specificities, particularly by colonialism, first under Spain and then under the United States. The making of 'workers of the world' then has historical roots that can be linked to colonial practices (Rodriguez & Schwenken, 2013: 380).

During the Spanish colonial period (1521–1898), men from the Luzon and Visayas islands were actively part of seafaring crews led by the Spaniards and other Europeans (Aguilar, 2014). They were first part of Spanish-led explorations of the New World that departed from the Philippines in the mid- to late-1500s. For example, native sailors from Cebu and Bohol were recorded to have joined Urdaneta's trailblazing voyage to the Americas. When the Spanish galleon trade between Manila and Acapulco was instituted in 1565, men from the Spanish Philippines joined the galleon crews and by the 1600s, they had formed the majority of the crews, recognized for their seafaring prowess but, like now, paid less than Spaniards and other Europeans working in the same positions. Native sailors also abandoned ship and settled in parts of the Americas. For example, sailors from the Spanish Philippines were known to have abandoned ship in Acapulco as early as the 16th century, migrating to and settling in other parts of Mexico and beyond, so much so that by 1763, a Filipino community had settled in Louisiana, in what would become the longest-standing permanent settlement of Asians in the United States (Fujita-Rony, 2003). Even before the galleon trade ended in 1815, 'Manilamen' (sic), as they had become known and as they called themselves, had spread beyond the Spanish realm, becoming part of multiethnic crews on international merchant ships that, for example, traded between Alaska and China, or in sandalwood in various parts of Oceania (e.g. Australia, New Zealand, Fiji and Tonga). After the Spanish colonial period, the Philippines continued to be a major source of seafarers. They were systematically recruited into the US Navy during the American colonial period and Filipino sailors are now probably as ubiquitous on the world's ships as Filipino domestic workers are in the world's homes, with the Philippines being one of the top three suppliers of sailors in the world (Aguilar, 2014). In tracing the continuities between the Manilamen and the Filipino sailors of today, one can see how Philippine labor was always '…immersed in the vortex of global capitalism and represent(ing) the vanguard of an emerging national proletariat … the Philippine workforce was, in the first instance, global before it became national' (Aguilar, 2014: 58).

Labor migration from the Philippines during the American colonial period (1898–1946) was structured largely by the colonial relations between the Philippines and the United States, and migration flows were mainly from the Philippines to the United States. The first wave of Filipino migrants to the United States began at the beginning of the 20th century. The ones who left were mainly Filipino men, many of them from Northern Luzon; they filled temporary labor needs in agriculture, first in Hawaii and eventually on the US West Coast (Fujita-Rony, 2003; Mabalon, 2013; Takaki, 1998). The second wave was made up mostly of Filipino professionals, many of whom were nurses (Ceniza Choy, 2003); they found entry to the United States through the US Exchange Visitor Program (EVP) in 1948, with major reforms in US immigration law in 1965 opening the door to a steady and significant flow of Filipino permanent migration to the United States, a flow that continues to this day. Rodriguez (2010: 6) has argued that 'institutional precursors to the contemporary labor brokerage state can be identified in the (American) colonial labor system, including the expansion of training programs, the role of labor recruiters, and the role of the state in facilitating out-migration'. For example, the Hawaiian Sugar Planters' Association (HSPA) was actively engaged in the recruitment of the first wave of Filipino migrants to the United States, and nursing recruitment agencies facilitated the migration of Filipino nurses. Bilateral agreements between the United States and the Philippines also allowed for labor transfers (through the EVP or the military) from the Philippines during a period of severe immigration restriction (Rodriguez, 2010: 6–9); and the beginnings of an 'empire of care', embodied by the immigration of Filipino nurses first to the United States and then to other developed countries, can be traced back to the Americanized system of nursing training that was instituted in the Philippines in the early 20th century (Ceniza Choy, 2003).

The evolution of state-sponsored labor migration in the 1970s can be traced to the shift from a strategy of import-substitution in the aftermath of political independence in 1946 to a strategy of EOI in the late 1960s (Gonzalez, 1998b; Tyner, 2000). 'One key to the Philippines' economic strategy was the discursive marketing of an "internationally attractive labor force"', i.e. a cheap and docile workforce prevented from unionizing and striking (Tyner, 2004: 30); this was crucial to the restructuring of the Philippine economy toward EOI and commercial agriculture. To produce an internationally attractive labor force, the Philippine government restructured domestic labor market conditions through the Presidential Decree 442 or PD 442. The code

> [...] permit[ted] employers to pay new employees only 75 percent of the basic minimum wage during a six-month 'probationary' period

[...]. By releasing workers after this period, multinational corporations effectively instituted a high turnover rate. [...] Denied access to traditional economic forms of subsistence production, yet more fully incorporated into the waged labor force, many Filipinos found employment opportunities unavailable in the Philippines, or untenable due to low wages. (Tyner, 2000: 136)

PD 442 also laid the foundations of labor migration (specifically in Articles 17.1 and 17.2) by mandating that the Philippine state would promote 'the overseas employment of Filipino workers through a comprehensive market promotion and development program and, in the process, [...] secure the best possible terms and conditions of employment of Filipino contract workers on a government to government basis' (Tyner, 2004: 33). Labor export was seen by the state as a means of resolving such unemployment and underemployment problems, while, at the same time, promoting Philippine development and alleviating balance of payment problems through remittances. In this way, the extremely destabilizing restructuring of the labor market that was an essential part of the country's export-led development strategy effectively made Philippine labor one of the 'natural resources' that the country could export.

With its labor force effectively considered as exportable 'commodities', the Philippines was one of the first Asian countries to respond to the labor needs of the oil-rich countries in the Middle East in the 1970s. What was intended to be a temporary solution to domestic unemployment and balance of payment problems, 'continued and expanded beyond the Middle East in response to the increasing demand for Filipino workers on the one hand, and the development of institutions and policies in the Philippines that enabled the state to seize opportunities in the global labor market on the other' (Asis, 2005: 26). In this regard, the role of overseas labor migration in the Philippines fundamentally shifted

[...] from a temporary solution to the critical low employment rate in the domestic market to an employment strategy that recognizes the role of overseas remittances in alleviating poverty, spurring investment and cushioning the impact of worldwide recession when private capital dries up. (Philippine Overseas Employment Administration, 2006a: 3)

Overseas employment has become a cornerstone of various administrations, figuring as an essential aspect of national development goals as elucidated in, for example, Medium-Term Philippine Development Plans (Tyner, 2004).

Officially, the Philippine state only 'manages' labor migration; it does not promote it. A DOLE 'White Paper' released in 1995 emphasized that

> Many people see opportunities abroad and want to benefit from them. And there are labor-market gaps in the global economy that are best filled by labor migration. The challenge to Philippine policymaking today is not one of exporting the country's labor surplus; it is *managing* effectively the *natural* process of labor migration – which will continue even if we ban the outflow of our workers. (DOLE, 1995 in Guevarra, 2003: 115, Guevarra's emphasis)

This report was later incorporated in the Migrant Workers and Overseas Filipinos Act (RA 8042) of 1995. It is important to note that the Philippine state's portrayal of itself as 'managing' labor migration is buttressed by a discourse that 'proposes that opportunities abroad are *natural* processes of globalization and that the desires and aspirations of Filipinos to work overseas are *natural* responses' (Guevarra, 2003: 115).

In managing this supposedly natural process of labor migration, the Philippine state has evolved a complex network of institutions that manage migration. The most important government institution for OFWs has been the Philippine Overseas Employment Administration (POEA), which oversees this official 'management' of overseas workers. The Philippine state, through the POEA, aggressively promotes migrant Filipino workers (Tyner, 2000). It has a marketing division that conducts market research on the locations where OFWs may go and the nature of the possible employment opportunities in these places. The POEA also seeks to develop 'friendly markets' for OFWs in the form of 'inbound marketing programs', where Filipino 'skills and talents' are showcased to foreign principals and employers invited to visit the Philippines, and 'outbound marketing missions', where POEA representatives are sent to existing and prospective labor destinations to explore opportunities and secure contracts (Guevarra, 2003).

The POEA works in tandem with the DOLE, the TESDA and the Overseas Workers Welfare Administration (OWWA). For example, in 2005, the POEA implemented the DOLE Labor Opportunities Program (DOLOP), which was designed as an 'in-bound marketing activity to promote the services of OFWs and showcase their skills and talents' (Philippine Overseas Employment Administration, 2006a: 15). TESDA is in charge of providing technical education to Filipinos, and now offers training courses that are designed to cater to the needs of overseas labor markets. The OWWA is the government agency responsible for providing welfare assistance to registered OFWs and their dependents. The POEA also licenses and regulates the thousands of privately owned overseas employment agencies in the country.

The POEA's 'management' of international labor migration has become the 'model for other labor-sending economies for the past two decades' (Philippine Overseas Employment Administration, 2006a: 3). More importantly, it is in this way that the export of labor from the Philippines represents the unprecedented convergence of interests between states and international capital, with the recruitment and deployment of migrant labor centrally organized and 'guaranteed' by the state (Aguilar, 2002).

Patterns of labor migration from the Philippines

If one were to look at the sheer number of OFWs that have been deployed by the state, overseas labor migration could be considered an enormously successful employment strategy. The number of OFWs has increased exponentially since labor migration was instituted in 1974. As can be seen in Table 2.1, only 36,035 temporary labor migrants were recorded to have left the country in 1975. Ten years later, 372,784 Filipinos left the country as migrant workers. By 2005, OFW deployment had almost hit the one million mark. By 2014, 1.83 million OFWs were deployed.

Table 2.1 also highlights an important pattern in labor migration from the Philippines: the increasing proportion of rehires among land-based workers. Rehires are defined as OFWs who go back to the same employer in the same country either because they have renewed their contracts for another term or are going back to the same employer after a vacation; they also include OFWs who are going back to the same employer in the same country but who were not registered with the POEA when they originally departed. Since 1992, more than 50% of the OFWs deployed every year were rehires; almost 66% of the OFWs who left the country in 2014 were rehires. This pattern 'indicates that the temporary labor migration of OFWs is gaining some stability – a case of temporary migration becoming more or less permanent – and the overseas employment experience is becoming longer' (International Organization for Migration, 2013: 3). This pattern is indicative of broader trends in global labor migration, namely, the turn to 'documented

Table 2.1 Annual deployment of OFWs and percentage rehires (1975–2012)

Year	Land based	Sea based	Total deployed	No. (%) rehires (land based)
1975	12,501	23,534	36,035	–
1976	19,221	28,614	47,835	–
1977	36,676	33,699	70,375	–
1978	50,961	37,280	88,241	–
1979	92,519	44,818	137,337	–
1980	157,394	57,196	214,590	–
1981	210,936	55,307	266,243	–
1982	250,115	64,169	314,284	–
1983	380,263	53,594	434,207	142,980 (37.6)
1984	300,378	50,604	350,982	166,884 (55.6)
1985	320,494	52,290	372,784	159,679 (49.8)
1986	323,517	54,697	378,214	152,812 (47.2)
1987	382,229	67,042	449,271	170,267 (44.5)
1988	385,117	85,913	471,030	202,975 (52.7)
1989	355,346	103,280	458,626	184,913 (52.0)
1990	334,883	111,112	446,095	164,883 (49.2)
1991	489,260	125,759	615,019	187,943 (38.4)
1992	549,655	136,806	686,461	289,062 (52.6)
1993	550,872	145,758	696,630	294,645 (53.5)
1994	564,031	154,376	718,407	305,012 (54.1)
1995	488,173	165,401	653,574	273,984 (56.1)
1996	484,653	175,469	660,122	278,592 (57.5)
1997	559,227	188,469	747,696	337,780 (60.4)
1998	638,343	193,300	831,643	419,128 (65.7)
1999	640,331	196,689	837,020	403,071 (62.9)
2000	643,304	198,324	841,628	398,886 (60.6)
2001	661,639	204,951	867,599	390,554 (59.0)
2002	682,315	209,593	891,908	393,638 (57.6)
2003	651,938	216,031	867,969	372,373 (57.1)
2004	704,586	229,002	933,588	419,674 (59.6)
2005	740,632	247,983	988,615	450,651 (60.8)
2006	788,070	274,497	1,062,567	470,390 (59.7)
2007	811,070	266,553	1,077,623	497,810 (61.4)
2008	974,399	261,614	1,236,013	597,426 (61.3)
2009	1,092,162	330,424	1,422,586	742,447 (68.0)
2010	1,123,676	347,150	1,470,826	781,710 (79.6)

Table 2.1 (Continued)

Year	Land based	Sea based	Total deployed	No. (%) rehires (land based)
2011	1,318,727	369,104	1,687,831	881,007 (66.8)
2012	1,435,166	366,865	1,802,031	976,591 (68.0)
2013	1,469,179	367,166	1,836,345	1,004,291 (68.4)
2014	1,430,842	401,826	1,832,668	943,666 (65.9)

Sources: International Organization for Migration (2013: 59); Philippine Overseas Employment Administration (2014).

circular migration...for sending and receiving countries' (Lindquist et al., 2012: 12) and the 'increasing formalization of migration management' (Lindquist et al., 2012: 11).

The majority of land-based OFWs are in the Middle East and Asia (see Table 2.2), in countries like Saudi Arabia, the UAE, Hong Kong, Singapore and Taiwan. The top five destinations of OFWs, namely, Saudi Arabia, the UAE, Qatar, Hong Kong and Singapore, have remained fairly consistent through the years. Saudi Arabia, the UAE and Qatar are not countries for permanent settlement. Those that do have pathways to citizenship or permanent residency as in the case of Singapore and Hong Kong have migration and citizenship regimes that exclude most of the OFWs who work there, i.e. domestic workers. These Middle Eastern oil-rich countries and affluent Asian economies demand a flexible and low-cost labor force to sustain their economic growth and support their own labor force. OFWs are also heading to North American and European destinations, such as Canada and Italy, where there are significant care deficits.

Table 2.2 Top 10 destinations of land-based OFWs (rehires and new hires) (2014)

Country	2014	Rehires	New hires
(1) Saudi Arabia	402,837	209,380	193,457
(2) United Arab Emirates	246,231	189,642	56,589
(3) Singapore	140,205	125,320	14,885
(4) Qatar	114,511	87,680	26,831
(5) Hong Kong	105,737	83,511	22,226
(6) Kuwait	70,098	33,367	36,731
(7) Taiwan	58,681	9,759	48,922
(8) Malaysia	31,451	16,611	14,840
(9) Bahrain	18,958	10,317	8,641
(10) Canada	18,107	11,690	6,417

Source: Philippine Overseas Employment Administration (2014).

Table 2.3 Deployment of new hires by sex (1992–2010)

Year	Male	Female	Not stated	Total
1992	128,380	132,213	–	260,593
1993	115,902	140,325	–	256,227
1994	103,953	155,066	–	259,019
1995	88,999	125,190	–	214,819
1996	94,408	111,653	–	206,061
1997	97,938	123,509	–	221,407
1998	86,195	133,523	6	219,724
1999	85,367	152,042	5	237,414
2000	70,427	174,768	7,835	253,030
2001	72,187	186,018	11,546	269,751
2002	77,850	197,441	10,837	286,128
2003	66,401	166,325	8,785	241,511
2004	72,355	209,372	86	281,812
2005	79,079	201,538	44	280,661
2006	123,668	184,416	38	308,122
2007	160,046	146,285	52	306,383
2008	174,930	163,324	12	338,266
2009	156,454	175,296	2	331,752
2010	154,677	185,602	–	340,279

Source: International Organization for Migration (2013).

Table 2.3 highlights another significant pattern in labor migration from the Philippines: the feminization of migrant labor. Since 1992, 'the gender distribution of newly-hired OFWs has been predominantly female' (International Organization for Migration, 2013: 202), with temporary declines in 2007 and 2008 due to the new guidelines of the Reform Package for Household Service Workers (see Chapter 3).

Women not only predominate labor migration from the Philippines in terms of numbers, they also end up in occupations that are highly gendered. As can be seen in Table 2.4, an overwhelming majority of new hires are deployed as household service workers (HSWs), i.e. domestic workers. Practically all of them are women. Again, this feminization of migrant labor from the Philippines is not entirely new. While the sailors

Table 2.4 Deployed overseas Filipino workers (new hires, top 10 occupational groups) (2010–2014)

Occupational group	2010	2011	2012	2013	2014
(1) Household service workers	96,583	142,689	155,831	164,396	183,101
(2) Nursing professionals	12,082	17,236	15,655	16,404	19,815
(3) Waiters, bartenders and related workers	8,789	12,238	14,892	14,823	13,843
(4) Caregivers and caretakers	9,293	10,101	9,128	6,466	12,075
(5) Charworkers, cleaners and related workers	12,133	6,847	10,493	12,082	11,894
(6) Laborers/general helpers	7,833	7,010	9,987	11,892	11,515
(7) Wiremen and electrical workers	8,606	9,826	10,575	9,539	8,226
(8) Plumbers and pipe fitters	8,407	9,177	9,657	8,594	7,657
(9) Welders and flame cutters	5,059	8,026	8,213	7,767	7,282
(10) Cooks and related workers	4,399	5,287	6,344	7,090	5,707
Other occupational categories	167,095	209,283	207,800	205,835	206,061
All occupational categories – total	340,279	437,720	458,575	464,888	487,176

Source: Philippine Overseas Employment Administration (2014).

during the Spanish colonial period and the first wave of labor migrants to the United States were men, the second wave of labor migrants to the United States was mostly nurses and mostly women. A similar pattern can be found in institutionalized temporary labor migration. Migrants in the 1970s were mainly men heading to Saudi Arabia to work in the oil fields. While this flow of male migrants still continues, since the 1980s, an ever-increasing proportion of migrants have been women, mainly working as domestic workers.

Language in the Philippine Labor Migration Enterprise

Language has always played an important role in the Philippine labor migration enterprise. The language skills of OFWs in English and, most recently, in the languages of their destination countries, has been a central part of the discourse of Filipino competitiveness in global labor markets, and of sustaining the OFW 'brand'. The importance of language in Philippine labor migration is such that the position and history of the Philippines as a labor-sending state has been considered to have influenced Philippine language policy significantly (Gonzalez, 1998a).

'Our labor force speaks your language'

Going back to the 2007 launch of the LSI, the then director Augusto Syjuco not only exhorted Filipinos to acquire foreign language skills, he also advertised the Pinoy 'workers of the world' whose

> [...] proven competence, ability, trainability and adaptability simply put them on a competitive edge. The growing need for *language-adept* workers can be easily filled by our Pinoy workers who take pride in *having the capacity and learning ability to learn languages easily*. (Technical Education and Skills Development Authority, 2007, emphasis mine)

Just two years before, in its 2005 annual report, the POEA had attributed the global competitiveness of OFWs (as evinced by the number of OFWs deployed) to 'the continued confidence of foreign principals to employ Filipino workers who are competent, highly trained, *English proficient*, with caring attitude and adaptable to work environment' (Philippine Overseas Employment Administration, 2006a: 8, emphasis mine).

These portrayals of OFWs are not significantly different from how the Philippine government depicted the Filipino labor force to potential foreign investors in a 1974 advertisement in the *New York Times*:

> We've put our house in order. You can't afford to overlook the new Philippines in surveying your Asian prospect this year. For the authoritarian government in Manila has put an end to political factionalism and social anarchy. Restored peace and order. Purged the bureaucracy of the inept and the corrupt. Freed economic policy-making from the constraints of extremist rhetoric. Result: the renewed

optimism of 40 million people and the resurgence of the national economy...
  We like multinationals...Local staff? Clerks with a college education start at $35...accountants come for $67, executive secretaries for $148...
  Our labor force speaks your language. Whether you're talking electronic components, garments or car manufacturing. National literacy was placed at 83.4% in 1973 (*English is the medium of instruction*) .... (Tollefson, 1991: 140, emphasis mine)

The representations of Filipino workers in these texts are striking in their similarities. They showcase the Filipino workforce as being ideal and desirable labor for foreign employers; they market the skills and the supposed particular qualities of Filipino workers that distinguish them from others; they all stress how Filipino workers know the 'other's' language: whether they be multinationals who speak English, or foreign employers who 'value' English proficiency or the worker's capacity to learn languages easily. However, there are also differences between the three passages. While the 1974 advertisement portrayed the Philippine labor force as a docile, cheap, highly skilled and therefore desirable workforce to transnational companies being enticed to locate themselves in the Philippines, the POEA represented OFWs as ideal transnational workers who are highly skilled and able to work practically anywhere in the world. Perhaps, most importantly, while English skills were a source of distinction for Filipino workers in the passages from 1974 and 2005, a 'natural' quality of being 'language adept' and thus of 'having the capacity and learning ability to learn languages easily' was portrayed as the competitive edge of Filipino workers in 2007.

The similar ways in which the Philippine labor force is portrayed underline the structural and historical continuities in the Philippines' location in the world system. Here, one can see how the Philippine state's strategy of capital accumulation by capitalizing on its labor force to attract foreign investment has been reconstituted into relying on its labor force to remit the capital the country urgently needs; in such a context, it is crucial that the labor force sustains its competitiveness. The shifts as to which language is portrayed as the competitive edge (from English only to an English-knowing multilingualism where the other language is the language of a destination country) and how language skills distinguish the Filipino worker (from being proficient in English to being 'language-adept' or proficient at learning languages) come at a time of 'expansion of capital' (Heller & Duchêne, 2012). The interconnected processes of market saturation, market expansion, distinction, tertiarization and flexibilization that Heller and Duchene (2012: 8–10) argue as underpinning the 'widespread emergence of discursive elements that treat language and culture primarily in economic terms' (Heller & Duchêne, 2012: 3) have been and are evident in the Philippines.

The history of English in the Philippines

English was introduced to the Philippines at the very beginning of the American colonial period when it became the *de facto* medium of instruction (MOI) in what has come to be considered as 'one of the most positive and enduring innovations brought by the American colonial government [...] the public school system' (Gonzalez, 1985: 91). The Americans opened the first public school on Corregidor Island, less than a month after Admiral Dewey destroyed the Spanish Navy in the Philippines in the Battle of Manila Bay on May 1, 1898. This apparent prioritization of education literally came on the heels of Spanish colonization, which had not succeeded in providing a good measure of public primary education (Churchill, 2003) and which had practically put the Spanish language only within the reach of the *mestizos* and *ilustrados*, the very elite of Philippine society. Only 2.46% of an adult population of 4.6 million spoke Spanish (Gonzalez, 1980).

It was mainly because of the public school education system and the use of English as the basis of all public instruction that English followed a very different trajectory from Spanish: it was disseminated more widely and entrenched far more effectively in state policies as well as in the public imagination (Hau & Tinio, 2003). Thus, '[...] at the tail-end of the American period (1898–1935), after only thirty-seven years, the 1939 Census reported a total of 4,264,549 out of a total population of 16,000,303 (or 26%) who claimed the ability to speak English' (Gonzalez, 1980: 26). Apart from the system of public instruction, Gonzalez (1980: 27–28) cited two other factors that contributed to the rapid spread of English and its swift ascent to the apex of the country's linguistic economy: 'the positive attitude of Filipinos towards Americans; and the incentives given to Filipinos to learn English in terms of career opportunities, government service, and politics'. English was also the official language of the civil service. Along with education, it was considered by the American colonizers to be the prerequisite for participating in the legislation, administration and leadership of the country. In this way, English came to be identified with the 'progressive' American ideals of 'enlightenment', 'democracy' and 'self-governance'. The grip of English was such that even when the 1925 Monroe survey noted that Filipino students had problems learning English and recommended the use of Filipino vernacular languages for teaching manners and morals, and despite various recommendations by educators to use the vernacular languages (Gonzalez, 1980), English remained the official language and the sole MOI during the American colonial period.

In analyzing the impact of this valorization of English during the American colonial period, Constantino (2002) emphatically argues that:

> The first and perhaps the master stroke in the plan to use education as an instrument of colonial policy was the decision to use English as the medium of instruction. English became the wedge that separated Filipinos from their past and later was to separate educated Filipinos from the masses of their countrymen. [...] With American textbooks, Filipinos started learning not only a new language but also a new way of life, alien to their traditions and yet a caricature of their model. This was the beginning of their education. At the same time, it was the beginning of their miseducation, for they learned no longer as Filipinos but as colonials. (Constantino, 2002: 181)

It must be emphasized that in his statement, Constantino (2002) outlined two devastating 'English effects'. Firstly, by providing Filipinos with a semblance of access to the colonial language, American colonizers ensured the 'forgetting' of the physical and symbolic violence wrought by colonization while guaranteeing a (misplaced) sense of indebtedness (*utang na loob*) from Philippine society (see, for example, Gonzalez, 1985). Tupas (2001b, 2003) calls this the 'problem of consciousness' in the Philippines where strategies of forgetting and erasure have effectively idealized the colonial history of the country and nullified the colonial accoutrements of English. Secondly, English became the marker of and the gatekeeper to an educated and privileged class. As both a resource for and a site of symbolic struggles, English became a central means by which access to valuable symbolic and material capital could be regulated during and after the American colonial period.

In the postcolonial era, this 'American legacy' of English shaped the landscape in which national language and bilingual education policies (BEPs) were debated and carried out. While there were strong sentiments for the search and declaration of a national language as early as 1903 (see Gonzalez [1980] for a comprehensive history of the search for and the debates around the national language), the call for the development of a national language based on Tagalog, renamed Pilipino in 1959 and Filipino in 1973 (Tupas, 2014), in the Commonwealth Act 570 of 1940 was met by much opposition from other language groups. As Hau and Tinio

(2003: 342) correctly point out, however, '[t]his opposition to Tagalog [...] should not be interpreted as a manifestation of ethnic conflict. The debate over Tagalog – one that continues to this day – reflects intra-elite rivalry and internecine battles over resource allocations that happened to be parceled out by region'. Not surprisingly, in this and other language debates in the country, the anti-Tagalog forces allied and continue to ally themselves with the pro-English lobby, particularly within the elite, thus ensuring the viability of the colonial language as a link within a social class that cuts across regional groups (Hau & Tinio, 2003), even at the peak of linguistic nationalism during the height of student activism in the 1970s.

In 1974, a year after the declaration that steps would be taken toward the development and formal adoption of a common national language to be known as Filipino, and the provision of English and Filipino as the official languages of the Philippines in the 1973 Constitution, a BEP was set in motion. Under the BEP, English was to be used as the MOI in science and mathematics, and Filipino was to be used for all other courses. This marked the first time that the supremacy of English was to be challenged by a local language. Ostensibly, the BEP was considered to be a compromise solution to the demands of nationalism and internationalism: Filipino would do the homework of identity while English would ensure that Filipinos would stay connected to the world (Gonzalez, 1998a). Arguably though, the BEP represented

> [A] political compromise between competing elites: the Tagalog-speaking elites who nevertheless were conversant in English and who took up the fight for Pilipino as the national language, and the non-Tagalog elites who were likewise conversant in English, but who feared that the imposition of Pilipino as the national language would put them at a disadvantage over resources necessitating competence in Pilipino. (Tupas, 2004b: 20)

It could well be argued that this compromise held fast in 1987 when the 1973 Constitution was revised in the wake of the 1986 People Power Revolution that toppled Marcos and Filipino was finally declared as the national language of the Philippines. As Hau and Tinio (2003: 344) note, 'the presence of a strong English-language lobby during the convention's deliberations secured the use of English in government and in the classroom'. The terms of the BEP were maintained with the provisions that Filipino would be accorded the primary position as the official language and that Congress could strip English of its official language status should circumstances warrant.

The making of English-speaking overseas Filipino workers

In 1974, when the BEP instituting Filipino and English as the media of instruction was put in place (Tupas, 2007), with the provision that steps would be taken toward the development of Filipino as the national language, the Philippine economy was already well into the process of becoming more fully incorporated into the global economy as a source of low-waged labor.

It was in this same year that the first batch of government-sponsored Filipino contract workers was deployed to the Middle East, an early indication of how the search for a national linguistic symbol of unity would soon be overtaken (see Tupas, 2007 for discussion), or had already been overtaken, by the insertion of the Philippines into the world system as a labor-sending country. The almost indisputable argument then was that English was necessary if the country was to participate in and fully benefit from the global economy. Arguably, in this light, the biggest losers were the Filipinos whose wages had been eroded by their incorporation into the global labor market, and whose varying levels of English competence differentially affected their entry as low-waged workers in an export-oriented, labor-intensive light industry financed by foreign capital (Tollefson, 1991).

In fact, already in the 1970s, the Philippine government had restructured the education system in accordance with the perceived needs of EOI. Restructuring the education sector was a vital complement to the changes that had been made to the labor sector. Major changes to the Philippine educational system can be traced back to martial law. According to Tollefson (1991):

> Various presidential decrees transformed the elementary and high school curricula into 'work-oriented' programmes to prepare you for participation in commercial and industrial enterprises [...] The goal was to ensure that the educational system would 'equip high school students with specific skills needed for industry and agriculture [...] In addition, beginning in 1976, the World Bank funded publication and distribution of millions of new textbooks and manuals through the Ministry of Education, Culture and Sports that were designed to help the system of education respond to the new economic policy. (Tollefson, 1991: 149)

These changes to the Philippine educational system were reinforced further through the institutionalization of the National College Entrance Examination (NCEE), which became the country's main educational stratifier:

> With standards set by the central government, the NCEE determined who among the high school graduates could go on to college, earn their degrees and most possibly become white-collar workers. Those who did not pass could either enroll in technical education certificate courses or start working on low-paying jobs because by then they would have been taught vocational skills in high school through institutionalized technical programmes. (Tupas, 2004a: 6)

These changes in Philippine educational policy translated to

> a renewed emphasis on English and a shift towards vocational and technical English training. The Marcos government's strong support of English was due primarily to its crucial role in meeting the labour requirements of the Philippine economy'. (Tollefson, 1991: 150)

The three main labor needs at that time were consistent with the country's policy of EOI financed and managed by foreign capital. They consisted of: (1) a large pool of workers for unskilled and semitechnical jobs in light manufacturing, assembly and the like; (2) office staff and middle managers able to work under the managers of transnational corporations investing in the Philippines; and (3) a service industry for foreign businesses, including maintenance crews, hotel staff and domestic workers (Tollefson, 1991). What the formal education system then produced was a multitiered skills-oriented population whose proficiencies in English were ordered accordingly (Tupas, 2001a, 2004a), with most students being educated for low-paying jobs requiring only basic English (Tollefson, 1991).

These differences reproduced the already glaring social and economic disparities in the Philippines. Those who learned English well and who had the skills to take up the better-paid white collar jobs were inevitably graduates of elite schools, with most of them coming from the well-off and landed families in the Philippines. Those who did not learn English well were usually from the impoverished areas of the country; they usually did not go on to college and they ended up in the large pool of semiskilled and unskilled workers in the manufacturing and service sectors. As Tollefson (1991: 151) pointedly states, 'the policy of using English in schools thus serves a dual purpose: it helps to ensure that a great number of students fail, and it produces the necessary number of graduates with appropriate English skills'. When overseas labor migration was formalized by the government in 1974 as a viable employment alternative and as a strategy of capital accumulation, many OFWs came from the group of semiskilled and unskilled workers.

The Philippine education system's pattern of producing a hierarchy of labor, with corresponding levels of English skills meant for an externally defined labor market, has intensified or even worsened with the institutionalization of overseas labor migration. As Toh and Floresca-Cawagas (2003) point out, the quality of education in the Philippines has continuously deteriorated over the years, and the educational system is unable to respond realistically and relevantly to social, economic and political demands in the country. This is most evident in the disparity between the degrees of most college graduates and the demand for such skills or expertise in the domestic labor market (along with the failure to create such demand), leading to a rise in the number of educated underemployed and unemployed who, in turn, may be funneled into overseas labor migration.

Former president Arroyo strongly articulated this push toward matching the goals of Philippine education with the demands of the global labor market. In a 2002 speech during Migrant Workers' Day, Arroyo argued that the increasing number of OFWs did not constitute a brain drain, because they benefited the country economically. As such, she urged the education system to 'produce and produce' the workers that are 'in demand' overseas:

> So when they say brain drain, I say, no, they are serving there but they are still serving here because they do not forget their families, their communities, and in this way our country also benefits. *The important thing is when we see the skills that are in demand, our school system should produce and produce. If there is a big demand for nurses, produce more nurses; if there is a big demand for I.T. workers, produce more I.T. workers*, because we need them here and other countries need them. They're an advantage there and they're an advantage here, so produce more because there is an overall increase in demand. (Arroyo, 2002, emphasis and translation mine)
> *(Kaya pag sinasabi nila brain drain, sabi ko, hindi, naglilingkod doon naglilingkod pa rin dito dahil hindi kinakalimutan 'yung mga pamilya, 'yung pamayanan, at sa ganung paraan pati 'yung bansa natin ay nakikinabang. Ang importante kung ano 'yung nakikita nating demand sa mga skills, an ating school system ay dapat produce nang produce. Kung malaki ang demand sa nurses, produce more nurses; kung malaki ang demand sa I.T. workers, produce more I.T. workers kasi kailangan din natin sila dito, kailangan sa ibang bansa. Kaya pakinabang kung nandoon, pakinabang kung nandito sila, so produce more because there is an overall increase in demand.)*

This dependence of the Philippine labor market on the demands of external markets is evident in how the Philippine government has continued to emphasize and support policies and skills training programs aimed at maintaining Filipinos' competitive edge in terms of linguistic resources.

This has been true in the case of English as proficiency in what is considered as the global lingua franca supposedly makes Filipinos 'ideally suited (for) any multi-racial working environment' (Philippine Overseas Employment Administration, 2006b). Thus, it is not surprising that there have been dire warnings that Filipinos are losing their 'competitive edge' over other countries because of their supposedly declining levels of English competence ('Filipinos' English skills on the decline', *Manila Times*, 2003; 'RP workforce losing edge in English', *Philippine Daily Inquirer*, 2004). A similar discourse has emerged in relation to outsourcing, and more specifically the call center industry (Salonga, 2010). Billed as the country's 'sunshine industry', it has expanded exponentially and now equals or even rivals labor export as an employment and income generator. While there were only two offshore call centers in the Philippines in 2000, there were over a thousand call centers in the country by 2010. The industry employs more than a million Filipinos and in 2012, it generated around US$12 billion in revenue (Salonga, 2010: 80–81). In its earlier attempts to attract businesses, the Philippines had been emphasizing the English proficiency of its workforce and, most especially, the 'Filipinos' familiarity and affinity for American culture and jargon' because of the country's colonial history ('The Philippines fights for US business', *Forbes*, 2003). These are supposedly the country's 'natural advantages' over India ('RP gets serious on outsourcing biz', 2003; 'US firms shifting call center operations to RP', www.inq7.net, last accessed the URL on 26 February 2003), advantages that would be its competitive edge in its bid to become one of, if not the top outsourcing destination in the world (Salonga, 2010: 189).

During the Arroyo presidency from 2001 to 2010, there were explicit pronouncements of a 'return to English'. In her first State of the Nation address in 2001, Arroyo made proficiency in English the major policy goal of the Department of Education. In January 2003, she followed this up by mandating a 'return to English' as the main MOI in Philippine schools. In September 2005, the House Committees on Higher Education and on Basic Education endorsed and sought the immediate approval of House Bill 4701 (HB 4701) which, among other things, would make it mandatory for English to be the official MOI in *all* academic subjects in high school (Rosario, 2005). This bill was passed almost a year later on September 21, 2006. While this bill was never implemented, the push for English during the Arroyo presidency affirmed just how the economic necessity of sustaining labor migration from the country has been and continues to be the most striking development in language policy and planning in the Philippines (Gonzalez, 1988, 1998a, 2004; Sibayan & Gonzalez, 1996).

Even with the implementation of Mother-Tongue Based Multilingual Education (MTBMLE) starting in 2009, in which the mother tongues are to be used as the primary media of instruction in all subjects from pre-school up to the end of elementary education (Gunigundo, 2010), the status of English as being absolutely essential for the continued competitiveness of Filipino workers has remained largely unchanged and unquestioned. In fact, supporters of MTBMLE have been careful to point out that using the mother tongue in the lower grades would help children learn English better in the upper grades (Tupas, 2009; Tupas & Lorente, 2014).

The making of skilled workers of the world

While the continued maintenance of the grip of English in the Philippines may be the most visible impact of labor migration on the linguistic economy and language policies of the country, the ways in which English is indexed or framed have shifted, especially with the state's renewed emphasis on deploying skilled migrants. So, while English proficiency, by and large, is still portrayed as a linguistic capital of OFWs, it is now also being depicted as their *minimum* linguistic capital or as their 'security language'. As a minimum requirement, it would seem that the ability to communicate in English is no longer sufficient to sustain the 'competitiveness' of OFWs.

Since the launch of the LSI in 2007, learning to speak another language, apart from English, has been touted as 'the next hot job skill' and 'an advantage in the global market' (Jaymalin, 2014). As of 2015, the foreign language courses offered by the LSI are: Basic English Language (100 hours), Basic Japanese Language and Culture (150 hours), Basic Korean Language and Culture (100 hours), Basic Mandarin Chinese Language and Culture (100 hours), Basic Arabic Language and Saudi/Gulf Culture (100 hours) and Basic Spanish Language for Different Vocations (100 hours). A total of 35 LSIs are listed on the TESDA website (TESDA Planning Office Labor Market Information Division, 2015). Not all of the courses may be offered in each LSI. The language courses offered by TESDA have no tuition fee; Filipinos 18 years and above can take the courses and priority is given to those who are pre-qualified to work locally and overseas. In 2013, 7341 trainees finished these language courses (Technical Education and Skills Development Authority, 2014).

Additionally, 'workplace communication skills' have become one of the 'basic competencies' in practically all of TESDA's training programs, from caregiving to game art development, from seafaring to housekeeping. This introduction of a communication skills element in all of TESDA's training courses may point to how the new work order where linguistic and communication 'skills' have come to dominate forms of work (Cameron, 2002) has, at least discursively, come to be inserted in the economies of labor in and labor migration from the Philippines. However, it is more likely that 'communication skills' here are 'skills terms' deployed for their 'strategic indexicality' (expressing alignment with corporate values) and 'denotational indeterminacy' (knowledge and practices referred to as skills are quite disparate) (Urciuoli, 2008: 211).

This representation of Filipino workers as 'skilled' workers who can work in 'high value jobs' and/or in premium positions in the marginalized occupational niches where they may gain a profit from being distinctive from the rest of the competition comes at a time when there seems to be ever-increasing competition in the global labor market from other labor-sending countries. While the Philippines was the first mover in the centralized management of labor export and is held up as the model for managing labor migration, other labor-sending countries like Indonesia, Sri Lanka and Pakistan have followed suit in centralizing the management of labor migration.

Also, some of the markets that were the traditional destinations of Filipino workers may now be saturated or may have restrictions. Shifts in the economies of the receiving country may also mean that Filipinos now face increased competition from citizens. This development is perhaps most marked in the case of migrant Filipino nurses whose traditional and desired destination was the United States. The Immigration Nursing Relief Act passed in 1989 sought to institutionalize the end of US hospitals' recruitment of foreign-trained nurses (Ceniza Choy, 2003) and there is a long waiting period for US immigrant visa approval and the completion of examination requirements (Guevarra, 2010: 111). Furthermore, large-scale shifts in the American economy have resulted in what the *New York Times* in a recent report called 'a shifting middle', that is, 'where industrial jobs have grown scarce, nurses and other health care professionals are increasingly leading the way to middle-income lifestyles' (Searcey *et al.*, 2015) with, it seems, more Americans opting for or moving to jobs in the health-care professions. There is a glut of nurses in the Philippines and they are heading to the Middle East and Singapore, as well as to Japan and Germany.

These shifts also come at a time when, as discussed in Chapter 1, labor migration is increasingly intensively mediated. In labor-receiving countries, language requirements are being imposed on temporary migrant workers before they migrate. In these cases, language proficiency serves as a defined border by being positioned as an 'objective' standard of qualification. This is the case in Korea, for example, where foreign workers have to take and pass the Employment Permit System Test of Proficiency in Korean (EPS-TOPIK), and where their ranking in the test determines whether they will be prioritized for employment in the manufacturing, construction, fish breeding, agriculture and stock breeding industries. Thus, it is perhaps no surprise that one of the free language courses that the LSI offers is Korean. There is also an emerging pattern of labor-receiving countries not just requiring language proficiency for entry but actually facilitating and even paying for the learning of the language in the Philippines before the migrants leave. This may be indicative of the selective permeability of nation state borders when they operate within a migration infrastructure (Meier & Lorente, 2014; Xiang & Lindquist, 2014). This is the case for the Triple Win project, a German project that aims to 'ethically recruit' 500 nurses from the Philippines for placement in German hospitals by 2016. Philippine nurses recruited for the project are required to have proof of a B2 level of German language proficiency before they can be deployed; the language learning of the nurses is sponsored by the German government and conducted by the Goethe Institut in the Philippines (Meier & Lorente, 2014). This is also the case for nurses and care workers who have been recruited to work in Japan (GMA News, 2014). The six-month Japanese language course is supposed to be followed by another six-month training program in Japan before the nurses and care workers are assigned to various hospitals throughout the country; they will eventually take the national examination for nurses or care workers (in Japanese), which will allow them to work and be paid at a similar level to Japanese nurses and care workers. Filipino nurses have also been recruited to work in Finland where they undergo intensive language training (Uutiset, 2012). Recently, part of this intensive training has also been done earlier, in the Philippines, before the migrants leave (Sunni, private correspondence, 2014).

This skillifying of migrant Filipino workers serves not only to ensure the profitability of the Philippine labor enterprise, it is also through this that the Philippine state can turn the laboring bodies of OFWs into bodies the nation can and should be proud of. Ensuring the competitiveness of OFWs is framed as the responsibility of the state, as it is the duty of the state to enable its citizens to take advantage of opportunities to work overseas should they choose to take the option.

Summary

This chapter has examined how the emergence of the Philippines as a labor brokerage state is linked to the durability of structures that can be traced back to colonialism. Language, as 'English', as 'foreign language' and as 'communication skill', is crucial to how the Philippines creates its position as the premier labor-sending country. The shift from 'English' to a growing emphasis on 'other' languages, skills in learning another language or 'communication skills', is the state's response to increasing competition and faster and more unpredictable changes to global labor markets, and it is how the Philippines sustains its position as a site of production where bodies can be scripted and transformed into globally marketable, made-to-order and profitable migrant labor for particular niches in the global labor market. This chapter has also shown the scale of the mechanisms (i.e. the education system, language-in-education policy, state-sponsored work training and labor migration institutions) by which the Philippine state intervenes in the labor market-related migration trajectories of its citizens. These mechanisms call attention not just to how states as power institutions construct particular representations of Filipino labor but also to how states legitimize the 'export' of migrant bodies for profit by ensuring that they have the supposed access to the linguistic resources they need in order to be more 'globally competitive'. The Philippine labor enterprise's project of ensuring the competitiveness of its migrant workers has material consequences: it reproduces inequalities within the state and reinforces the state's marginal role as the provider of made-to-order, readily deployable, flexible workers in the global labor market. The next chapter focuses on how the Philippine state scripts HSWs, i.e. domestic workers, who constitute the largest proportion of OFWs.

3 Assembling the 'Supermaid': Language and Communication Skills for 'Vulnerable Occupations'

On a Friday afternoon in December 2009, I watched around 60 Filipino women seated in closely packed rows in an air-conditioned room on the fifth floor of the main building of the Overseas Workers Welfare Administration (OWWA) in Pasay City. They listened to a lecturer, a turbaned man dressed in a long white *kurta* with a microphone in hand. It was the second day of a three-day OWWA Arabic Language and Culture Training, one of the requirements of the Comprehensive Pre-Departure Education Program (CPDEP) for first-time migrant household service workers (HSWs). The women attending the training were bound for destinations in the Middle East: Bahrain, Dubai, Kuwait, Oman, Qatar, Saudi Arabia and the United Arab Emirates. Aside from Arabic, five other language and culture trainings were being offered, four of them reflecting major destinations of Filipino HSWs: Cantonese (Hong Kong), Hebrew (Israel), Italian (Italy) and Mandarin (Singapore and Taiwan). The fifth language and culture training being offered was for English, which 'being universally spoken is considered to be the security language' (OFW Tribune, 2012). The language and culture training is intended to 'help (HSWs) get along in the day-to-day association with employers and foreign nationals' (Overseas Workers Welfare Administration, 2008) and 'help (them) adapt easily to their country of destination' (Overseas Workers Welfare Administration, 2007).

An OWWA staff member later gave me a copy of the material that was being used during the training and had been distributed to the women: a mimeographed booklet entitled 'Arabic Language and Culture Familiarization'. Written in Filipino were brief textbook-like introductions to Arabic countries and to Arabic society, culture, religion and food. The rest of the booklet was made up of tables of words, phrases or sentences. Each table had four columns: a 'transliteration' of the Arabic word in the

Latin alphabet, a Filipino translation, an English translation and the words written in Arabic script. There were tables for numbers; days of the week; months; tastes; personal, demonstrative and interrogative pronouns; and a few examples of how to use them. There were also tables that listed words for food (vegetables, fruits, kinds of meat), family members, common illnesses, parts of the house, furniture and objects in the house, and caring for the sick. A table entitled 'household chores' was made up entirely of imperative sentences like *Itbakhiy al'aan* (You cook now), *Igsiliy al-malaabis* (Wash the clothes) and *Ah-dhiriyl laban lit-tifl* (Prepare (a) milk for the infant). Another list entitled 'daily conversations' listed formulaic utterances deemed important for a migrant Filipino HSW in the Middle East, including questions like *Min ayna Ji'ti?* (Where are you going?) and *Ayna Assifara?* (Where is the embassy?); requests like *Hatiy liy ka'san minas shai* (Please give me a cup of tea); announcements that meals are ready like *Al-futuwru jaahiz* (The breakfast is ready); and other basic phrases like *Ana a'asifa* (I am sorry), *Ana mareedha* (I am sick) and *Ana mushtaqatun Li Ahliy* (I miss my family).

In the last few pages of the booklet was a list entitled 'some of the dos and don'ts in the Middle East' that was written in Filipino: *Magaral ka ng Arabic dahil ito ang susi upang lalo kang mapalapit sa mga tao sa gitnang silangan* (Learn Arabic because this is the key to your becoming close to people from the Middle East); *Huwag patulan ang amo kapag nagalit dahil madali din naman mawala ang galit ng mga Arabo. Mas nakakabuting tumahimik ka na lang.* (Don't retort back when your employer gets angry because the anger of Arabs easily dissipates. It would be better if you just kept quiet); and *Magpakabait ka, dahil pag mabait ka sa kanila mabait din sila sa 'yo* (Be good, because if you are good to them, they will also be good to you).

The Arabic Language and Culture Training is a concrete instance of when the Philippine state scripts Filipino workers, and the booklet I collected could be considered an artifact of such a script. The OWWA language and culture-specific training is one of the requirements of the Reform Package for Household Service Workers (HSWs) that was instituted by the Philippine Overseas Employment Administration (POEA) in 2007. Only first-time HSWs (i.e. domestic workers) are required to go through the training; OFWs who are deployed to all other occupations are not required to go through the training. This is because Filipino domestic workers (FDWs) are probably the most extensively 'branded' and, for that matter, scripted Filipino bodies circulating in the global marketplace (Guevarra, 2014). This may reflect the anxieties that are triggered when the figure of the Filipino is identified and is perhaps even conflated with particular personhoods, or particular bodies. Aguilar (1996: 126) has argued that this anxiety over FDWs is actually 'shame' and that this is felt by the elite, upper and middle classes of Philippine society '…who detest the thought that the country has become, in their mind, the servant of the world. It is as though the nation is at the bottom of a global pecking order, a position that magnifies their sense of inferiority a thousand fold'. In this regard, then, 'the bodies of domestic (workers) have become sites for the construction of and contestation over the national body abroad. (DW)-bodies serve as objects of the nation's struggle for subject-status on the global scene' (Tadiar, 1997: 165).

Protecting the Filipino Domestic Worker

The export of women as domestic workers has always been highly controversial and highly contested in the Philippines. Non-government organizations (NGOs), scholars and grassroots migrant activists, among others, have long decried the Philippine state's role in 'facilitating women's migration as low wage workers in gender-typed and gender-stereotyped jobs that make them especially vulnerable to exploitation and sexual abuse' (Rodriguez, 2010: 93). These 'anxieties' would probably not have been addressed had it not been for the Flor Contemplacion case in 1995, which triggered such outrage that the Philippine state had to confront and address the anxieties over Filipino women's migration as domestic workers in order to legitimize its program of labor export. Flor Contemplacion was an FDW in Singapore who was sentenced to death in 1995 for allegedly murdering a fellow FDW and the child she was taking care of. Many Filipinos believed she was innocent and that she had been set up to take the fall for a Singaporean. Diplomatic efforts to stop her execution were futile. In this sense, the shape of the discourses branding the FDW can be traced back to the state's response to the crisis precipitated by the Flor Contemplacion case.

At the height of the case, a state-appointed body called the Gancayo Commission was appointed to evaluate the impact of women's migration on the Philippines. The Commission came to the following conclusion:

> [T]he saddest reality as found in the mission is the irreparable damage that has been inflicted to the reputation of the Filipina woman in the international scene because of the indiscriminate deployment of our women as domestic helpers and entertainers. Our nation has gained the embarrassing reputation that we are a country of DHs, entertainers, and even prostitutes…It is said that even in a certain dictionary the latest definition of the word 'Filipina' is a 'housemaid'. (Rodriguez, 2010: 93–94)

After their findings, the Commission introduced the notion of 'vulnerable occupations' as a special category of state protection (Guevarra, 2010: 38). These occupations included domestic work and entertainment work. Following this policy inclusion, the state assumed the posture of a governing body that was responsive to and could appease its public – by being able to protect migrant women – even as it continued to profit from the participation of these women in 'vulnerable' occupations. One of the primary outcomes of the Gancayo Commission's findings was the introduction of 'gender-sensitive' programs 'empowering' migrant women. The introduction of such programs could be read as the state's recognition of the risks faced by migrant Filipino women abroad and of the necessity of protecting them. But it can also be read as a way of addressing the anxieties and the 'shame' engendered by the image of the FDW. Read this way, the protection of the FDW had become tantamount to protecting the nation brand.

Just how the Philippine state proposed to construct, regulate and protect the nation brand (via protecting the FDW) is encapsulated in Republic Act 8042 (RA 8042), also known as the Migrant Workers and Overseas Filipinos Act of 1995, which was passed soon after the execution of Flor Contemplacion. RA 8042 mandated many policies for better 'protecting' migrant women, but it also declared that 'the State recognizes that the ultimate protection to all migrant workers is the possession of skills. Pursuant to this and as soon as practicable, the government shall deploy and/or allow the deployment only of skilled Filipino workers' (Republic of the Philippines, 1995). This was further strengthened by RA 10022 in 2010.

The twinning of protection with the possession of skills should be highlighted here. By making this move, the Philippine state not only sought to create a competitive and desirable brand of Filipino workers, it equated the 'protection' of migrants with equipping them with skills, where 'the possession of such skills by Filipino workers abroad is their best protection from any abuse or maltreatment' (Marcelo, 2007). By doing this, it effectively passed the responsibility for protecting the brand and for protecting the OFW to the 'vulnerable' workers themselves (Urciuoli, 2008; Urciuoli & LaDousa, 2013).

The Supermaid: Rebranding Filipina Domestic Workers

The most recent development in branding the FDW came in the form of the 'Reform Package Affecting Household Service Workers (HSWs)' by the POEA on February 5, 2007. Under the then president Gloria Macapagal Arroyo, it was advertised and framed as part of the 'Supermaid' program

Assembling the 'Supermaid' 57

Figure 3.1 Advertisement for Supermaid program, 30 August 2009 (Source: www.ellentordesillas.com/2009/08/30/shaming-the-shameless/)

(see Figure 3.1). The notion of 'supermaids' was originally introduced by Arroyo in August 2006 during a roundtable discussion on job and livelihood opportunities, especially for workers who were then returning from war-torn Lebanon. The president said that the government had put in place livelihood opportunities and a training program to upgrade the skills of Filipinos going abroad as domestic workers so that they would not just be ordinary domestic workers but 'supermaids' (Dalangin-Fernandez, 2006). This skills-upgrading training would produce Filipino supermaids who 'can administer first aid, attend to emergency procedures such as evacuation when there is a fire, *can speak the language of the country of employment*, aside from performing the usual chores of housekeeping and cooking' (Dalangin-Fernandez, 2006, emphasis mine). The possession of such skills would not only entitle Filipino domestic workers to receive higher salaries (Syjuco, 2007), but it would also 'help (HSWs) adapt easily to their country of destination' (OWWA Performance Highlights, 2007) and 'help (HSWs) get along in the day-to-day association with employers and foreign nationals' (OWWA Performance Highlights, 2008).

Under the new guidelines, would-be FDWs (now called 'household service workers') with visas issued after December 16, 2006, would have to meet the following requirements: a minimum age of 23, a minimum entry salary of US$400, a 216-hour Technical Education and Skills Development Authority (TESDA) NC II Certificate for Household Services and attendance at an OWWA country-specific language and culture orientation. In its Governing Board Resolution 8 rationalizing the introduction of these guidelines, the POEA reproduced the discourses of RA 8042: 'migrant workers for deployment require the highest degree of protection owing to their gender and the vulnerable state of their employment', and 'the State recognizes that the ultimate protection to all migrant workers is the possession of skills and familiarity with the country and language of their employers and host governments'. In seeking acceptance for these new requirements, the POEA further argued that 'the certification one gets from this training would enable a household help to apply for a higher job level in hotels ...HSWs must welcome the training program. We are adding more value to the skills of our HSWs'. Upgrading the skills of domestic workers would translate to Filipinos being given a premium by employers, i.e. 'they would be able to earn more'. These requirements applied only to the HSW; it did not apply to any of the other OFWs.

The introduction of these new guidelines was met by a storm of protest from recruitment agencies and workers. At least 8000 workers, most of them women applying for overseas jobs as domestic workers, held a protest rally on January 15, 2007, at the Liwasang Bonifacio and in front of the DOLE offices in Intramuros, Manila, protesting the new guidelines ('More rallies vs hiring policy for Pinoy DH', www.gmanetwork.com, 2007). In Hong Kong, about 5000 FDWs marched on the streets on January 28, 2007, to demand the immediate scrapping of the new POEA guidelines ('5T Pinoy maids march in Hong Kong vs. new deployment rules', *Cebu Daily News*, 2007).

Recruitment agencies, workers and migrant NGOs protested the $400 minimum wage, arguing that this would effectively price Filipinos out of the market for domestic workers. The groups also complained about the steep costs of the TESDA NC2 training and the OWWA country-specific language and culture orientation, the fees for which ranged from ₱5,000 to ₱10,000, and the additional amount of time (approximately 27 days) it would take for them to complete the training.

Domestic workers and some migrant groups also questioned the government's capacity to enforce the salary guidelines and its motivation for collecting more fees for additional certificates, the general sentiment being that this was another 'money-making scheme' of the government. The Department of Labor and Employment (DOLE) and the POEA responded by highlighting that the guidelines were intended to raise the working conditions of disadvantaged Filipino HSWs globally, and that the issue had been 'hijacked' by recruitment agencies who stood to lose their profitability because of the 'no placement fee' guidelines (DOLE, 2007). The $400 minimum salary would help secure a premium niche for Filipino 'supermaids' and, hopefully, better working and living conditions for them ('Superpay for supermaids', *Manila Times*, 2007). The additional training that Filipinos would go through would also enable them to apply for 'higher-level' service jobs in, for example, hotels and restaurants.

Table 3.1 Differences between the PDOS for OFWs and the CPDEP for HSWs

Pre-departure orientation seminar (for overseas Filipino workers who are not HSWs)	Comprehensive pre-departure education program (for migrant HSWs)
Compulsory 8-hour (1 day) seminar that is country specific (and in some cases skill specific). The seminar is composed of the following modules: • Migration realities – code of conduct for OFWs, possible challenges of work abroad • Country profile – laws, culture and customs of the host country • Employment contract – rights and responsibilities of workers as per their contract • Health and safety • Financial literacy • Government programs and services • Travel procedures and tips	Compulsory 4- to 7-day program specific to migrant household service workers, jointly conducted by accredited NGOs, private PDOS providers and OWWA. The program is composed of • 1 day PDOS (with the same topics as OFWs); HSWs and OFWs going to the same country attend the same PDOS • 3–6 days language and culture training in Arabic (for Middle East-bound workers, Cantonese for Hong Kong-bound workers, Hebrew for Israel-bound workers, Mandarin for Taiwan and Singapore-bound workers, Italian for workers bound for Italy, and English. The Mandarin training lasts for 6 days. All other trainings last for 3 days. • Stress management course

Source: Batistella and Asis (2011).

Since 2009, the language and culture training of the HSW reform package has been expanded into the CPDEP, which incorporated the one-day Pre-Departure Orientation Seminar (PDOS) that had been required of all OFWs since 1983. The formalization of the CPDEP, on top of the requirements imposed by the 2007 HSW reform package, hints at the very different ways in which FDWs were being enregistered compared to other OFWs. Table 3.1 summarizes the differences between the PDOS and the CPDEP.

As can be seen in Table 3.1, only FDWs are required to go through language and culture training and a stress management course before they leave the country. Implicitly, the reform package and the additional requirements were a means of regulation: they were supposed to have the effect of lessening the number of Filipino women who would leave the country to work as foreign domestic workers overseas. While there was a momentary decline in the number of women leaving the country as domestic workers in 2007 and 2008, soon after the introduction of the reform package, the number of HSWs actually increased and more than doubled between 2009 and 2012 (Batistella & Asis, 2011).

Scripting the Supermaid

With regard to the new language and communication requirements set by the POEA for FDWs, they echoed the emerging discourse of competitiveness for OFWs discussed in Chapter 2: (1) the ability to communicate in English is considered to be a 'minimum requirement'; (2) 'workplace communication skills' are considered to be a basic skill of HSWs and, indeed, is one of the basic modules of the TESDA Household Service Worker NC II Program; and (3) some knowledge of a 'foreign' language, i.e. the language of the destination country, is necessary, as seen in the requirement that prospective domestic workers undergo country-specific language and culture training with the OWWA. The Filipino 'supermaid', as constructed by these new POEA guidelines, is an English-knowing multilingual, knowledgeable of the language (e.g. Cantonese for Hong Kong, Arabic for the Middle East) and culture of the household she is going to work for, and with competent 'workplace communication skills'. In the next section, I take a closer look at what these requirements actually translate to.

Workplace communication skills

The TESDA NC II Household Services Training is supposed to run for at least 216 hours or around 2 and a half months. Students, that is, prospective HSWs, pay the costs for the training. To be qualified to enroll in the TESDA NC II Household Services training, the trainee must at least be 'a high school graduate, [...] able to communicate in English; and [...] be physically, emotionally, psychologically, and mentally fit'. As mentioned in Chapter 1, English is portrayed as the minimum requirement here. The TESDA NC II training can be conducted by TESDA or by any of the private school or training programs licensed and regulated by TESDA. Figure 3.2 is from the TESDA training regulations for certification; workplace communication skills is a basic competency and the regulations outline in detailed Tayloristic fashion the units, elements and criteria for this basic competency. Not included in the figure are the 'range of variables' and the 'evidence guide' for workplace communication skills that are broken down and specified. Workplace communication is not the only competency that is outlined in this way; in fact, of all the competencies, it is the one that takes up the least number of pages in the training guidelines. All of the basic, common and core competencies are detailed in the same way. Such competencies include 'cleaning the living room, dining room, bedrooms, toilet and kitchen;

SECTION 2 COMPETENCY STANDARDS

This section gives the details of the contents of the basic, common and core units of competency required in **HOUSEHOLD SERVICES NC II**.

BASIC COMPETENCIES

UNIT OF COMPETENCY	:	**PARTICIPATE IN WORKPLACE COMMUNICATION**
UNIT CODE	:	500311105
UNIT DESCRIPTOR	:	This unit covers the knowledge, skills and attitudes required to gather, interpret and convey information in response to workplace requirements.

ELEMENT		PERFORMANCE CRITERIA
		Italicized terms are elaborated in the Range of Variables
1. Obtain and convey workplace information	1.1	Specific and relevant information is accessed from *appropriate sources*
	1.2	Effective questioning, active listening and speaking skills are used to gather and convey information
	1.3	Appropriate *medium* is used to transfer information and ideas
	1.4	Appropriate non-verbal communication is used
	1.5	Appropriate lines of communication with supervisors and colleagues are identified and followed
	1.6	Defined workplace procedures for the location and *storage* of information are used
	1.7	Personal interaction is carried out clearly and concisely
2. Participate in workplace meetings and discussions	2.1	Team meetings are attended on time
	2.2	Own opinions are clearly expressed and those of others are listened to without interruption
	2.3	Meeting inputs are consistent with the meeting purpose and established *protocols*
	2.4	**Workplace interactions** are conducted in a courteous manner
	2.5	Questions about simple routine workplace procedures and matters concerning working conditions of employment are tasked and responded to
	2.6	Meetings outcomes are interpreted and implemented
3. Complete relevant work related documents	3.1	Range of *forms* relating to conditions of employment are completed accurately and legibly
	3.2	Workplace data are recorded on standard workplace forms and documents
	3.3	Basic mathematical processes are used for routine calculations
	3.4	Errors in recording information on forms/documents are identified and properly acted upon
	3.5	Reporting requirements to supervisor are completed according to organizational guidelines

Figure 3.2 Excerpt from the Training Regulations for Household Services NC II

washing and ironing clothes linen and fabric; preparing hot/cold meals/food; providing food and beverage service'. The training regulations also specify how the competencies should be taught in terms of 'learning outcomes, methodology, assessment approach'.

As discussed in Chapter 2, workplace communication skills are a component in all of TESDA's training courses and like the other courses, 'communication skills' here are 'skills terms' deployed for their 'strategic indexicality' (expressing alignment with corporate values) and 'denotational indeterminacy' (knowledge and practices referred to as skills are quite disparate) (Urciuoli, 2008: 211). The descriptions of the workplace communication skills could well have been taken from a business communication textbook or other similar texts; they are generic and 'what such texts suggest is not so much a process of translation across languages as the global spread and relocalization of certain language practices' (Pennycook, 2010: 112).

But how were these descriptions relocalized into certain language practices? Deboneville (2014: 73–74) gave an example of what the TESDA guidelines translated to. The scene he describes here is from his field notes in April 2013 as he observed the assessment of several students in a TESDA-certified training school. The students were being assessed on what was called the 'Russian table setting'. The assessment was conducted in English.

> Dressed in a T-shirt, jeans and a pair of sneakers, covered by a green apron, a net for hair and cloth on the arms, a few dozen candidates waited in the corner of a room decorated as a dining room while the teacher sits at the table.
> – 'Number five, your turn!' says the teacher.
> The candidate runs in without saying a word. She goes to the cabinet where the dishes are stored and scans the different objects with a distraught air.
> – 'Faster, faster!', roared the teacher. 'Your employer is hungry!'
> The candidate quickly takes a few dishes before heading to the table and begins to put the dishes under the eyes of the evaluator.
> – 'What are you doing? [pause] First, you must say: "Excuse me ma'am/sir, are you ready for dinner?" Be polite, and then, when you are setting the table, say "Sorry ma'am/sir". Do it again!'
> – Candidate incorporates the recommendations of the instructor.
> – 'Okay, what's next?' asks the teacher.
> – Looking down, the candidate returns to the buffet and grabs the silverware, then the glasses.
> – 'Stand up properly', ordered the instructor. The candidate stands suddenly. The candidate takes the pitcher of water and begins to fill the water glass.
> – 'Stop. What did I tell you? First you ask your employer, "Excuse me ma'am/sir. Would you like some water?" Go. And don't forget to smile. Always put a smile on your face. It's important for your employer!'
> – 'Excuse me ma'am. Would you like some water?', the candidate said with a timid smile.
> – 'OK next! Number six'.

The language and culture-specific training

Apart from knowing English and having workplace communication skills, Filipino 'supermaids' are also constructed to be knowledgeable in the language and culture of the destination country. This means being able to understand Cantonese if they are heading to Hong Kong, Arabic if they are going to any of the countries in the Middle East, etc., and possibly Mandarin Chinese if they are going to Singapore. Six language and culture familiarization courses are currently being offered: Arabic, Hebrew, Italian, Cantonese, Mandarin and English. The 20-hour courses (Arabic, Hebrew, Italian, Cantonese and English) last for three days. Of these 20 hours, only 16 actually go to training in language and culture, as four hours are devoted to a stress management workshop which seeks to prepare would-be domestic workers for problems they may face with the families they leave behind in the Philippines and the families they will work for in their various destinations. In 2007, 129,159 OFWs ready for deployment underwent the country-specific language and culture training as part of their pre-departure orientation seminar. In 2008, 60,979 would-be foreign domestic workers were trained in basic spoken and written Arabic, Cantonese, Mandarin, Italian, English and Hebrew, ostensibly to help them in their day-to-day interactions with their foreign employers (Overseas Workers Welfare Administration, 2009). In 2011, 127,165 HSWs on new contracts underwent the training and in 2012, 156,452 HSWs attended the training.

In the booklets used for the language and culture familiarization program, the following topics are covered: introduction to the destination country and culture (i.e. religion, government system, traditions and food), introduction to the destination country's alphabet and numbers, greetings, vocabulary lists for vegetables, fruits, tastes, kinds of meat and parts of the body, parts of the home, household chores and family members. Expressions and words used for caring for the sick and describing common illnesses are also given, as is a list of specific cultural dos and don'ts in the destination country. Obviously, the OWWA orientation will not be sufficient to make would-be 'supermaids' proficient in the language of their destination countries, but this development reinforces the image of migrant Filipino workers as being 'flexible' and able to work with anyone, whether or not they speak English.

Similar to household Spanish booklets for employers of Spanish housekeepers in the United States (Divita, 2013; Schwartz, 2006), the expressions selected for the booklet constituted a limited register explicitly meant to facilitate transactional communication; many of the expressions

Qatti'iy addajaaj	Hiwain mo ang manok	Cut the chicken.	قطعي الدجاج
Qatti'yl laham	Hiwain mo ang karne	Cut or slice the meat.	قطعي اللحم
Igsiliy al-malaabis	Labahan mo ang mga damit	Wash the clothes.	إغسلي الملابس
Najjhifiyl gurfa	Maglinis ka sa kuwarto	Clean the room.	نظفي الغرفة
Najjhifiyl hammam	Linisin mo ang kubeta	Clean the toilet.	نظفي الحمام
Alliqiy al-malaabis	Isampay mo ang mga damit.	Hang the clothes.	علقي الملابس
A'tiniy maa'	Bigyan mo ako ng tubig.	Give me water.	أعطيني ماء
A'tiyniy ka'san minas shay aw al-qahwa	Bigyan mo ako ng isang basong tsa o kape.	Give me a cup of tea or coffee.	هاتي لي كأسا من الشاي
Ath-imiy al-awlaad	Pakainin mo ang mga bata	Feed the children.	أطعمي الأولاد
Qawwiy al-malaabis	Plansahin mo ang mga damit	Iron the clothes.	كوي الملابس
Ah-dhiriyl laban lit-tifl	Gawaan mo ng gatas ang sanggol.	Prepare a milk for the infant.	احضري اللبن للطفل
Irmiy azzubaala	Itapon mo ang basura	Throw the garbage.	إرمي الزبالة
Najjhifiy al-mawkit	Linisin mo ang carpet	Clean the carpet.	نظفي الموكيت
Rattibiy al-karaasiy	Ayusin mo ang mga silya	Arrange the chairs.	رتبي الكراسي
Agliqiyl baab	Isara mo ang pinto	Close the door.	أغلقي الباب
Iftahiyl baab	Buksan mo ang pinto	Open the door.	إفتحي الباب
Igsiliy assuhoun	Hugasan mo ang mga plato	Wash the plates.	إغسلي الصحون
Igsiliy al-akwaab	Hugasan mo ang mga baso	Wash the glasses.	إغسلي الأكواب

28

DINING PREPARATION تجهيز الطعام
PAGHAHANDA SÀ PAGKAIN

Transliteration	*Filipino*	*English*	*Arabic*
Najjhifiy Maa-idatas sufra.	Linisin mo ang mesang kainan.	Clean the table.	نظفي مائدة السفرة
Dha-iy githaa' attawila alayha.	Ilagay mo ang mantel sa mesa	Put the table clothe.	ضعي غطاء الطاولة عليها
Dha-iy assuhoun wal-akwaab wal-malaaiq wal ash-waak alal maa'ida.	Ilagay mo ang mga plato, baso, kutsara at tinidor sa mesa.	Put the plates, glasses, spoons and forks on the table.	ضعي الصحون والأكواب والملاعق والأشواك عليها
Ah-dhiriy attha-aam.	Dalhin mo ang mga pagkain.	Bring the foods.	أحضري الطعام
Ah-dhiriy al-aruz wal-khubz wal-laham wad dajaaj was samak wal-khadraawaat.	Dalhin mona ang kanin, karne, isda at gulay.	Bring the rice, bread, chicken and vegetables.	أحضري الأرز والخبز واللحم والدجاج والسمك والخضروات
Ah-dhiriy alfwa-akih	Dalhin mo ang mga prutas	Bring the fruits.	أحضري الفواكه

أعضاء العائلة
A'adhaa'ul aa-ila
Ang mga miyembro ng pamilya / Family members

Translitera-tion	*Filipino*	*English*	*Arabic*
Ab / Waalid	Tatay	Father	والد/أب
Umm / Waalida	Nanay	Mother	أم/والدة
Akh	Kapatid na lalaki	Brother	أخ
Ukht	Kapatid na babae	Sister	أخت
Ibn	Anak na lalaki	Son	ابن
Ibna	Anak na babae	Daughter	ابنة
Amm	Tiyohin sa ama	paternal uncle	عم
Amma	Tiyahin sa ama	paternal aunt	عمة
Khaal	Tiyohin sa ina	maternal uncle	خال
Khaala	Tiyahin sa ina	maternal aunt	خالة

Figure 3.3 Excerpt from the Arabic Language and Culture Training booklet

were one-way directives meant to be understood by the domestic worker. More importantly, the booklets modeled a relationship between domestic workers and their employers where the domestic worker is a passive participant on whom the burden of understanding the employer is placed (Figure 3.3).

It is not just through 'skills' that the responsibility for protecting the nation brand is passed on to FDWs. Migrant women are inducted into an ethic of self-discipline, arguably another aspect of the script of servitude, as the 'brand ambassadors' of the Philippines. There are sections in the CPDEP where trainers go over a list of dos and don'ts particular to the countries they are going to (see Figure 3.4). These dos and don'ts always include exhortations to be 'polite' and to 'learn and understand your host country's language'. Topics that can and cannot be discussed in conversations with employers or locals are highlighted, as are acceptable and unacceptable ways of dressing, among other things.

Aynal bawwaba	Saan ang pintuan?	Where is the gate?	أين البوابة؟
Aynal Mustashfa?	Saan ang ospital?	Where is the hospital?	أين المستشفى؟
Ayna Assifara?	Saan ang embahada?	Where is the embassy?	أين السفارة؟
Ma isma assafeer?	Anong pangalan ng ambassador?	What is the name of the ambassador?	ما اسم السفير
Hal Al qunsul Mawjud?	Nandito ba ang kunsul?	Is the consul around?	هل القنصل موجود.
Hal Maaka Hawiya?	May I.D. ka ba?	Do you have Identification Card?	هل معك هوية؟
Hal Indaka fulus? Noqud?	May pera ka ba?	Do you have money?	هل عندك فلوس؟
La tataakh khariy.	Huwag kang paluh.	Don't be late	لا تتأخري.
Itbakhiy al'an	Magsaing kana ngayon.	Please cook now.	اطبخي الآن
Najjhifiy alhammam	Pakilinis mo ang kubeta.	Please clean the comfort room.	نظفي الحمام
Hatiy liy ka'san minas shai	Bigyan mo ako ng isang basong tsa.	Please give me a cup of tea.	هاتي لي كأساً من الشاي.
Hatiy liy ka'san minal maa'.	Bigyan mo ako ng isang basong tubig.	Please give me a glass of water.	هاتي لي كأساً من الماء.
Al-futuwru jaahiz	Ang almusal ay handa na.	The breakfast is ready.	الفطور جاهز
Al-gada'u jaahiz	Ang pananghalian ay handa na.	The lunch is now ready.	الغداء جاهز
Al-ashaa'u jaahiz	Ang hapunan ay handa na	Dinner is now prepared.	العشاء جاهز
Igsiliy Al malaabis	Labahan mo ang mga damit	Wash the clothes	اغسلي الملابس
Ruddiy alaa Al haatif	Sagutin mo ang telepono	Answer the telephone	ردي على الهاتف
Id-habiy Ila Baqqala	Punta ka sa tindahan	Go to the grocery	اذهبي إلى البقالة

Ath-imiy al awlaad	Pakainin mo ang mga bata	Feed the children	أطعمي الأولاد
Naamiy Al aan	Matulog ka na.	Sleep now	نامي الآن
La tudkhiliy ahadan fil manzil	Huwag ka magpapasok ng sino man sa bahay	Don't let anybody enter the house	لا تدخلي أحداً في المنزل
Agliqiy al-baab	Isara mo ang pinto	Close the door	أغلقي الباب
Iftahiy al bab	Buksan mo ang pinto	Open the door	افتحي الباب

Some of the Dos and Don'ts in the Middle East
(Ang mga dapat gawin at hindi dapat gawin sa gitnang silangan)

Ang mga dapat gawin

- Igalang mo ang kultura at tradisyon ng bansang pinagtatrabahuhan mo;
- Magpakabait ka, dahil pagmabait ka sa kanila mabait din sila sa'yo;
- Maging masipag, mapagkatiwalaan at tapat sa trabaho at amo;
- Mag-aral ka ng Arabic dahil ito ang susi upang lalo kang mapalapit sa mga tao sa gitnang silangan;
- Kapag binati ka nila ng ***Assalamo Alaykum*** sumagot ka ng ***wa Alaykumus Salam;***
- Manatiling nakatakip ang buhok at nakasuot ng mahabang damit habang nagtatrabaho;
- Ipakita mo na gustung gusto mo ang kultura nila;
- Mag-tanong tungkol sa relihiyon at kultura nila dahil gustung gusto nila ito;
- Lagi kang mag-pasalamat sa kanila tuwing may binibigay sila sayo sa pamamagitan ng pag-sasabing ***SHUKRAN!***
- Kapag may Makita kang produkto nila , purin mo ito sa pamamagitan ng pag-sasabing, ***maa shaa-Allah***

Ang mga hindi dapat gawin

- Huwag magsuot ng mga damit na nakikita ang mga kili-kili, pusod likuran , tiyan at iba pang maselang bahagi ng katawan;
- Huwag maging malapit sa among lalaki upang hindi madaling makursunadahan;
- Huwag gawing biruan ang pagbating *Assalamu alaykum* katulad ng pagsasabing" malay ko sa'yo' dahil ito'y insulto sa kultura nila
- Huwag basta hawakan ang Qur'an dahil ito'y banal na salita ng Allah maliban na lang kung emergency at ipinag-utos ng amo;

Figure 3.4 Dos and don'ts in the Middle East, excerpt from the Arabic Language and Culture Training booklet

Summary

The reform package for HSWs sheds some light on the process by which the Philippine state deals with the national anxieties produced by an embodied nation brand while also protecting these 'vulnerable workers'. The Philippine state does this by multiplying, intensifying and, for that matter, formalizing the scripts of FDWs, especially in the form of the language and culture-specific training and workplace communication skills that are part and parcel of the training in household services that FDWs are required to go through. The language training that FDWs explicitly (in the case of language and culture-specific training) or implicitly (in the case of TESDA training in household services) go through scripts them as passive and docile workers who perform efficiently and avoid problems with their employers because they have been trained to know what is expected of them, linguistically and otherwise. In this way, the Philippine state assembles a particular worker and it legitimizes this assemblage by drawing on a 'national' discourse of protecting its 'vulnerable' citizens, even as it displaces this responsibility to the citizens themselves. The next chapter shifts from the Philippine state to transnational maid agencies in Singapore and the mechanisms they employ to differentiate and style transnational domestic workers in general and FDWs in particular.

4 Marketing Domestic Workers: Maid Agencies in Singapore

Maid agencies are ubiquitous institutions in the lives of Filipino transnational domestic workers, especially at the critical juncture when a Filipino woman seeks employment overseas as a domestic worker. A migrant woman who is working as a domestic worker in Singapore for the very first time (often referred to as a 'first-timer') may avail herself of their services in the source countries where, for a 'placement fee' or a 'recruitment fee', maid agencies 'process' her for deployment. Domestic workers pay for the recruitment fee by taking up a loan with the maid agency. Employers are then obliged to be a part of this loan scheme by deducting a certain amount from the salaries of their domestic worker on behalf of maid agencies (or if employers had to pay an agency fee then employers are sometimes advised to deduct the amount from their domestic worker's salary). This means that domestic workers may not be paid (except for a token allowance) for the first two to eight months of their initial two-year contract in Singapore. In 2007, the 'recruitment fee' was between S$1300 and S$2400, depending on where the 'first-timer' is from. In 2010, the Ministry of Manpower (MOM) capped the agency fees charged to domestic workers on two-year contracts at a maximum of two months' salary. This cap, though, only applies to agencies in Singapore; it does not preclude the possibility that an agency based in the Philippines may charge such a fee.

Such 'processing' may include: producing bio-data and videotapes of the applicant that will be shown to prospective employers, ensuring (at least on paper) that she meets the age, health and educational requirements of the receiving country and that she has the necessary travel documents, and arranging her air ticket once an employer has been located. A first-timer who comes to Singapore as a 'direct hire', that is, as a domestic worker who has been hired directly by an employer without having to go through a maid agency, will usually still need some of the services of maid agencies. Depending on the arrangements with the employer, a maid agency may take care of processing the direct hire's requirements and travel papers in the Philippines, and/or her medical checkup and work permit in Singapore. The domestic worker may again approach an agency for assistance in 'transferring' (thus the term 'transfer maid') to a new employer toward the end of her two-year contract with her current one. The relationship of the domestic worker to the maid agency is not limited to these junctures: they may also approach the agency for assistance in dealing with a difficult employer and/or in instances of abuse; they may work for the agency 'part-time', either training first-timers or recruiting more domestic workers from their communities (for which some agencies pay a fee for every successful deployment); they go there when their contracts with current employers are extended and they have to renew their work permits. Maid agencies may (again, for a fee) also 'sponsor' domestic workers who wish to become 'freelancers' in Singapore. 'Freelancers' are domestic workers who do not live with their employers and who work part-time on a full-time basis; maid agencies sometimes act as their employers 'on paper'. 'Freelancers' are also called 'part-timers'. These ongoing and ambiguous relationships that domestic workers may have with maid agencies are especially illustrative of the mediating function of maid agencies.

Transnational Maid Agencies as Mediating Institutions

Transnational employment agencies or labor brokers that specialize in the recruitment and placement of migrant workers such as maid agencies are considered to be a key gatekeeping industry in labor migration (Bakan & Stasiulis, 1995). In her dissertation on the transnational labor brokering of nurses and domestic workers from the Philippines, Guevarra (2003) argues that

> [...] labor brokering is a social process that acts as a form of capitalist labor control insofar as it is both a subject-making strategy and a disciplinary process that designates and disciplines the types of workers suitable for specific labor processes. It is a process that is labor-specific [...] and is [...] based on particular naturalized, gendered and racialized ideologies about work and individuals suited for specific tasks. The work activity of labor brokering is also a process of negotiations that emerge from labor brokers' relationships with the Philippine state, foreign employers, prospective workers, and NGOs, all of which contribute to the formation of a unique transnational arena of labor export. (Guevarra, 2003: ix)

The centering and mediating functions of labor brokers (among them maid agencies) can be gleaned from the previous paragraphs. Firstly, the activity of labor brokering configures individuals from labor-exporting locales into specific, made-to-order types of workers bound for labor-importing markets. In the process of producing these specific types of bodies (Tyner, 2004), labor brokers act as gatekeepers of value and meaning, especially when they construct gendered and nationality-based stereotypes of migrant workers in an exercise of positioning their 'products' within their niche in the global labor market (Rahman, 2003). This construction of stereotypes is consistent with the centering function of institutions that 'almost always involves either perceptions or real processes of homogenisation and uniformisation: [...] the (real or perceived) reduction of difference and the creation of recognisably "normative" meaning' (Blommaert, 2005: 75).

Secondly, the transnational and interscalar nature of labor brokering in the current era of globalization means that labor brokers maintain and negotiate simultaneous relationships with various institutions and actors in the migration process whose interests may be in conflict with each other; they are in between the sending and the receiving country, and in between the prospective migrant worker and the prospective employer. In a presentation of his work on labor agents in China, Xiang (2005) variously described agents as being the 'indispensable bad guys', 'spin doctors' and 'scapegoats'. Labor brokers are practically unavoidable in the process of labor migration: they translate labor quotas into meaningful 'packages' for would-be migrants while, at the same time, they 'package' migrant workers into marketable 'products' for prospective employers; they also take care of the everyday nitty-gritty details related to the recruitment, deployment and employment of migrant workers (Xiang, 2005).

As transnational labor brokers, maid agencies perform these centering and mediating functions. It must be highlighted here that as mediating institutions, maid agencies are unique from states as they act as intermediate nodal points between global flows and national boundaries, and between national linguistic hierarchies and local linguistic markets. In the same manner, maid agencies operate transnationally and intranationally, though not in the same centralized manner that is associated with multinational companies. Instead, it seems that they operate in a network of transnational alliances, structured by supply and demand. A maid agency in Singapore that takes care of the placement and the 'processing' of a Filipino domestic worker (FDW) once she arrives in Singapore very likely works with several employment agencies in the Philippines (mainly Manila) that recruit Filipino women and 'process' them for deployment to Singapore. Intranationally, the roles of maid agencies are very much shaped by the structural position of the state in which they are based, i.e. labor sending or labor receiving, in the flows of labor migration. Here, I focus on maid agencies in Singapore as a labor-receiving country.

Maid agencies in Singapore

In Singapore where, as of 2015, approximately one in five households has a domestic worker, labor brokering is a cutthroat industry where 1146 registered employment agencies are specifically engaged in the recruitment and placement of domestic workers.[1] The exponential increase of domestic workers in Singapore (from around 28,000 in 1986 to 218,300 in 2014) has been accompanied by increasing numbers of maid agencies and, consequently, stiffening competition among them. In such a demand-driven market, the competitiveness of maid agencies has come to depend more and more on their capacity to offer 'viable products' (Tyner, 1999). This is reflected in the number and the kinds of advertisements placed by maid agencies in the local newspapers. Rahman (2003) has traced the patterns of these advertisements for domestic workers in the classified section of the *Straits Times*, in terms of both their volume and content:

> In December 1983, there was only a handful of advertisements offering the services of live-in Filipina maids listed under the 'Situations Wanted' column. These advertisements were small and consisted of only a few lines without any graphics or agency names. In 1986, a 'Domestic Help Available' column first appeared in the classified section. Advertisements published in these columns were larger in size with graphics and maid agency names written in bold, indicating the entry of bigger and more serious players in Singapore. [...] In the early 1990s, maid agency advertisements continued to grow in both volume and size. These advertisements emphasised the services offered by agencies, such as free medical check-ups, guarantee periods, training, work permit renewals and cancellation options, etc. By the mid 1990s, maid agency advertisements started to intensify. [...] It was during this time that personal qualities such as submissiveness/obedience, loyalty, language ability, intelligence and personal hygiene, started becoming a focus of the advertisements. (Rahman, 2003: 73)

One can see how, with increased competition, maid agencies came to rely more and more on the construction and commodification of the domestic workers as products. The profitability of maid agencies, though, does not hinge on the construction of marketable 'products' that can sustain a sufficiently speedy turnover of the 'stock' alone, it also depends on the availability of a supply of migrant women that fit the mold of and are ready to be deployed as domestic workers. Given this, maid agencies have come to rely on careful marketing strategies through which they employ both their centering and mediating functions.

70   Scripts of Servitude

Figure 4.1 Posters on the glass door of a maid agency in Lucky Plaza

Such careful marketing strategies are manifest, for instance, in the posters shown in Figure 4.1. Taken in Lucky Plaza, a shopping center along Orchard Road in Singapore that has a significant number of maid agencies as well as commercial establishments (e.g. stores, remittance agencies and restaurants) that cater to Filipinos working and living in Singapore, the picture shows three A4-sized posters pasted on the glass door of one of the many maid agencies in the shopping center.

In Figure 4.1, starting from the left, the first two posters (henceforth 'Poster A' and 'Poster B') are in English and have the headings 'Domestic Helpers Available' and 'Quality Maids for Transfer', respectively. The rightmost poster (henceforth 'Poster C') has the heading 'Meron expat at local employers dito' ('There are expatriate and local employers here'), which is in a mixed code of Filipino and English; the rest of the text is predominantly in Filipino.

Poster A highlights in bold letters the countries of origin ('Philippines, Indonesia, Sri Lanka') of the domestic workers it has 'in stock'. In the rest of the poster's text, the maid agency advertises: (1) the wide range of domestic workers it has available by emphasizing their various countries of origin and their various profiles experience-wise, as the domestic workers available may be 'first-timers' or 'transfers' ('Experienced at home or abroad e.g. Malaysia, Singapore or Middle East or both'; 'girls who have completed or will soon complete their term'); (2) the value-added qualities and skills that their domestic workers have ('experienced'; 'We have girls suitable for childcare including midwives'; 'English'; 'Of course our Filipinas speak English, but some of our Indonesian girls also speak English and one can even speak Cantonese! How about that?'); and (3) the competitive services it offers ('interview and video', 'prompt arrival', 'personal interviews can be arranged'). Furthermore, the agency emphasizes how it has *personally* selected the domestic workers ('We screen and interview our own girls and do the video-taping').

In Poster B, the maid agency advertises the 'quality' of the transfer maids it has on its listings by enumerating the features that count as 'quality' and, at the same time, emphasizing again the range of 'quality maids' it has available. Desirable features include: '2 or more years' experience' as a domestic worker; occupational and/or educational backgrounds as 'midwives', 'teachers', 'college graduate' or 'high school graduate'; and perennial availability ('available now or later'). Guevarra (2003: 384) points out how labor brokers encourage domestic workers to display such educational and occupational backgrounds as an added export value. However, labor brokers also 'condition domestic workers that their "domestic" individual duties will vary because they are subject to each employer's needs'. The advertisement assures clients that, given this range of quality maids available, there is a 'maid to order' ('There is a maid for every job!') whether the employers want a 'cook, nanny, private nurse or just plain maid' and whether the domestic worker is already with the agency or not ('If we do not have them on file, we'll find them').

Finally, as pointed out earlier, Poster C is almost entirely in Filipino except for the heading, which borrows the terms 'expat' and 'local employer' from English:

*Meron **expat** at **local employers** dito!*
Libring [sic] video sa gustong magtrabaho
Tinuturuan namin kayo dito kung ano ang sasabihin sa mga tinatanong
Matutulungan namin ang inyong kaibigan at kamag-anak na gustong magtrabaho dito
Magtanong lang sa loob

(There are expatriate and local employers here!
We provide free video to those who want to work
We teach you what to say and how to answer questions
We can help your friends and relatives who want to work here
Just go inside and ask)

In Poster C, the maid agency advertises its services to FDWs. It highlights the range of employers, both local and expatriate, that form its clientele, and the various forms of 'assistance' it provides to those who would like to work as domestic workers whether they are already in Singapore or still in the Philippines. Such 'assistance' includes videotaping the (prospective) domestic workers for free and 'coaching' them on what to say and how to answer questions, presumably in the videotaping sessions and/or in interviews with employers.

Using Hymes' (1974) components of speech as an analytical matrix, it is obvious that the addressees of Posters A and B are the prospective employers whereas the addressees of Poster C are the FDWs; both groups are, in essence, clients of maid agencies and securing a readily available supply of and sufficient demand for their 'products' depends on how satisfactorily (though not equally) the maid agencies portray themselves as meeting the needs of both parties. The juxtaposition of the three posters on the glass door of the maid agency in Lucky Plaza is, therefore, iconic of the mediating and centering functions of maid agencies, that is, of how they juggle the multiple and competing demands of prospective employers and FDWs and how they establish the norms expected of domestic workers and employers.

It would seem that the success of this juggling act rests on the maid agencies' ability to speak to the addressees exclusively: Posters A and B are in English because they are ostensibly for employers whereas Poster C is mostly in Filipino because it is ostensibly for FDWs. However, if one considers that FDWs are English-knowing bilinguals (Pakir, 1999), then Posters A and B are not speaking exclusively to prospective employers. Because they can read and understand English, FDWs also 'hear' what they are expected to do for their employers (e.g. 'cook, nanny, private nurse or just plain maid'); they are privy to how long it will take for them to be deployed ('In most cases, our girls can arrive in 7–10 days') and how they will be presented to employers (through videotaping and arranged interviews); they are made aware of what the maid agency considers as the value-added skills and qualities of 'ideal' domestic workers. Employers, however, cannot 'hear' Poster C in the same way. Because Poster C is mostly in Filipino, much of what the maid agency says to FDWs remains hidden from employers and the little they might 'hear' because of the English borrowings would probably be things about the maid agency that they already know (e.g. that there are 'expat' and 'local employers' and that the agency uses 'video'). This makes it feasible for the maid agency to reassure the FDWs who they address in Poster C that they will be 'coached', that is, that they will be taught what to say and how to answer questions, presumably for interviews; as in Poster A, the maid agency assures employers that the maid agents have personally screened and interviewed the domestic workers, and that personal interviews can be arranged with them.

The posters illustrate how, as institutions, maid agencies exercise both centering and mediating functions. In terms of their centering function, maid agencies put into place the script of servitude, influencing what employers should expect of their domestic workers and reinforcing how domestic workers should not have expectations of their employers (Guevarra, 2003). They also produce specific types of workers by generating indexicalities to which domestic workers are compelled to orient, especially as they are bound to the implicit expectations of employers. In terms of their mediating function, maid agencies practice complex and convoluted juggling acts between institutions and actors in the arena of transnational domestic work that have contrasting and contradictory concerns. As shown in the case of the posters, one of the ways by which they successfully do this is by selectively concealing and revealing their activities and practices to the addressees and hearers of their message.

Positioning Products

The centering function of maid agencies in Singapore is especially apparent in the ways that they appropriate English in their representations of domestic workers. As part of this function, maid agencies in Singapore have established 'English' as a prominent value-added skill of the 'ideal' domestic worker (see Poster A in Figure 4.1, for example). In doing so, they have, among other things, effectively segmented the market into domestic workers who can speak in English and domestic workers who cannot speak or have a limited knowledge of English, establishing a hierarchy where English-speaking domestic workers are at the top and domestic workers with limited or no English-speaking ability are at the bottom.

Representations of Filipino domestic workers in Singapore

This segmentation is reflected in how the English language skills of domestic workers are generalized according to nationality in their bio-data, the information sheets of domestic workers such as the one shown in Appendix 1. These bio-data are often available online and they are also compiled in thick folders at maid agencies.

The bio-data includes information on the personal details of the domestic worker, her work experience, her linguistic and domestic skills, and the tasks she is willing to perform. The segmentation is also reflected in

Table 4.1 Generalized levels of English proficiency among transnational domestic workers in Singapore[a]

Maid agency	Filipinos	Indonesians	Myanmar
Nation Employment Pte Ltd.	Good SG experience, college education. Fair when DW has no overseas experience	Fair when DW has overseas/SG experience. Little	Fair with SG experience. Little
Homekeeper International Pte Ltd.	Good	Fair. Little	Little
United Channel Employment Agency	Fair	So-so/poor	Fair
JPB International Services Pte Ltd.	Very good/good	Fair	Fair
Crislo Employment Agency	Good	Fair/little	Fair
MPL Employment Agency	Fair	So-so	Good (no off day, no phone), fair, so-so
SLF Green Maid Agency	Excellent/ good/fair	Good/fair	Good/fair

[a] The data were drawn from my own online survey of maid agencies. The maid agencies selected were 7 of the top 10 agencies in Singapore by placement volume, i.e. number of foreign domestic workers placed with employers in 12 months (MOM source). Three were not included because two (Jack Focus and Charisha) had no online data of domestic workers and, in the case of one agency (Best Home Employment Agency), there were no details about the level of proficiency of the domestic worker. The survey was conducted in January 2015.

the prevailing stereotypes of transnational domestic workers in Singapore, which are summarized in Table 4.1.

The hierarchy of domestic workers, on the other hand, is best seen in claims by maid agencies and in the widespread public perception in Singapore that FDWs have higher starting salaries[2] *because* of their English language abilities (Lorente & Tupas, 2002). Though not comprehensive, Table 4.1 illustrates the segmentation that maid agencies observe when they assign levels of English proficiency to domestic workers. As Yeoh and Huang (1998a) point out, there is no objective yardstick for measuring language ability, instead it is filtered through the lenses of nationality. Thus, Filipinos are credited as having 'good', 'very good' and 'fair' English language abilities while Indonesians have 'fair fluency in English' (if they have overseas experience) or they have 'little' or 'so-so' English. Domestic workers from Myanmar seem to have similar levels of proficiency as the Indonesians. These nationality-based levels of English proficiency are employed by maid agencies in the nationality-based stereotypes they construct of domestic workers. No objective yardstick seemed to be used for determining whether a Filipino had 'good' or 'very good' English either. Gina, who was tasked with transferring bio-data from the Philippines into a uniform template provided by her maid agency (see Appendix 1 for a sample of a bio-data sheet provided by a maid agency) while she waited for an employer, told me that she was told to check 'good' if the applicant finished high school or came from a rural area, and 'very good' if the applicant had some college education.

As can be seen in Table 4.2, FDWs are stereotyped as having a good command of English and as being naturally hardworking, quick to learn, competent, etc., but they are also portrayed as being bold and streetwise and therefore unreliable, dishonest and more assertive. On the other hand,

Table 4.2 Stereotypes of Filipino, Indonesian, Myanmar and Sri Lankan transnational domestic workers in Singapore

Nationality	Positive stereotypes	Negative stereotypes
Filipino	Most naturally hardworking, quick ability to learn, competent, meticulous, and possess more initiative, possess **good command of English**, honest and hygienic	Bold and streetwise, hence unreliable, dishonest and more assertive, more demanding, very difficult to handle
Indonesian	Docile, compliant, simple and homely, submissive, poses no social problem, good with household chores	Slow learners, forgetful, **poor command of English**, naive, not streetwise, not familiar with city living
Myanmar	Cheapest, less demanding, sweet natured in temperament, easy to work with, compliant	Speak **little to no English**, receive no training before arriving in Singapore, underage
Sri Lankan	Responsible, helpful/pleasing, obedient and shy	Dark skinned, too 'blur', too slow, backwards, has poor hygiene, **very poor command of English**

Source: Rahman *et al.* (2005: 243, emphasis added); The Asian Parent Singapore (2014).

Indonesian and Sri Lankan domestic workers who have a poor or very poor command of English are relationally stereotyped as the 'others' of FDWs. Thus, Indonesian domestic workers who have a poor command of English are supposedly docile, compliant, simple, homely, etc., but they are also considered to be slow learners, naive and not streetwise. Likewise, Sri Lankan domestic workers are stereotyped as responsible, helpful, obedient and shy but also too slow, backward, confused or 'blur' (i.e. a Singlish term for being confused, vague or dimwitted). In doing this, maid agencies produce specific types of domestic workers for the specific needs of employers. They would, for example, market FDWs as being ideal nannies because aside from being efficient housekeepers, they can also act as tutors to the children. On the other hand, Indonesian domestic workers are often marketed as being ideal for those who just want a 'plain maid' who can be trained and who does not have too many demands. In this way, each 'product' is 'styled' at different price points and as having its own inherent advantages and risks; employers can then choose a 'made-to-order' domestic worker that would fit their needs and budget.

It is significant to note that certain groups of qualities ascribed to domestic workers seem to coincide with their supposed level of English ability. Qualities such as intelligence ('quick ability to learn'), competence ('competent, meticulous, more initiative') and modernity ('hygienic', 'bold and streetwise') co-occur with a good command of English, whereas qualities such as ignorance ('slow learners', 'too "blur"'), backwardness ('naive', 'backwards', 'poor hygiene') and being 'traditional' ('docile', 'compliant', 'simple and homely', 'submissive', 'helpful/pleasing', 'obedient and shy') tally with a poor or very poor command of English. This pattern of co-occurrence that is certainly not peculiar to stereotypes of domestic workers nor to Singapore alone may reflect two things: firstly, the adherence of certain discourses to English (see Pennycook, 1998) and secondly, the space-specific distribution and value of linguistic and semiotic resources (Collins & Slembrouck, 2005).

Firstly, the adherence of discourses of modernity and progressiveness to English, which, as Pennycook (1998) shows, have a historical continuity with colonialism, has become part and parcel of many semiotic economies and has, in the process, been appropriated in other niches, such as in the construction of the stereotypes of domestic workers in Singapore. That intermediate-level institutions such as maid agencies can legitimately segment the market in this manner and assign a higher (economic) value to FDWs is indicative of how they are drawing from and are embedded in the linguistic and semiotic economies of more encompassing and powerful centering institutions such as, in this case, the Singapore state. As said earlier, the stereotypes of domestic workers reflect the orders of indexicality in Singapore's semiotic economy, where modern and progressive 'qualities' are prominent and where they adhere to English. Aside from reflecting the semiotic economy, the higher 'value' that is assigned to English-speaking FDWs also indicates a linguistic economy at the macro-level, where English has highly important functions across many domains and is thus valued more than Bahasa Indonesia, Sinhalese or Tamil, which would have limited or no function at all in Singapore. Singaporean Malays would be able to communicate with Indonesian domestic workers, but maid agencies cannot afford to focus on a limited segment of the market. Sri Lankan domestic workers would speak Sinhalese and/or Tamil. As such (and also because of their supposedly common cultural backgrounds), they are 'marketed' almost exclusively to Singaporean Indian families who are very likely to be able to speak in Tamil. Again, this makes the marketability of Sri Lankan domestic workers limited.

The relative values of English linguistic capital

This brings us to the second point, that of the space-specific distribution of valuable linguistic and semiotic resources. The emphasis on the linguistic and semiotic economies of *receiving* states in labor migration in the previous section is intentional. While one may be tempted to consider the higher value assigned to FDWs in Singapore as proof of how English is the 'competitive advantage' of migrant Filipino workers, this may be a short-sighted conclusion. As Koven (2004: 271) shows in her paper on the sociolinguistic capital of the children of Portuguese migrants in France, the life possibilities of migrants are 'structured by sociolinguistic norms centered within two socially stratified [...] nation-states'. English is no exception to this; it is not intrinsically valuable and the *recognition* of the 'English advantage' of migrant Filipino workers depends very much on the linguistic and semiotic economies of the contexts in which migrant Filipino workers are inserted. As such, the value of linguistic capital is relative, that is, it may vary enormously across spaces because when 'sociolinguistic items travel across the globe, they travel across *structurally different* spaces, and will consequently be picked up differently in different places' (Blommaert, 2003: 612, emphasis in original). In the case of migrant Filipino workers, the mobility of their supposed 'linguistic capital' (even if it is the 'world language') is still contingent on how they are positioned by centering institutions in the receiving states.

For example, in the case of how FDWs are portrayed in Poster A (see Figure 4.1), while the maid agency enacts its centering function by affirming that Filipinos do have the value-added skill of being able to communicate in English ('Of course our Filipinas speak English'), it also suggests that 'English' is not a skill that is exclusive to Filipinos and that Indonesians may know languages (which Filipinos may not know) that may make them 'ideal' for certain employers ('but some of our Indonesian girls also speak English and one can even speak Cantonese. How about that?'). In this way, they meet the demand for English-speaking domestic workers (which are constructed as 'ideal'), and they are able to continue 'sourcing' and 'marketing' domestic workers from various 'stocks' by not making English the exclusive skill of Filipinos, i.e. by also assigning the skill only to a limited number of Indonesians. Thus, while Filipinos may still maintain an edge in this regard, it is an edge that is not exclusively assigned to them. The recognition of English skills has to be 'flexible' if the maid agency in Singapore is to profit from labor brokering. In this regard, the specific distribution and valorization of linguistic resources in Singapore incapacitates and displaces Indonesian domestic workers who usually do not learn English in the Indonesian school system. The portrayal of Indonesians as 'blur' can be traced to this. With limited skills in speaking and understanding English, much less in reading and writing in English, it is no surprise that they would be perceived as 'slow to learn' and 'docile'.

The relative value of the linguistic capital of FDWs becomes even more apparent when one compares the stereotypes of domestic workers in Singapore with the stereotypes of domestic workers that maid agencies in Canada have been instrumental in putting into place (Table 4.3). Canada is one of the leading destinations of migrant Filipino women. Domestic workers

Table 4.3 Prevailing stereotypes of foreign domestic workers in Canada

Nationality	Positive stereotypes	Negative stereotypes
European	Highly trained, ideal as nannies, **ideal accents in English** (especially if the nanny is British) **or may be potential second or foreign language 'teachers' to children** (if nanny is French, German, etc.), able to interact and teach children	Takes privileges for granted, demanding, open
Filipino	Naturally docile, passive, hardworking, quiet, shy, 'knows her place', excellent housekeeper, respectful of authority	Unskilled, unintellectual, **strong accent in speaking English**, easily intimidated by children and parents

Sources: England and Stiell (1997); McKay (2005).

arrive in Canada under the Live-in Caregiver Program (LCP), where they are entitled to 'landed status'. Landed immigrants can apply for citizenship after residing in Canada for three years. Since the early 1980s, Filipino women have replaced Caribbean women as the domestic worker migrants of choice. They predominate the LCP migration stream (McKay, 2005).

As has been argued earlier, intermediate-level institutions such as maid agencies draw from and are embedded in the linguistic and semiotic economies of macro-level centering institutions such as states. As such, maid agencies in Canada exercise their centering function by segmenting the market, not along the lines of whether the domestic workers know English or not, but rather along the lines of the prestige of their English *accents*. This would reflect the linguistic and semiotic economy of Canada where accents closest to that of the idealized 'native' English speaker (the British) are desirable and 'strong accents' in English are devalued. In Canada's linguistic economy, the value of French outside of Quebec is also increasing as bilingualism (English–French) is becoming more and more commodified (see Heller, 2002). Other 'Western' languages such as German, though without any function in Canada, may still index the prestige of their places of origin, making them desirable 'additional' languages. In such a linguistic economy, Filipino would have no value: it has no communicative function across different domains and it would not be prestigious as it indexes a 'Third World' country.

Given this, it is not surprising that FDWs in Canada seem to be the 'Indonesians' in the labor market. FDWs who supposedly have strong accents when they speak English are portrayed as being 'naturally docile, passive, quiet, shy and respectful of authority', but they are also considered to be 'unskilled, unintellectual and easily intimidated' and are thus marketed as ideal housekeepers but not as ideal nannies. On the other hand, European domestic workers who have ideal accents in English or who could potentially teach the children an additional language are portrayed as being demanding but highly trained, and they are marketed as ideal nannies. Maid agencies in Canada also portray Filipinos as being willing to work for wages that are lower than those a European woman may demand (England & Stiell, 1997; McKay, 2005; Pratt, 1997). Thus, the discourse of the 'English advantage' that favors FDWs in Singapore where they are 'competing' with Indonesians who have limited or no English knowledge now works to their relative disadvantage in Canada where their accents in English are measured against the British, and where Filipino (and the other Philippine languages) is measured against, for example, French and German.

One must note here that while the discourses that adhere to English have basically remained the same, their relocation within Canada's semiotic economy means that it is now *accents* in English that matter. Accents and 'the use of specific varieties "sets" people in a particular social and/or physical place [...] and confers the attributive qualities of that place to what they say' (Blommaert, 2005: 223; see also Lippi-Green, 1997; Urciuoli, 1995). As such, a domestic worker's 'relative worth' is tied to her accent, which in turn is tied to her country's position in the world system. It comes as no surprise then that in the stereotypes of domestic workers in Canada, 'Third World' women such as the Filipinos are the 'others', identified as having 'strong accents' and ascribed the characteristics of ignorance ('unintellectual'), backwardness ('unskilled') and 'traditional' values ('docile', 'shy', 'respectful of authority'). European women, on the other hand, are identified as having 'ideal' accents or languages and they are considered to be 'highly trained', 'able to interact and teach children' and 'demanding': they seem to be practically Canadian.

Styling the Domestic Worker

The production of nationality-based stereotypes that draw from the linguistic and semiotic economies of *receiving* states is not the only means by which maid agencies appropriate the discourse of 'English advantage'. Maid agencies also exercise their mediating and, more evidently, their centering functions when they ensure that English is performed and 'done' by the domestic worker within the margins of what I call, the script of servitude. In this way, maid agencies produce their own indexical order – their own hierarchy of linguistic forms, styles and repertoires – which is niched, that is, it is specific to domestic workers.

In the case of maid agencies, the nationality-based stereotypes of domestic workers that were discussed earlier are part and parcel of the script of servitude: such stereotypes are inflexible and they are oftentimes durable discourses that construct the 'ideal' domestic workers; they neutralize individual differences and universalize certain characteristics (e.g. domesticity, accents and skills in English), naturalizing and rationalizing the marginalization of domestic workers in the process. In addition to producing nationality-based stereotypes, maid agencies also produce and employ other discursive and highly structured means – texts, activities and interactions – through which they directly outline and enforce the specifics of the script of servitude.

In using such discursive and highly structured semiotic instruments, maid agencies seek to 'style', linguistically and otherwise, domestic workers according to the demands of their subordinate and servile roles in the script of servitude. The maid agencies' linguistic 'styling' (Cameron, 2000b; Rampton, 1995, 1999) of domestic workers involves controlling and regulating the performance of their language skills where the goal is 'to preempt any choice of means to ends by the people actually engaged in a given activity' (Cameron, 2000b: 341). Though controlling linguistic behavior is certainly not the only means by which maid agencies 'style' domestic workers according to the script of servitude, it is a crucial instrument in its performance. The migrant woman not only has to look and act like a domestic worker, she must speak like one.

The migrant woman/prospective domestic worker must also speak in English. However, the indexicalities that adhere to being able to speak the language are not compatible with and therefore cannot be transferred into the script of servitude. As such, maid agencies prescribe and at the same time impose 'the way in which particular speech acts should be performed, the choice of address terms/salutations and the consistent use of certain politeness formulae' (Cameron, 2000b: 324), among other guidelines. In doing so, they establish a singular speech style and a standard linguistic repertoire *in English* that index the subordinate position of the domestic worker. By reassigning the functions of particular speech acts, address terms, politeness formulae and the like, maid agencies resignify the meanings and values of English, restricting their interpretation in accordance with the script of servitude. In this way, the indexical order to which domestic workers are, in one way or another, compelled to orient to, is *niched* (Blommaert, 2003): such linguistic practices are limited to and expected of domestic workers. It must be noted here that these practices also regulate the domestic worker's performance of gender. As will be shown later, domestic workers are not supposed to present themselves as sexually attractive women. They are 'de-sexualized'; they perform gendered labor as workers and servants and not as women.

Maid agencies produce and enforce the script of servitude by adapting various disciplinary practices in which the English language skills and the linguistic behavior of migrant women are standardized and 'stylized' to fit the requirements of their position as domestic workers. Such disciplinary practices include: (1) scripting the domestic worker's performance of the script of servitude in videotaped 'interviews'; and (2) 'coaching' the domestic worker to display linguistic deference during, for example, pre-employment 'training' sessions. Each disciplinary practice mentioned has its own 'techniques', but the functions overlap and complement each other. The following sections of this chapter will focus on these two disciplinary practices because they highlight how the linguistic behavior of domestic workers is 'disciplined' and how maid agencies produce their own niched indexical order in the process. Domestic workers undergo these disciplinary practices at different temporal and geographical points in their transnational journeys. The order in which the practices are discussed (and the data that will be used) reflects the order in which a first-timer would undergo or experience them. Usually, a first-timer would first submit her bio-data before undergoing a videotaped 'interview' in the Philippines (both of which are sent to Singapore). When the first-timer already has an employer, then she may be explicitly coached on linguistic deference in pre-departure 'training' in the Philippines and/or while waiting for her employer to pick her up when she is already in Singapore. A 'transfer maid' may also have to resubmit her bio-data and go through a videotaped 'interview' when she is looking for a new employer. The first-timer's initial deployment is the (dis-)juncture where the most pronounced reconfigurations of linguistic forms, functions and meanings by maid agencies take place, as they 'translate' migrant women of heterogeneous backgrounds into monochromatic domestic workers.

Performing the script of servitude

The production of personalized videos of prospective domestic workers is an important aspect of the recruitment practices of maid agencies. It is a practice that maid agencies continue to engage in, though they now also advertise interviews via Skype or by phone. These videos of 'qualified applicants' are usually produced and compiled by labor brokers in the Philippines before they are sent to partners in Singapore who make them available to prospective employers. Because employers in Singapore usually do not interview the applicants in the Philippines, these videos (and to a lesser extent, the bio-data) are intended to enable them to evaluate, if not to select, the appropriate domestic worker to be employed, and then to come up with a shortlist of domestic workers. According to the maid agencies in the Philippines that Guevarra (2003: 356) interviewed:

> [...] the purpose of these videos is to primarily allow foreign employers to 'see' different applicants and evaluate their communication skills. [...] employers need to know that they can speak English and that they can do so with a minimal 'accent' in ways that would facilitate 'good quality' communication between them and their maids. (Guevarra, 2003: 356)

The videos give the prospective employers a chance to 'see' the domestic worker up close and in action, the physical appearance of the domestic worker being an important aspect of determining the health, well-being and 'looks' of the 'commodity' they are selecting. According to Guevarra (2003: 357), 'some labor brokers expressed unhesitatingly that for many employers, the physical appearance of the domestic worker they want to bring into their household is important. For instance, while some do not want a domestic worker who is 'too attractive' because of wives' fears about their husbands getting seduced by her, others do not want a domestic worker who has any visible facial and/or general physical deformities'. This emphasis on how the domestic worker looks was also evident in my interviews. Nelma, for example, said that her employers told her she had been selected because she 'looked young' (the couple had a young child) whereas Precy was chosen because she 'looked kind'. Pearly, on the other hand, was disappointed when, after seven years of working for the same employer, she was told they had selected her because, in her video and pictures, she had short hair.

Even as the videos can be used by employers to assess the domestic worker's looks, it is questionable whether employers are able to or intend to assess the domestic worker's English communication skills given the brevity of the videos. The videos that maid agencies make of domestic workers are highly structured performances and scripted and rehearsed speech events. This is evident in Example A, which is a transcript of the video of 'Maid 778' and which, for the purposes of the discussion, has been numbered sentence by sentence. This video was made available online on a maid agency's website.[3] 'Maid 778' was described to be 'a graduate in education, good English, cheerful, lively, pleasant and decent'. The video was shot against a generic white background. Detsie ('Maid 778') was wearing a round-necked white shirt with her hair pulled back in a clean ponytail. She looked directly at the video camera as she spoke:

Example A. Detsie's ('Maid 778') video transcription

(1) Good afternoon, sir, madam.
(2) This is Detsie de Vera, 22 years old, single and came from the province of La Union.
(3) I am one of the members of the Iglesia ni Kristo.
(4) We are four in the family.
(5) I have two brothers and one sister.
(6) My brother is already married and my little sister is still studying for her college.
(7) I have finished my bachelor of secondary education, last 2002, major in mathematics.

(8) Though I don't have the experience in going abroad, I can assure you that I can be a good maid, an honest, hardworking housemaid and babysitter of yours.
(9) I have experience or I was used to take care of my nephews and nieces especially when their parents are busy working because they are both working.
(10) So I need to prepare for their food, prepare for their clothes.
(11) That's why I can assure you that I can do anything though I am so small.
(12) I am just four feet and ten inches in height.
(13) I can do what other people can do.
(14) Ma'am if you will choose me as one of your maids, I promise to do my very best just to serve you with all my heart.
(15) Thank you.

As a speech event, this 'narrative' can be parsed into at least four parts. First, there is an opening formulaic salutation (Line 1) where the 'applicant' greets her prospective employers ('Good afternoon') and addresses them using formal and polite forms ('sir, madam'). The second part is the lengthiest section of the 'narrative' where the 'applicant': (a) lists her personal details, all of which may be found in her bio-data (e.g. name, age, marital status, province of origin, religion, order of birth in the family and educational background) (Lines 2–7); and (b) talks about her experience as a domestic worker, or failing that, her experience that can be related to the work of a domestic worker (Lines 8–13). The third part which, in the case of Detsie, somewhat overlaps with the second, consists of the speech act that is akin to service slogans and which I will call a 'service guarantee' (Lines 11–14). The notion of a 'service guarantee' is most evident in Line 14 ('Ma'am if you will choose me as one of your maids, *I promise to do my very best to serve you with all my heart*', emphasis added). Finally, the speech event ends with a closing politeness formula (Line 15).

With some variation, the same sequence of speech acts can be found in Example B, which is a sample of the script that a maid agency in the Philippines provides to first-timers. According to Guevarra (2003), who observed these videotaping sessions in the Philippines, applicants are supposed to memorize the script and customize it based on their own individual information. The script is provided to them a couple of days before they are videotaped. During the videotaping session itself, 'they must recite *every detail* of this script and deliver it in a form of public "speech" without any mistakes *and* without making unnecessary changes to it' (Guevarra, 2003: 361, emphasis in original).

Example B. Pilar's script (Guevarra, 2003: 362–363)

(1) Good day Sir, Madam.
(2) I'm Pilar Gutierrez, eldest in the family and a college graduate.
(3) I took up bachelor of science in elementary education.
(4) I'm employed as a domestic helper and babysitter to Mr. Ramon Abaya since January 12, 1990 to the present.
(5) I can do all the household chores such as cooking, cleaning all parts of the house and babysitting.
(6) Upon waking up early in the morning, I'll fix my bed first and take a bath then I'll proceed to the kitchen to cook and prepare breakfast for my employer and for the needs of their children.
(7) After they finish eating, I'll start to wash all the used dishes, utensils, plates, clean the gas stove and mop the floor.
(8) In the bathroom, I'll scrub the tiles, toilet bowl, put some detergent and rinse it to dry.
(9) In the living room, I'll remove all the dust in the displays, furnitures, appliances, and I vacuum the carpet or the floor.
(10) In the bedroom, I'll change the curtains, change the dirty pillows, bedcover and pillowcases.
(11) In cooking, I can cook Filipino food but I'm willing to learn how to cook Chinese dishes.
(12) I do marketing once a week.
(13) I do the laundry and ironing twice a week.
(14) In babysitting, I could babysit newly born babies and above age.
(15) My duties and responsibilities to them is to give them a bath, give them food, and vitamins, change their diapers, clothes and treat them as my own brothers and sisters.
(16) The reason why I wanted to work in Hong Kong is to earn money to support my parents and for my future needs.
(17) I guarantee you that I'm hardworking, honest, responsible, obedient, loyal, and I promise to finish my two years' contract.
(18) Thank you very much.

The additional part in Pilar's script is the insertion of the reason why she would like to work overseas (Line 16). Otherwise, Pilar's script observes the same sequence as Detsie's: she greets her prospective employers (Line 1), enumerates her personal details and goes into detail about her experience as a domestic worker in the Philippines (Lines 2–15); she then states the reason why she wants to work overseas (Line 16) before giving a 'service guarantee' (Line 17: 'I guarantee you that I'm hardworking, honest, responsible, obedient, loyal, and I promise to finish my two years' contract') and closing with a 'Thank you very much' (Line 18).

In terms of communicating the speech acts that are valorized by maid agencies, the frequent use of politeness formulae ('Good afternoon', 'Good day', 'Thank you very much') and of very formal address terms ('sir', 'madam') in the scripts of the personalized videotapes indicates that they are part of a speech style which, as will be shown later, is prescribed by maid agencies to domestic workers. Their function is to index the domestic worker's consistent deference to her employer; they also signify the highly asymmetrical relationship between the domestic worker and her employer. But the scripts are not just about the maid agencies establishing a normative speech style that is 'appropriate' for domestic workers, they are also (and arguably, mainly) about the maid agencies communicating the marketability of their 'products' by appropriating and controlling the voices of the applicants. Again using Hymes' notions of speaker–hearer and addressor–addressee as an analytical matrix for the speech event in Examples A and B, the crucial realization is that the speaker and the addressor are not one and the same. The speaker is evidently the prospective domestic worker and the hearers and addressees are apparently the prospective employers since the entire message is targeted at them. But the addressors, the actual senders of the message, are the maid agencies, the hearers would include both the prospective domestic workers and the prospective employers, and the speakers, the prospective domestic workers, are, in this regard, but 'mimic maids'.

This ventriloquism is especially manifest in the second and third parts of the speech events where the applicant enumerates her personal details and talks about her domestic worker-related work experiences, and where she gives a 'service guarantee'. In these parts of the script, the applicant does more than just repeat the personal details and work background she has that would already be in her bio-data; instead, her discourse is styled so that she addresses and responds to the specific concerns of prospective employers. In Detsie's case (Example A), for example, her script addresses the concerns that prospective employers may have over her lack of experience as a domestic worker in the Philippines and overseas, and her possible lack of physical stamina and strength because of her smallness. As such, she reassures them that she can be 'a good maid' (Line 8), that she 'can do anything' (Line 11) and that she 'can do what other people can do' (Line 13). For Pilar (Example B) who is already an experienced domestic worker, her script includes highlighting her work routine to prospective employers (Lines 5–15), the establishment of a work routine being a primary concern of many employers. The detail in which she describes her tasks communicates to prospective employers not only what she can do, but also *how* she will specifically perform domestic tasks (Guevarra, 2003). Finally, the maid agency communicates that the selection of the 'product' comes with a 'service guarantee'. This is framed in the form of, among other ways, promises that the domestic worker will be emotionally involved ('I promise to do my very best to serve you *with all my heart'*, Example A, Line 14) and that the domestic worker will not run away, switch employers or change her mind in the middle of a contract ('I promise to finish my two years' contract', Example B, Line 17). The 'service guarantees' of domestic workers are, in some cases, backed by the maid agencies' guarantees of 'free replacements' should the employer be dissatisfied with the domestic worker.

A memorized script is not the only kind of text that a 'mimic maid' can perform in the personalized videotape. The applicant may be asked to answer questions instead. However, such videotaped question and answer interactions where the applicant may look like she is independently answering questions are also controlled scripts, as illustrated in Adora's case. Adora had been working in Singapore since 1994 and as a first-timer she had gone through the agency route. I interviewed her together with Beth who was a 'direct hire' but who had 'insider knowledge' of the whole process because her mother, also a domestic worker, was helping a maid agency recruit new 'applicants'. I asked Adora, in particular, about how she was videotaped:

Adora: First, you get this [pause] silly uniform. And make your hair short.
BL: They cut your hair?
Beth: No, they make you. You don't have to wear jewelries right? [Adora nods]. You don't have to wear make-up.
Adora: No make-up and your fingernails must be short. *And then they... just ask basic questions like 'what do you know about children?', about your cooking and more basic questions.*
BL: Just basic?
Adora: Yeah. Of course, I stand there [breaks into laughter]. You stand up there with your most... It was just so [laughter]. And then I remember, like, you know, it was quite hilarious...
BL: How long does it take?
Adora: Shouldn't be 10 minutes. It's a short one really. Really short.
Beth: I remember ... ngiti ngiti ka lang [you just smile and smile].
Adora: Yeah, you have to smile [laughs].
BL: *Do they give you instructions before you do it?*

Adora: *They say, uhhhhhmmm, the same questions like the interviewer ask you.*
Beth: And then you answer it.
Adora: *Just like a little hint or you have to say this or you have to say that.*
Beth: Then you have to smile. You don't have to make a long face or whatever ... you just have to impress them [laughs].

(emphasis added)

Just as Detsie and Pilar (in Examples A and B) probably had to memorize the script they delivered in their video, Adora had *rehearsed* her answers to the questions she was asked. As she noted in her interview (in italics), she answered the same 'basic' questions that she had been asked off-camera and she was 'coached' on what she should be saying. This affirms the highly controlled and 'disciplined' manner in which the personalized videos of domestic workers are produced.

Apart from showing how maid agencies control the text that is delivered during the videos even when (and perhaps, especially when) the applicant appears to be answering questions on her own, Adora and Beth's 'narrative' also shows how maid agencies regulate what the applicants look like, styling them to fit the employer's expectations of how a domestic worker should look. Adora's experience is widespread; for the videos (as well as the pictures in the bio-data), applicants are often required to wear maid uniforms and to cut their hair short or to at least wear it in a ponytail; they are not supposed to wear make-up and all jewelry must be removed; applicants are also instructed to smile – all because the applicant must 'impress' the prospective employer. My interviewees' narratives of how they were videotaped by maid agencies were often accompanied by much laughter and hilarity. The women I interviewed indicated to me that they were *aware* of why the maid agency was asking them to speak or act in a certain way. The women were also aware of the importance of their performance in these videos and they told me that they did their best not to laugh or 'act funny' in front of the camera.

Indeed, while the overt aim of the personalized videos may be to 'impress' a prospective employer into hiring an applicant, it must be pointed out that, as hearers of the speech event, both the applicants who perform in the videotapes and the prospective employers who will view the videotapes are socialized into the behaviors, linguistic or otherwise, that are expected of them in their particular roles in the script of servitude. The applicants are introduced to a deferential speech style that indexes their subordinate position; the prospective employers are primed to expect deference from their domestic workers. The applicants are prepared for the domestic tasks that they will be performing and the manner in which these tasks will be performed; the prospective employers may come to assume that they are 'buying' tireless, multitasking and efficient domestic 'machines'. The applicants are 'told' to finish their contracts and to be emotionally attached to their employers; the prospective employers presume that it is guaranteed that the domestic worker will work for them, no matter what.

Displaying servitude

The practice of disciplining the language production of prospective domestic workers may continue up to the time when the domestic worker is already in Singapore and waiting for an employer. When Emily, one of my students at the Bayanihan Center, first came to Singapore in 1991, a representative of the maid agency that had recruited her from the Philippines picked her up from the airport: 'My agent try his best to make me feel comfortable; he talked to me while he is driving back to his home. He did ask me a lot of questions, *trying to find how polite I am to answer all his questions*' (emphasis added). Emily's interpretation of the agent's questioning as an inconspicuous assessment of her ability to speak and answer questions politely is hardly atypical. With some variations, these disguised tests for politeness were not the only means by which maid agencies showed interest in and, for that matter, ensured that the domestic worker would be 'polite'. Within the confines of the maid agency,[4] the maid agents also coach, train and discipline the domestic workers to perform deference, linguistic and otherwise. The kind of deferential behavior that is expected of domestic workers is best summarized by Figure 4.2, a photograph of an A4-sized poster tacked onto the glass doors of a maid agency in Lucky Plaza. Intended for an audience consisting of both domestic workers and employers, it again serves the function of socializing both parties into their expected roles in the script of servitude. However, the poster is also striking for the iconic way in which it lists the rules that delineate the role of a 'servant'.

In the poster shown in Figure 4.2, each of the letters of the word 'servant' is arranged vertically on the page. Each letter stands for the beginning of a phrase or sentence that together spell out what is expected of a 'servant'. Among this list of dos and don'ts is a list of rules that specifically govern the linguistic behavior of the domestic worker, what she says and how she speaks being an important aspect of performing servility. Specifically, the maid agency indicates that the domestic worker should be 'very polite and always greet [her] employer'; she should be 'attentive and ask if not sure of [her] work'; and finally, she is told to 'never argue with [her] employer'. The maid agencies not only prescribe speech styles, they also recommend limiting one's opportunity to speak or, more specifically, to interact with

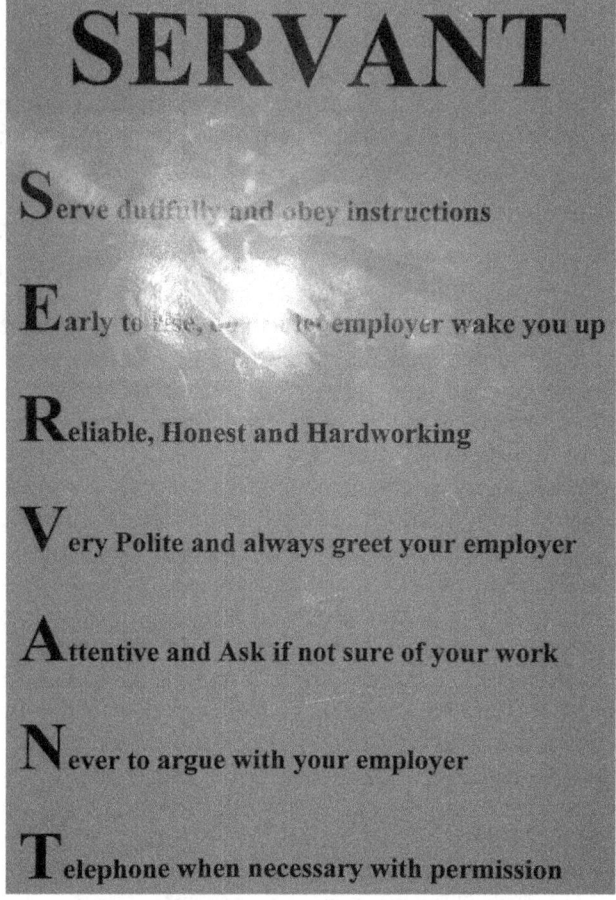

Figure 4.2 Rules posted on a glass door of a maid agency in Lucky Plaza (Note: The text for the first two rules reads as follows: 'Serve dutifully and obey instructions; Early to rise, do not let your employer wake you up')

others ('Telephone when necessary with permission'). Gina, one of my interviewees, came to Singapore in 1998. She mentioned to me that, in her agency, domestic workers were not only given a list of dos and don'ts (e.g. 'You must not speak to your neighbors'; 'You must not gossip or use the phone'; 'Before you sleep, say good night') to read while waiting for their employers, they were also asked to supposedly practice their English by reading the list aloud. This is part of how maid agencies style the domestic workers to perform the script of servitude. By reading the rules aloud, they ostensibly show that they can read and speak in English, but at the same time, the exercise of reading aloud may be meant to drill them (and to show employers that they are being drilled) on the rules they are supposed to observe as domestic workers.

If the domestic workers were already introduced to a highly deferential speech style evinced by the constant use of salutations, politeness formulae and very formal address terms ('sir', 'madam') in their videotaped interviews as applicants, when they are with the maid agencies, they are frequently and didactically told to be 'polite'. The domestic workers I interviewed and spoke to in my fieldwork often narrated how maid agencies conducted orientations (usually lasting two to three days), supposedly to prepare and train newly arrived women (from the Philippines, Indonesia, Sri Lanka and Myanmar) for their jobs as domestic workers. Amidst whirlwind lectures and demonstrations on subjects such as elderly care, childcare, cooking, electrical appliances and housework, the women were given *explicit* instructions, not only regarding how they should address their employers and the politeness formula or salutation which they should use, but specifically *when* they should perform such acts of politeness. In Tina's case, the maid agency emphasized how such acts should be among the first things she should do in the morning:

> Ma'am and sir, *turo 'yan sa agency, sabi ng nagturo sa amin* [Ma'am and sir, they taught us that at the agency, the one who taught us said ...], 'Alright, first thing when you wake up and see your employers, say 'Good morning, Madam', 'Good morning Sir'. (Tina)

Such instructions were subsequently reinforced by the instructors' constant references to the domestic workers' potential employers as 'your madam', 'your ma'am' and 'your sir'. Quite possibly, newly arrived Filipino women would already have an idea about the terms by which they should address their employers. Their possible sources would range from their own informal networks, that is, through relatives, neighbors, town-mates and/or friends who are already working in Singapore and who may have written or spoken about their madams, ma'ams and sirs, and from their own experiences as a good number of the FDWs I have met in Singapore had previously worked in the service sector – as waitresses, as 'helpers' in middle- and upper-class households, as hotel personnel, etc.

At the same time, the maid agencies also emphasized that while the domestic worker was expected to constantly perform such verbal acts of politeness, she should not expect the same token from her employers:

> *Di na 'ko nag-expect, sabi ng agency huwag mag-expect ng* thanks for your work, *ng* greeting *na* 'Good morning', *na tawagin kaming* 'Auntie'. [I didn't expect anymore, the agency told us not to expect thanks for our work, greetings like 'Good morning', that we be addressed as 'Auntie'.] (Tina)

Many of the FDWs I listened or spoke to perceived an unspoken warning in the instructions given by the maid agencies during the orientations and briefings, that is, to expect more from the employers or to expect acknowledgement and recognition was to overstep the boundaries between domestic worker and employer. The penalty for this was the ire of the employers or even the risk of losing a job that is oftentimes the sole means of livelihood for their families back in the Philippines.

From these narratives and observations, one can reasonably surmise that maid agencies have interests beyond just finding out whether domestic workers would be able to speak politely or not. One could also say that what maid agencies require of would-be domestic workers is more than politeness 'motivated by a speaker's desire to save face, his or her own face or the hearer's' (Scarcella & Brunak, 1981). By instructing the women to perform verbal acts of politeness that, in turn, are to be ignored or unacknowledged by their employers and by binding their linguistic behavior to the precariousness of their jobs, maid agencies manipulate the linguistic behavior of the women they have recruited and initiate them into a crucial aspect of servitude, namely linguistic deference (Weix, 2000). With this particular brand of linguistic deference reinforcing and being reinforced by the women's supposed training in or even supposed natural inclination for domestic work, maid agencies effectively style women who satisfy the employers' preferences and oftentimes their demands for submissive and obedient workers, workers who politely, uncomplainingly and silently do the 'dirty work' (Anderson, 2000).

Apart from prescribing highly formal address terms and politeness formulae to domestic workers, maid agencies also train them to respond minimally to their employers. Unlike call center operators who are instructed to use minimal responses such as words of acknowledgement supportively so that the conversation flows freely (Cameron, 2000b), domestic workers are taught to use minimal responses only affirmatively, the point being not only to show attentiveness to and/or comprehension of the instructions of the employer, but also to confirm their subservient status vis-à-vis the employer. As the poster in Figure 4.2 emphasizes: '*Never* to argue with your employer' (emphasis added). Not only are domestic workers supposed to use minimal responses only in an affirmative way, they are also told to speak minimally, to talk only when they are spoken to by their employers or, at most, to talk only if they are not sure about their work (and nothing else). In doing this, the maid agencies highlight the highly restricted linguistic repertoire that the domestic worker is supposed to use when communicating with her employers.

Gina, who arrived in Singapore in 1998, told me that her maid agency back then made them practice 'Yes, ma'am; No, ma'am; OK, ma'am' over and over again. She laughingly 'blamed' the constant rehearsal of these words of acknowledgement as the reason for her 'muteness' during her initial encounter with her first employer. She recreated the conversation that occurred when she first met her employers:

Maid Agent (MA): Oh, greet your employer.
Gina: Good morning, ma'am. Good morning, sir.
MA: You be good ah!
Gina: Yes, ma'am.
MA: Don't talk so much.
Gina: Yes, ma'am.
MA   (to employers): She can understand but she cannot talk so much, just newcomer, she's shy.

Assuming that Gina's retelling of the event captures the way in which the exchange was framed and its primary intent, one sees that though the interaction overtly involves the domestic worker and the maid agent most of the time, it was primarily intended as a performance for Gina's employers. The addressor and the speaker is the maid agent, the domestic worker and her employers are the addressees and the hearers, though, in such a setting, the domestic worker speaks as a 'mimic maid', repeating what she has been told to say by the maid agency. The interaction between Gina and the maid agent is very much a performance where the maid agent shows that she/he is a 'good' maid agent by showing that she/he can admonish the domestic worker to act like a domestic worker ('behave', 'don't talk so much'). His/her statements invite only an affirmative and minimal response from the domestic worker. Gina kept to her role in the script of servitude by being 'mute' and answering only with a 'Yes, ma'am', indicating her politeness, docility and willingness to do whatever her employers say. When the maid agent finally speaks to the employers, the domestic worker's answers are interpreted as shyness, a kind of self-effacing quality that would be desirable in a domestic worker.

Summary

In this chapter, I have examined how transnational maid agencies in general and maid agencies in Singapore in particular do much of the work of translating and 're-embedding' migrant domestic workers into their niches in a local labor market. To do this, maid agencies in Singapore use particular techniques or mechanisms to style the English language skills and verbal behavior of foreign domestic workers in general and transnational FDWs in particular according to a script of servitude, which is a function of the restricted and highly regulated boundaries of foreign domestic work in Singapore. Maid agencies in Singapore draw from national and racial stereotypes and from the indexicality of English to segment the market for foreign domestic workers, giving the impression that there is always a supply of the 'right' domestic worker who has the specific personal qualities an employer is looking for and who is naturally appropriate for the specific tasks (e.g. take care of children, take care of elderly, clean the house) the employer has for her. Furthermore, maid agencies in Singapore also socialize foreign domestic workers into their roles, training them in scripts that perform subordination and deference. In doing this, maid agencies not only reproduce national and racial hierarchies, they also reinforce – to a large extent - national scripts for migrant domestic workers while ensuring that the market is sufficiently segmented and the domestic workers are sufficiently differentiated (e.g. via personal qualities or English skills) for them to profit. The next two chapters focus on the scripts of FDWs themselves.

Notes

(1) This is based on a search of employment agencies for foreign domestic workers on the MOM website. The search was conducted on February 15, 2015. Not all of the maid agencies may be active, i.e. placing one maid per month for the last 12 months: 420 of the agencies had 0 FDW placement volume, meaning they had not placed a domestic worker in the past 12 months; 150 had placed more than 200 (considered major agencies). Of these 150 major agencies, 38 had placed 500 or more, and of these 38, 10 had placed a thousand or more domestic workers in the past 12 months.
(2) Until the end of 2006, the starting salary of FDWs was S$350 as compared to S$280 for Indonesian domestic workers and S$220 for Sri Lankans. By 2015, the salaries of Filipino and Indonesian domestic workers were converging, perhaps partly as a result of the Philippine and Indonesian governments mandating a minimum salary for foreign domestic workers in 2006 in the case of the Philippines and 2014 in the case of Indonesia. Starting salaries were based on the online survey of maid agencies. Filipinos with no overseas experience had S$500 as a starting salary,

Indonesians S$450 and Myanmar between S$420 and S$430. Starting salaries for those with overseas experience could be higher.

(3) The availability of video clips online is supposedly for the convenience of the customers who can now surf for their domestic workers in their own time. Maid agencies that have websites usually put up the bio-data of domestic workers online. Some indicate that videos are also available for viewing in the maid agency. The videos were taken from maidcity.com, the online presence of Jobuzz Consultants, an employment agency; it no longer posts videos of maids online.

(4) While waiting for employers or while finalizing the requirements of their work permits, domestic workers usually stay in the homes of the maid agents where they are supposedly 'trained'. Such an arrangement is very much subject to abuse. From the stories that my interviewees told me and from my many encounters with FDWs in my fieldwork, the 'training' usually consisted of doing the household chores in the maid agent's home and this was often accompanied by verbal and psychological abuse. Also, the domestic workers are usually not provided with decent beds and meals while they are with the agency. The domestic workers I spoke to recalled sleeping on the floor, getting only one packet of instant noodles to eat per day (and this was sometimes shared) and sometimes being punished (e.g. made to stand in the corner of the maid agency) for the slightest error, real or imagined. The domestic workers who are waiting for employers usually spend their days either in the maid agent's home or in the office of the maid agency where they may be put 'on display'.

5 The English-Speaking Other Looks Back

Anna was a Filipino domestic worker (FDW) I met in Singapore on a Sunday in April 2001, on what would turn out to be the first day of my PhD fieldwork. It was my first day as a volunteer teacher in the Filipino Overseas Workers in Singapore (FOWS) skills training program. I had been tasked to teach English to FDWs who had enrolled in the nursing aide course. Anna was one of my students and she, along with two other women, had stayed behind in the classroom as the rest of the students took a 15-minute break. In the course of talking about her employer, Anna told me that her employer's 'bad English' was one of the reasons why her English had deteriorated in Singapore:

> She had an anecdote about the 'bad English' of her employers. One time, her employer's husband called to say they would not be home for dinner and then he instructed her '...so you eat yourself'. 'Eat myself, sir?! But where do I begin? My foot?! My finger?!' She repeated the punchline, much to the amusement of her two classmates (and me). She complained about the English used by her Singaporean employers and said that she had been forced to learn to speak Singlish because when she spoke 'good English' or *'yung English ba na parang yung sa atin'* (the English that's like what we speak back home), her employers would say 'Ha? Cannot understand you'. (Field notes, 1 April 2001)

Anna's joke about her employer's English was the first of many jokes I heard in Singapore that poked fun at the English of Singaporean Chinese employers. Anna had earlier described her employer as a 'perfectionist' who was always correcting her; the joke was a temporary reversal of that pattern as Anna was showing how she knew 'better' English than her employer. Tellingly though, I never heard FDWs make fun of the English of their white 'expat' employers, even though they sometimes laughed at themselves for 'running out' (*nauubusan*) of English or complained about their difficulty in understanding their employers' accents. The rather consistent differences in how FDWs talked about the English of their Singaporean Chinese employers versus the English of their white 'expat' employers were among my first inklings that FDWs constructed and assigned distinctive scripts to different employers in Singapore. Just as maid agencies in Singapore (Chapter 4) created a hierarchy of foreign domestic workers indexed by English and based on nationality and race, FDWs too had a hierarchy of employers indexed by English and based on racial essentializations. Furthermore, Anna's complaint about her Singaporean Chinese employer's English, the distinction she drew between her 'good English' (or 'the English that we speak back home') and her employer's English, and her feeling that she had been 'forced to learn Singlish' suggest that FDWs do have a template for what they consider to be 'good English' and that their having that English was instrumental to how they positioned themselves, not just vis-à-vis their employers but also vis-à-vis domestic workers from other countries who were working in Singapore. FDWs' notions of 'good English' were intertwined with their scripts for employers and their scripts for themselves.

The Idea of 'Good English'

The FDWs I interviewed may have had different English proficiencies but they all seemed to share similar notions of what was and what was not 'good English'. Concomitantly, they shared similarly strong views about who could speak 'good English' and who could not. They invested meanings in these evaluations, constructing images and inferring causal relationships from the way people spoke, and in the process highlighting the legitimacy and value of their English vis-à-vis the English known and spoken by others. This demonstrates how 'good English' is not so much a clearly defined system of grammatical rules as it is a potent semiotic resource that can be variably appropriated by centering institutions and individual agents. As Urciuoli (1996) rightly noted, 'good English' is a powerful *social* fact.

How did the participants define 'good English'? The FDWs' self-evaluations of their English before they migrated as well as their stories about their initial linguistic dislocation in Singapore and their (former) Singaporean employers are telling in this regard. The FDWs' notion of 'good English' was to a certain extent premised on a prescriptive linguistic ideology where the values of linguistic purity (*'puro Ingles'*) and proximity to American English (or more specifically, to an American accent) were paramount, but the FDWs also valued authenticity, that is, sounding Filipino. I shall discuss these points below.

Good English is *'puro Ingles'*

When the participants talked about using English in the Philippines, they described situations where they used what they referred to as 'pure English' or *'puro Ingles'*, that is, the exclusive or sole use of English in conversations. By this, they meant that English was the only code in use in the interaction. For example, Beth who had worked as a reservation officer in a travel agency specializing in inbound Korean tourists told me that she used English extensively and *exclusively* when dealing with the tourists. But she later laughingly recounted a conversation she had with her mother, a domestic worker in Singapore, when she was still in the Philippines; she had used 'some English' and her mother had said she was not used to hearing English anymore because all she ever used in Singapore was Singlish. Fe and Gina who had worked as service crew in fast-food chains in Manila told me they used 'pure English' only when they had customers who were foreigners. Yet, the menus in fast-food chains in the Philippines are in English, and Fe and Gina would have used English words when repeating the orders of their customers. Some of the participants also told me that they used English *only* during their English subjects in school, even though they also said that their teachers would use Taglish or a 'mix' of their mother tongues and English when teaching other subjects. This notion that speaking in 'English' refers only to speaking exclusively in English draws from an ideology where languages are considered to be discrete entities and what is valuable, i.e. what is considered to be a display of proficiency (and, therefore, as signifying wealth and authority), is the capacity to produce the 'pure', unmixed linguistic code. This separation of languages was enforced in schools that the participants attended, as in Del's case where, in her words, 'must be you speak in English inside the school. That's why very difficult to communicate. We can speak in English because we must be put the fine so we force ourselves to speak in English'. Del was referring to the common practice in schools of fining students if they were caught not speaking in English. While the intention of this may be to ensure that students are immersed in an English-speaking context while they are in school, it is apparent from Del's narrative that, in a multilingual situation like the Philippines, this was not only 'difficult' but also rather 'artificial' with students forcing themselves to speak in English; its effectiveness is also, as one can see from the short extract, questionable. Not only did this practice reinforce the ideology that only 'pure English' could be considered English, it also reinforced the superior position of English vis-à-vis other languages.

This notion that 'good English' is *puro Ingles* played a significant role in the participants' self-evaluation of their use of English when they were still in the Philippines. Participants who indicated that they spoke '*carabao* English' or 'trying hard English' often referred to their experiences of being unable to speak entirely in English. This led to their feeling of being 'really conscious' (Adora) when speaking in English and feeling like they were being strangled whenever they had to use English in the Philippines (Nelma). In contrast, participants who had indicated that they could speak English well before they migrated talked about how they were '*direduretso*' (literally, 'straight') when they had to speak in English. During their interviews, the FDWs often referred to me as an example of someone who could speak 'good English' because my English was 'straight' and, according to them, 'nice to listen to' ('*masarap pakinggan*'). The FDWs subscribed to the value of *puro Ingles* and measured the value of their English against this yardstick. What exactly did 'nice to listen to' mean?

Singlish is not 'good English'

Once in Singapore, the participants used a similar scale to evaluate Singlish.[1] Whether they claimed they spoke 'good English' back in the Philippines or not, the participants defined 'good English' by identifying Singlish as a very good example of what 'good English' is not. The FDWs I interviewed thought Singlish was 'horrible' and 'not nice'. Some even used the same words they had employed to describe their 'trying hard' English when they were still in the Philippines, i.e. Singlish was 'funny' or '*carabao* English'.

When I asked them why they thought Singlish was not 'good English', they cited how words were 'interchanged' or 'chopped up' in Singapore English and how Singaporeans used 'shortcuts' such as 'Can or not?' or 'What you want?' They also pointed out that Singlish was 'not really English' because of the 'lah', 'lor' and other non-English expressions that peppered Singlish. In explaining why Singlish was not 'good English', the FDWs pointed out specific features, as can be seen in Jocel's case:

> **Jocel:** I don't like it. It's horrible to hear. In the rule of English, there's no 'lah'. No other country does that except here in Singapore. I don't like how they rhyme.
> *Ayoko. Masagwang pakinggan. In the rules of English, there's no 'lah'. No other country does that except here in Singapore. Ayoko 'yung rhyme nila ba.*

In explaining why Singlish is 'horrible to hear', Jocel picks out two particular features – 'lah', a lexical item, and 'rhyme', by which she might have been referring to the rhythm of Singlish (see Brown, 2000). She then reframes Singlish, taking it out of its local context in Singapore and comparing it 'globally' to the 'rules' of English and the use of English in 'other countries' ('No other country does that except here'). In this context, whether Jocel knows the rules of English or not, and whether she has indeed been to other English-speaking countries or not, is irrelevant; what is important is that she appropriates these scales semiotically.

The Singaporean pronunciation and accent figured prominently in the FDWs' explanations for why they thought Singlish was 'bad' English. For example, Beth cited the 'funny' pronunciation of 'h' and 'eight', which had given her difficulties when she first arrived in Singapore (see Chapter 6). Jo, who worked for a Chinese Singaporean employer for almost seven years, pointed to the lack of the rhotic /r/ in Singlish:

> **Jo**: I don't like it because they don't have /r/ [rhotic *r*]. Then their accents are different, funny. It's like they're copying but it's not appropriate to them or they can't quite copy.
> *Ayaw ko kasi walang /r/. Tapos iba 'yung accent nila, funny. Parang nanggagaya lang sila pero hindi naman bagay or hindi naman nila magaya-gaya.*

There are several things at work here. Jo highlights a feature of Singlish, i.e. the lack of a rhotic *r*, to call attention to the 'different' and 'funny' accents of Singaporeans. She then evaluates the Singaporean accent as a poor copy of presumably 'real' English by describing it as indexing speakers who are 'copying but it's not appropriate to them or they can't quite copy'.

This notion that the Singaporean accent is a poor copy of a 'real' English accent was consistently evoked by the FDWs I interviewed. Furthermore, they positioned their accent and pronunciation (the 'Filipino accent') as being superior to the Singaporean accent. In the excerpt below, Jocel had just told me that she did not like the 'accent' in Singaporean English; I had argued back that Filipinos had accents too.

> **BL**: But we Filipinos also have accents, right?
> *Pero may accent din tayo na mga Pinoy di ba?*
> **Jocel**: We can handle the accent in English, but they, they can't handle it, maybe it's in their tongues.
> *Tayo, kaya natin 'yung accent ng English pero sa kanila, di nila kaya, nasa dila na yata nila.*

One can see here how Jocel attributed the superiority of the Filipino accent to the Filipinos' *innate* ability to better handle the English accent. They positioned the Filipino accent as being close to or as being like the 'American accent', to which they attributed the positive qualities of clarity and being 'nice to listen to'. When I asked Nelma and Loida why they did not like the Singaporean accent, they both indicated their preference for the American accent:

> **Loida:** Because it's [Singlish] different. If you're not used to it, you won't understand. We have the American accent, that's why we can be easily understood and we speak clearly. Their accent is Chinese. I really prefer our accent. Because our English is straight, it's nice to listen to.
> *Kasi iba eh. Kung di ka sanay, di mo maintindihan. May American accent tayo kaya madaling maintindihan saka clear tayo magsalita. Sila Chinese ang accent nila. Prefer ko talaga 'yung accent natin. Kase straight 'yung English natin, magandang pakinggan.*
> **BL:** How do you feel about Singlish?
> **Nelma:** I just don't like it. I don't want to follow it. It's not nice. I don't want sing-song. I like the American accent because I'm used to it and it's nice to listen to.
> *Basta, ayoko talaga. Ayokong sundin. Hindi maganda. Gusto ko walang sing-song. American accent ang gusto ko kasi na-used to it na ako saka magandang pakinggan.*

By positioning the Filipino accent as being 'nice to listen to', 'straight' and close to or like the 'American' accent in its clarity, the FDWs assign the symbolic values of authenticity and 'purity' to their English, positioning it as *the* linguistic capital vis-à-vis Singlish.

This pattern of positioning the Filipino accent as being like the American accent and, as such, as superior to the Singaporean accent, is not peculiar to the 19 FDWs I interviewed. In the survey I conducted with 111 FDWs (see Chapter 1 for details), the same pattern emerged. One of the most striking results of the survey was the respondents seeming dislike of the Singaporean pronunciation of English as compared to the Filipino and the British pronunciation. When asked to rate their liking of the three different accents on a scale from 1 to 5, with 1='strongly agree' and 5='strongly disagree', the respondents indicated that they liked their own pronunciation best (1.88), followed by the British (2.46) and finally the Singaporean (3.78) pronunciation.

The respondents were also asked to rate how much they agreed that certain speakers spoke 'good English'. Interestingly, the respondents ranked themselves third (2.30), although it must be noted that they followed very closely behind Filipinos in general (2.04). American and British speakers had the 'highest' mean (1.87). On the lower end were Singaporeans (3.07) and Indonesian domestic workers (3.37).

The FDWs' dislike of the Singaporean accent and their negative evaluation of Singaporeans' English were further corroborated by the results of a comparison between those employed by locals and those working for expatriate employers based on their measures of 'linguistic accommodation', that is, on whether they (a) would like to speak like their employer; and (b) thought their present employers spoke 'good English'. FDWs with expatriate employers expressed a much higher desire to speak like their employers (2.30; $n=30$) as compared to those who worked for local employers (3.11; $n=56$); the former group also showed a stronger belief that their employers spoke 'good English' (1.71; $n=31$) as compared to the latter group (2.39; $n=56$).

Glo rationalized her evaluation of Singlish as being 'bad English' by pointing out that the English in Singapore is not what would be expected of a country where English is supposed to be the lingua franca. Tellingly, she contrasted this to the Philippines where only those who had an 'education' could be expected to use English.

> **Glo**: If this were in the Philippines, this would be acceptable because not everybody got the education you had but coming from a country wherein the normal norm for you to understand each other is English, this is quite an irony. Because they will ask you, 'You're eating, can or not?' Ha?
> *Kung sa Pilipinas ito, 'yung English na 'to acceptable eh, kase not everybody got the education you had pero coming from a country wherein ang normal norm for you to understand each other is English, this is quite an irony. Kase tatanungin ka, 'You're eating, can or not' Ha?*

The FDWs also perceived Singlish to be a resource that they would not be able to mobilize; Singlish would not have any value to them if they moved outside of Singapore, whether they went back to the Philippines or migrated to another country to work, an aspiration which many of the participants had. Beth, for example, told me that she did not want to speak Singlish because she would be ridiculed back in the Philippines:

> **Beth**: And then they will laugh at you really when you go back to the Philippines. I have a cousin here working [...]. He's a computer engineer. So every six months, he go back to the Philippines just to visit the family. And then sometimes, he speaks English there that's Singlish, my relatives would laugh; they would really laugh at him.

For Adora, she did not want to use Singlish because she was 'looking forward':

Adora: And then, uhm, no there's a word in there. Uhm, or maybe because I look forward, like I don't want to be, I don't want to be like saying these...words, you know, forever [...].

Adora's comment suggests that for FDWs, Singlish is not just 'bad English'; it also indexes their being domestic workers, and their having 'lost' their English and their voices (see Chapter 6). The FDWs' positioning of their English as being 'good English' and Singlish as 'bad English' may not just be a symbolic assertion of legitimacy, but also a claim to a preferred future where, as Adora so aptly puts it, they won't be 'saying these words forever'.

'You have to use your own accent'

The FDWs I interviewed ostracized other FDWs who adapted 'prestige' accents, e.g. British, American or Australian accents. This was evident among some of the participants. When we started talking about their English class at the center and about their classmates, a number of them drew my attention to their classmates who did not use their 'own' accents. Interestingly, in evaluating the English accents of their fellow FDWs, the participants seemed to value an 'authentic' accent, one that was Filipino. This is in contrast to the scale that they used to evaluate Singlish where the Filipino accent's proximity or similarity to the American accent was valued.

In the course of my interview with Fe and Gina, they started talking about one of their classmates who they described as 'trying hard' to perform a British accent:

Fe: The English just makes my hair stand because [...] the accent is just trying hard!
'Yung English kasi nakakatayo ng balahibo kasi [...] 'yung trying hard 'yung accent!
Gina: And it doesn't match them [laughs].
Na di naman bagay, kumbaga [laughs].
BL: But everyone has accents, I have an accent.
Pero lahat ng tao may accent eh, ako may accent.
Fe: But you have to use your own accent! You don't need to copy others, right?
Pero you have to use your own accent! You don't need to copy others ano?

FDWs in my class who were perceived to be 'flaunting' their English skills were labeled as 'show offs', 'OA' (i.e. overacting) and pretentious:

Jo: It's like some Filipinas, it's like they're showing off. Like A. in class. The group doesn't like her because it's like she's too pretentious, too OA. The impression of her is just because she's good in English, she's showing it off! Her Tagalog doesn't have an accent!
Parang 'yung mga ibang Pilipina, parang pinagmamayabang. Gaya ni A. sa klase. Ayaw sa kanya sa grupo kase parang masyado syang maarte, masyadong OA. Ang impression sa kanya eh porke't marunong siyang mag-English, pinagmamayabang niya! E 'yung Tagalog naman nya, wala namang accent!

According to Peng, in Singapore, it did not matter whether an FDW had a degree or if she was fluent in English; in the end, they were all domestic workers. This may explain why 'non-Filipino' accents were derided and the FDW was perceived as having pretensions of not being a Filipino, and as denying being a domestic worker:

Peng: Even if you're a graduate and you have a degree from Manila, please keep that under the table. That's just back home, here you're still a maid. Your degree is your advantage over us who did not finish, but here we are all the same.
Kahit graduate ka, may degree ka from Manila, please keep that under the table. Sa atin lang yun, ilagay mo sarili mo na katulong ka pa rin. 'Yung degree mo, yun ang advantage mo sa min na hindi nakatapos, pero dito pare-pareho tayo.

A Hierarchy of Desirable Employers

The FDWs' script of 'good English' played an important role in their hierarchy of desirable employers as well as the extent to which they could use their English as a means of subverting, however temporarily, the employer–domestic worker relationship. While the variety of English their employers spoke and their perceived fluency in English was not the deciding factor in whether FDWs liked their employers or not, English seemed to be one of the few sanctioned sites where they could, to varying degrees, display their feelings toward their employer and visibly contest their subordinate role.

The FDWs I interviewed had quite a clear hierarchy of desirable employers, with Singaporean Chinese at the bottom and white expatriate employers at the top. Paul (2011), who found a similar pattern with FDWs in Singapore and Hong Kong, argues that this stereotyping that the FDWs employ reproduces racial hierarchies with the FDWs distancing themselves from local Chinese employers and aligning themselves with expatriate white employers. I would add that the racial stereotyping that FDWs employ and that is rationalized and reinforced by 'good English' highlights the bind of agency (Butler, 1997) experienced by FDWs, that is, while they may be able to rewrite their scripts of servitude and temporarily resist the immediate context of their marginalization, in doing so, they also reconstitute and reproduce enduring structural conditions.

Singaporean Chinese employers

The FDWs I interviewed said that there were huge differences between Singapore Chinese and white expatriate employers. All of the FDWs said that, by and large, they preferred (or they would prefer, in the case of those working with Singaporean Chinese) working with expatriates, though they did qualify that not all expatriates are good employers. It must also be noted that the participants did say that not all Chinese employers were 'bad', but the worst Chinese employer was significantly worse than the worst expatriate employer.

Adora and Beth said that the biggest difference between Singaporean Chinese and expatriate employers was the degree of 'freedom' they had. According to them, Chinese Singaporean employers had a tendency to 'control' the FDWs and to not want them to succeed:

BL: What was it like changing from Chinese to expat?
Beth: It's a big difference [...] in terms of freedom [...] because in Chinese, they're like degrading you. It's like they don't want you to succeed and they want to control you. They want you to become a maid. Whereas with expat employer, you have your own freedom but it depends. In my case, I have more freedom, I have more freedom to go out, it's not like with the Chinese when even when I was doing office work, I cannot just go out to buy something else outside. I still have to ask permission from them and they still ask me why.

It's a big difference [...] in terms of freedom [...] because in Chinese they're like degrading you. Parang ayaw ka nilang umasenso saka hawak-hawak ka pa rin. Gusto ka nila ikatulong. Whereas with expat employer, you have your own freedom but it depends. In my case, I have more freedom, kumbaga I have freedom sa paglabas-labas, hindi kagaya 'yung Chinese kahit na office work 'yung ginagawa mo, I cannot just go out to buy something else outside. I still have to ask permission from them and they still ask me why.

Beth: The same with my first employer, especially the wife. She wants to be recognized all the time. It's the type like, that's my madam, that's my boss. And then when you're out, she always says that's my maid. She always go out and then she always takes you with her and you have to carry her things and then she says 'this is my maid'. That's how she is. Even with her friends because, you see with my first employer, the wife was a stewardess. But when she got married, her husband was not like her friends. Her friends married rich Singaporeans, she married an ordinary man. So she wants to show off that she has two maids. Sometimes she gets asked 'who's that?'. Because the other maid who was with me in the house, she looked Chinese and they always mistake them as sisters and she always says 'that's my maid!' (laughs).

The same with my first employer, especially the wife. She wants to be recognized all the time. Yung tipo bang, that's my madam, that's my boss. And then when you're out, she always says that's my maid. She always go out and then she always takes you with her and you have to bitbit her things and then she says 'this is my maid'. Ganun siya. Kahit yung mga friends nya kase ano 'to my first employer, the wife was a stewardess. But when she got married yung napangasawa nya not like her friends. Yung friends nya married rich Singaporeans, siya she married an ordinary man. So she wants to show off that she has two maids. Yun pag tinatanong ng maids nya 'who's that?'. Kase yung kasama ko sa bahay nun, mukhang Chinese and they always mistake them as sisters and she always says 'that's my maid!' (laughs).

This lack of 'freedom' with 'Chinese' employers and their supposed tendency to 'look down' on domestic workers was a consistent stereotype that all the participants and FDWs I talked to had. Pearly, for example, told me that it was only after four years that her 'Chinese' employer finally gave her two Sundays off and these were given only after she pleaded with them to let her study at the center. Del told me that in the six years that she worked for a Chinese family with elderly parents, she only got a half day off every other Sunday and she had to cram all her activities (remitting money, attending church, buying phone cards and personal items, etc.) into those half days. Linda was very emotional when she told me that:

Linda: Even if you know English, if your employer is Chinese, they still treat you the same. You're still a maid, it doesn't matter if

> you know English [...] With Chinese families, when you're a maid, you're really just a maid. That's how they look down.
> *Kahit na marunong kang mag-English kung Chinese amo mo, wala rin, ang trato sa 'yo ganun pa rin. Katulong ka pa rin, it doesn't matter kung marunong kang mag-Ingles [...] Pag Chinese family talaga, pag katulong ka, katulong ka lang talaga. Ganun sila mag-look down.*

Glo had also been told by her sister-in-law who was working in Singapore when she arrived that with Chinese employers, 'you cannot voice out your own opinion, no matter how you say you are right [...]. They would never accept [...]'. That the Chinese thought domestic workers should behave according to their whims was often cited as one of the reasons why Chinese employers would cancel contracts and buy return tickets back to the Philippines for FDWs without first notifying them about it.

Singaporean Chinese employers' restrictions on the FDWs' freedom was coupled with what the participants viewed as a lack of trust in them. Fe, for example, said her Chinese employer would claim that she had called the house and that Fe had not answered the phone. She attributed this to her employer's suspicions: '...in the mind of the boss, if they are not there, the helper will go out and have fun, or the helper will use the personal items of the employer' (*Ang isip ng boss, pag wala sila, ang katulong maglalakwatsa, o ang katulong gagamitin ang gamit ng amo*). According to Fe, her employer would also voice her suspicions of her indirectly (*parinig*), something that really irked Fe because she thought her employer was treating her as if she were 'just a maid' when in fact, she was very observant. In this excerpt, Fe reports what her employer said and what her response was:

> **Fe:** 'You know my friend ah, my friend ah, their maid ah, wash the clothes ah, they just wash their clothes together with the rest and then ah, the clothes together and then they just wash together with the clothes of the maid' (in a colloquial Singlish accent). I said that I would not wash my clothes. I said 'No, no matter what you do, I will not include my clothes with yours, no matter what you do, even if you pay me.' I told her in front.
> *You know my friend ah, my friend ah, their maid ah, wash the clothes ah, they just wash their clothes together with the rest and then ah, the clothes together and then they just wash together with the clothes of the maid.' Sabi ko na hindi ako maglalaba ng damit ko. Sabi ko 'no, kahit anong gawin nila, hindi ko isasali ang damit ko sa inyo, kahit anong gawin niyo, kahit bayaran ako. Sinabi ko in front.*

BL: What's their reaction when you talk to them that way?
Anong reaction nila pag kinakausap mo sila ng ganyan?

Fe: They're quiet. Because you are confronting them. They seem to really think that you are stupid but they do not know that you have been observing them. They seem to think that we are just maids, but they do not know that beforehand whatever it is that they thought about you, you've thought worse about them. You've thought about it and so you are ahead of them.
Tahimik sila. Kasi kino-confront mo sila. Talagang kumbaga kala nila tatanga-tanga ka, di nila alam na nagmamasid ka sa kanila, yun bang parang kala nila maid lang tayo, di nala alam na beforehand pa kung anong naisip nila sa yo, mas grabe pang naisip mo sa kanila, naisip mo na, kaya naunahan mo na sila.

Fe's story is telling, not just for what she says her employer does, but also for how she reports it. When she reports the speech of her employer, she does so with a colloquial Singlish accent and she punctuates the speech, somewhat exaggeratedly, with many 'ahs', a particle characteristic of colloquial Singapore English. She then switches back to Filipino to recount what she said and to highlight how she confronted and silenced her employer. This script where FDWs perform or attribute Singlish to their Chinese employers while portraying themselves as either being able to talk back or being in a somewhat superior position to their employers was a consistent pattern in the stories the participants told me.

In households where the employers predominantly used Singlish, the FDWs could claim to be the ones with 'good English', to the point that they would sometimes correct their employers' English. As it was rare that the FDWs could overtly correct their employer's English, they sometimes used the children as an excuse to impose the use of 'correct English' on the household. Nelma, for example, adjusted to the Singlish of her employers but she also tried to regulate the Singlish spoken by the children by telling them to remove their 'lahs' when they were at home:

BL: How do you feel when you use Singlish?
Anong feeling mo pag napapa-Singlish ka?

Nelma: It's OK because you really need to adjust. But as for the kids I'm taking care of now, I'd like to remove their 'lah'. S$1 for every lah. I tell them that here at home, they have to 'fix' their language. I'd be a millionaire if they paid for each 'lah'.
OK lang kase kelangan naman talagang mag-adjust ka. Pero 'yung alaga ko nga ngayon, gusto kong tanggalin 'yung 'lah' nila eh. $1

ang bawat lah. Sabi ko, dito sa bahay ayusin niyo naman salita nyo. Milyonaro na sana ako kung may bayad bawat 'lah' nila eh.

Linda told me that she once explicitly corrected her employer's English by arguing that if the employer kept 'pronouncing' English in the wrong way, the children would follow:

> **Linda**: My first employer, the sauce, sauces even if there's just one. Watch, watches. Once, I really told him/her off. I really don't like it. That's not the way to pronounce. If you pronounce that way, the children will follow.[2]
>
> *'Yung una kong amo, 'yung sauce, sauces maski isa lang. 'Yung watch, watches. Minsan sinabihan ko talaga. Ayoko talaga. Hindi yan ang pag-pronounce. Pag ganyan ka mag-pronounce, susunod 'yung mga bata.*

The FDWs' imposition of 'correct English', in the interests of their employers' children, was not questioned. There could be a convergence of interests here that allows the FDWs to assert their 'good English'. FDWs may be genuinely concerned about the children; at the same time, by highlighting the children, they are also able to implicitly call attention to the fact that, in the household, they are the ones with the linguistic capital. For the employers, increasing the linguistic capital of their children would be their paramount concern, given that they are living in a country that runs regular campaigns reminding its citizens to 'speak good English' so as to bolster their and the country's competitiveness. This theme crops up again in a later section where I discuss how the FDWs portray themselves as being 'more than just maids'.

A display of 'straight English', or even just the suggestion that they had a claim to 'standard' English, was risky as it could mean repercussions from the employer, especially when it was the employer himself/herself who was challenged. Glo, with whom I had a close relationship, often told me about her travails with her new employers, a Japanese-Australian couple; the Japanese wife was not proficient in English. One day, she told me, the husband suggested that the wife learn English from Glo:

> **Glo**: My male employer said to my female employer, 'Why don't you learn English from Glo?' That made things so difficult! Now the woman asks me to do all sorts of things, I even have to pour water for her even if the pitcher is right in front of her!
>
> *Sabi ba naman ng amo kong lalaki sa babae, 'Why don't you learn English from Glo?' Ang hirap kaya nun no?! Kung anu-ano tuloy ang inuutos ng babae sa akin, pati ba naman 'yung water sa pitsel pinapapour niya kahit na nasa harapan niya!'*

While the FDWs' rejection and stigmatization of certain varieties of English may rarely be explicitly demonstrated in the face of their employers, their presence in the household may still change the linguistic economy in that particular space. Sometimes, the presence of an English-speaking FDW who can speak English and who can potentially make a claim to being able to speak the 'standard' seemed to 'silence' some employers who were not fluent in English. For example, Pearly, who said that her female employer was more fluent in Chinese than in English, told me about her employer's silence whenever she told the children not to follow the 'lah lah lah' of Singlish:

> **Pearly**: Sometimes there's lah lah lah but we try not to use it. I say that the children might follow if they hear it. I tell them to try not to use it. When my female employer hears that, she's just quiet. That's because my female employer answers in Chinese even when she is spoken to in English. I hear her when she's teaching piano, even when she's spoken to in English, she seems to steer it to Chinese.
> *Minsan lah lah lah pero we try not to use it. Sinasabi ko na baka sundan ng mga bata pag narinig nila. I tell them to try not to use it. Pag naririnig ng amo kong babae, tahimik lang siya. 'Yung amo kong babae kase, kahit na kinakausap siya sa English, sasagot siya sa Chinese. Naririnig ko 'yan pag nagtuturo siya ng piano, kahit na English ang salita sa kanya, parang iniisteer ba niya to Chinese.*

The lack of a common language, i.e. English, between the FDW and an employer could also render the employer temporarily 'voiceless', that is, unable to communicate with the FDW. This was something that the FDWs said they sometimes liked because it meant they would not be ordered around or scolded all the time. For Loida, for instance, her female employer's incapacity to speak in English meant that she had to rely on her employer's children to translate instructions for her. This sometimes meant waiting for the children or the husband to come home. It also meant that Loida was left to take care of the household chores with very minimal supervision:

> **Loida**: The woman was Chinese so if there were children at home, they would translate. If it was just the two of us, we'd talk through action or I'd chop up the words, ½ Chinese, ½ English. Even the man, he was not very fluent in English. [...] My female employer could not talk so what was my job, was my job. I just took care of everything because she could not talk to me.
> *Chinese 'yung babae so pa may anak siya sa bahay, sila 'yung nag-tratranslate. Pag kaming dalawa, nag-uusap kami through action or*

china-chop-chop ko 'yung words, ½ Chinese ½ English. Pati 'yung lalaki, hindi rin gaanong marunong mag-English. [...] 'Yung amo kong babae, di nakakapagsalita so 'yung sa akin, akin na lang. Ako na'ng bahala sa lahat kasi hindi niya ako makausap.

As her employer could not give her explicit instructions, Loida could do things her way. She told me of an instance when her female employer wanted to tell her how to wash the laundry. Because the two of them could not communicate, Loida went ahead and washed the laundry as she always did. Only when her male employer came home did her female employer finally manage to 'tell' her to wash the men's and women's clothes separately. Jocel and Myrna whose first employers were also 'Chinese' had similar stories. They said it was sometimes to their advantage because this meant that they only discussed the most important things and the employers could not 'nag' them about their work.

While the FDWs may rarely denigrate Singlish in their public scripts, i.e. when they are face-to-face with their employer, the English spoken by their employers was definitely, as I said in the introduction, the topic of many of their jokes. On the occasions when I would have lunch with my students as well as some of the FDWs who attended classes at the Bayanihan Center, they would regale their friends and me with stories and jokes about the English of their employers. This was a constant source of amusement in all of my English classes and in my interviews as well.

Jo: Like a friend of mine, she said someone was told, 'Eat dog!' when they meant 'Feed the dog!' This one, my friend was laughing so hard when she told me. Someone was supposedly told, 'Clean chicken!' but actually they meant 'Clean kitchen!' She supposedly went through the whole kitchen looking for the chicken to clean.
Like 'yung isa kong kaibigan sabi may sinabihan daw na 'Eat dog!' eh ang ibig sabihin pala e 'Feed the dog!'. Ito, tawang-tawa 'yung kaibigan ko nung kinuwento niya. May sinabihan daw ng 'Clean chicken!' pero actually 'Clean kitchen!' ang ibig sabihin. Hinahulughog daw niya 'yung buong kusina sa kakahanap ng manok na lilinisin.

These jokes among FDWs are not confined to Singapore. Lan (2003), whose research is on FDWs in Taiwan, reports that FDWs make fun of the English of their employers. Constable (1997) also mentions the same phenomenon among FDWs in Hong Kong. I had heard similar jokes from FDWs who used to work in the Middle East. The jokes have the same pattern. They are usually related to job directions given to migrant domestic workers by their employers [...]. English directions like [these] often lead to miscommunication. As a consequence, the domestic worker often fails to perform the duty; in some cases, they even consciously twist the order as a way of resistance. (Lan, 2003: 154)

As such, in one version of the 'Eat dog' joke that I heard, and which had all the trappings of an urban legend, I was told that the FDW had actually cooked the dog that was the household pet. FDWs also told me that they were sometimes asked to 'Broom the floor' (i.e. sweep the floor) or to 'Bring down the staircase' (i.e. bring down the ladder). To some degree, these 'jokes may temporarily reverse the pattern of domination and subservience between employers and workers or between local Chinese and overseas workers' (Constable, as cited in Lan, 2003: 154).

Some of the FDWs seemed unable to mobilize their claims to 'good English' with Singaporean employers who required them not to speak Singlish at home. Gina who, earlier in the interview, had been poking fun at how Singaporeans pronounced certain words, told me later that her current employer required her not to speak Singlish at home. She found this to be 'difficult'.

Gina: My employer wants me to use 'where', 'we', 'what', complete sentence because the kids will follow [...] so you have to know how to use 'where', 'what', 'did you'. 'I would like to speak to' not 'I would like to talk to' [...] It was that hard!
'Yung employer ko, gusto niya gamitin mo 'yung where, we, what, complete sentence kasi mahahawa 'yung mga bata [...] Kailangan alam mong gamiting 'yung where, 'yung what, did you, I would like to speak to hindi I would like to talk to [...]. Ganun kahirap no!

Yet, even when the Chinese employers seemed to speak standard Singapore English, FDWs like Gina still tended to portray them as being unreasonably strict and prescriptive about grammar or lexical choice (e.g. 'speak' vs. 'talk'), or they were portrayed as being arrogant or, at the very least, overly confident about the correctness of their English. This was the case for Myrna.

Myrna: My female Chinese employer, she was even the one who criticized me. The one who is not good is the one who criticizes! She thought she was good. (BL: What was your reaction when she criticized you?) I didn't react because I knew I was better than her. I just told her that our Englishes were different: theirs is British English, ours is American English.

> 'Yung amo kong Chinese na babae, siya pa 'yung namimintas. Kung sino pa 'yung di marunong, siya pa 'yung namimintas. Feeling niya, siya 'yung magaling. (BL: Ano 'yung reaction mo pag pinipintasan ka niya?) Wala e alam ko namang mas magaling ako sa kanya. Sinasabi ko na lang sa kanya na magkaiba 'yung English namin: 'yung sa kanila British English, 'yung atin American English.

'White' expat employers

In contrast, the FDWs portrayed most of their white expatriate employers as being 'progressive', not 'looking down' and treating them as 'equals'. The participants had a lot of stories about how their expatriate employers did not closely monitor or supervise them at work, allowing them to do their tasks independently. Their expatriate employers supported them when they wanted to attend classes at the center, etc. In the hierarchy of employers in Singapore, expatriates were definitely at the top.

One of the most striking things that white expatriate employers did, and which the FDWs looked at favorably as part of the script of expatriates, was that they preferred to be called by their first names.

> **Adora**: At first, I call them Mr and Mrs. Then after a week, they said they don't like it; call us by our first name. At first, I get difficulty because I'm not used to it because you know they're your employers and you have to say sir or ma'am. I always said Mr and Mrs but they don't like it because I don't know.
>
> **Beth**: Expats are like that. 'Call me by my first name.' I heard it's because it's degrading to them (to be called sir/ma'am or Mr/Mrs).
> Mga expat ganyan eh. 'Call me by my first name.' Kase nakakadegrade sa kanila, I heard.

In their stories, the participants cast white expatriate employers in a favorable light, showing how being allowed to call their employers by their first names was more than just a symbolic leveling of the relationship between the domestic worker and employer, white expatriate employers treated them as equals. Edna, who was the only full-time part-timer among the participants, said that her white expatriate employers seemed to treat her work as equal to theirs, that is, that her job was a job like theirs was.

> **Edna**: Even those who I work part-time for, it seems that they level their work to mine. I had an American employer before. He's a bachelor, whatever it was he was working on he would tell me.

> On Saturdays, if his girlfriend was not around, he would call me, tell me what went on in the office, ask me how I was. He would teach me what I should do. He would give ideas. Because one time I said to him: 'I have an employer who's always stealing my time.' He said to me: 'He's consuming your time.'
>
> *Kahit na yung mga part-time na trabaho, it seems na nilelevel nila sa akin yung trabaho nila. May American na amo ko noon. He's a bachelor, kung ano yung kanyang trinatrabaho, sinasabi nila sa akin. Saturday yun, kung wala yung kanyang girlfriend, tatawagin nya ako, sasabihin niya kung anong nangyari sa kanyang office, tinatanong nya kung kumusta ako. Tinuturuan nya ako kung anong gagawin ko. Nagbibigay sya ng ideas. Kase sabi ko sa kanya: 'I have an employer who's always stealing my time.' Sabi niya sa akin: 'He's consuming your time.'*

Arguably, Edna was doing emotional labor in listening to her employer's stories about his work, especially when his girlfriend was not around. But to Edna, her American employer's opening up to her about his work, asking her about how she is and teaching her what to do (including correcting her choice of words) are signals of a more equal, more 'level' relationship. From their stories, it seemed to me that FDWs had 'conversations' with their expatriate employers, while they had instructions from and fights with their Chinese employers. For Marivic, conversations and sharing stories with her Australian employer were a regular thing and one of the main reasons why Marivic considered her employer to be kind (*mabait*). When I had asked her why she considered her employer to be kind, Marivic told me what a regular day with her employer was like:

Marivic: …After our lunch, she would call me and say 'Come and have a cuppa with me', the woman, the man is at work. Then we'd share stories with each other like she would ask me what my family background is, she would ask me 'if you want to ask me something about my family'. Then, when it's our dinner, after our dinner, after I have put the kids to bed, she would invite me to have a drink. We'd drink gin and tonic, even with my male employer if he has arrived. Then we'd share stories; that's our conversation; that's how we communicate…Our conversations would reach an hour. Then, if I'm in a hurry, she would say: 'Marivic, it's alright. You can do it tomorrow.' Unless, she has a call, then she excuses herself. That's everyday: we talk for one hour; we exchange ideas about the house, what's nice, the children, food. Yes, it's like that.

> *After lunch namin tatawagin ako, sasabihin 'Come and have a cuppa with me', 'yung babae, 'yung lalaki nasa trabaho. Tapos nagkukuwentuhan kami like tinatanong niya kung ano yung family background ko, tinatanong niya ako 'if you want to ask me something about my family'. Tapos, pag dinner naman namin, after namin mag-dinner, pag nalagay ko na yung mga bata sa bed nila, tatawagin naman ako ng amo ko na mag-inom, inom kami ng gin and tonic, pati yung amo ko na lalaki kung dumating na. Tapos yun kuwentuhan kami; tapos ganun ang conversation namin; ganun kami mag-communicate...Umaabot ng isang oras ang usapan namin. Tapos pag nagamamadali ako, sasabihin niya 'Marivic, it's alright, you can do it tomorrow.' Unless na lang pag may tawag na siya, ayun nag-eexcuse na siya. Everyday yan: one hour kami nag-uusap, nag-eexchange ng ideas about yung bahay, anong maganda, yung mga bata, pagkain. Oo ganun.*

It must be pointed out that Marivic was still the one who put the children to bed. Marivic would still be the one who would wash the glasses used for the gin and tonic the next day (a task that could add to her other tasks for the day). Presumably, Marivic prepares the lunch and the dinner. But Marivic really valued how she seemed to be treated as an equal, how she was somehow 'allowed' to do the same things as her employers did: a cup of tea after lunch, a gin and tonic after dinner, conversations about what would be best for the home.

The FDWs never made fun of the English spoken by their white expatriate employers. In fact, their expatriate employers' imposition of 'standard' English on the household was something they did not question. This was true whether their expatriate employers were 'native' English speakers (e.g. American, British or Australian) or 'non-native' speakers (e.g. French). Glo, who considered herself to be fluent in English, had an American employer who minimized her communication with the children on Mondays because, according to Glo, she knew that Glo would have a 'hangover' from talking in Singlish on her day off, the day before. She was told: 'If you can't talk plain English on Mondays, don't talk'. Glo told me that she understood this because her priority was the children and this was especially important because the children were studying at the Tanglin School (an international school).

> **Glo**: With my first employer, my priority was the children and the kids were studying in Tanglin so it was really British English. [...] So I cannot speak with them in a sing-song manner. I could never

talk with them with the expressions of the Chinese, the lahs, ok lahs and cannots. You really have to speak straight English.

Dun sa unang amo ko kasi, parang ang priority ko dun bata tapos sa Tanglin pa nag-aaral kaya talagang British English. [...] So I cannot speak with them in a sing-song manner. I could never talk with them with 'yung mga expression ng mga Chinese, 'yung mga lah, ok lah, cannot. You have to really speak straight English.

Del, who considered her English back in the Philippines to be *carabao* English, faced a similar situation with her former French employers who would point out to her that she was using a 'Singaporean word':

Del: I learn a lot ma'am, you know why? When I work in my France language [referring to French employer], my language I use the Singaporean word. That's why my madam say: 'Oh, you're using the Singaporean word.' 'I'm sorry, ma'am.' I stay with them for six months. I learn how to speak English also.

Del now faced pressure with her Dutch employers who told her that she must learn how to speak 'good English' because she was teaching the children:

Del: My first kid 1 ½ years old. I talk to her English and then she learn to me [...] I teach the children. She learn Dutch language so must be I give to her pronunciation English [Parents speak to the child in Dutch, Peng speaks to the child in English] [...] My madam say 'must be you know how to speak English clearly because the children learn from you'. That's why oooohhhh, must be my pronunciation also.

A Hierarchy of Domestic Workers

In their narratives, the participants also pointed out to me how their knowledge of English made them more than just maids. There were two ways in which they did this. First, they positioned themselves as 'not just doing household work' by emphasizing how they did things beyond the scope of a 'maid', e.g. tutoring the children and doing office work. Second, they compared themselves to the Indonesian foreign domestic workers and designated the Indonesians as the 'real maids'.

More than just a maid

The FDWs portrayed their 'good English' as instrumental to their being asked to do jobs beyond 'just' household work, something which all of them viewed positively. Jocel summarized to me the difference English makes by pointing out that if a domestic worker did not know English, she would be confined to doing household chores:

> **Jocel**: If you're a helper, they'll think that you can do a better job, you can help in the business if you can speak English [...]. Because I can speak English, they automatically think I can do other things. (BL: For example?) Like tutoring the kids or helping out in the business. If you don't know how to speak in English, you just do household chores.
> *If you're a helper, they'll think na you can do a better job, you can help in the business if you can speak English [...]. Because I can speak English, automatically isipin nila na kaya ko ang ibang trabaho. (BL: For example?) 'Yung pag-tutor sa mga bata or pagtulong sa business nila. Kung di ka marunong sa Ingles, trabahong bahay ka lang.*

This was further confirmed when I asked the FDWs I interviewed why they thought their employers hired them. They were quick to emphasize that they were not hired to do only household chores. Among the various roles that FDWs undertook in households, their additional duty as a tutor to the children was the one that cropped up the most in the interviews. Adora, for example, said her first employers hired her because she would be able to speak in English to their two young children, aged one and six years. The same was true for Connie whose first employers were a couple who spoke 'broken English'. In this family, Connie not only taught the children English, she also evaluated the English tutors the children had:

> **Connie**: Actually, they were thankful that I was good in English and I could teach the children. So sometimes, last time, they had an English teacher who'd come to the house who was Chinese Singaporean. But to me, her standard also is not very good. So after she'd left, my employer would ask me: 'So how is she doing?' So I had to be honest, I said: 'In my own opinion, not very good.' So they had to change the teacher [...].
> *Actually, thankful sila na marunong akong mag-Ingles and then matuturuan ko 'yung mga bata. So sometimes, last time, 'yung may English teacher sila nun na nagpupunta eh Chinese Singaporean.*

> *But to me, her standard also is not very good. So pag umaalis na siya nun, tinatanong ako ng amo ko: 'So how is she doing?' So I'm kind of, so I had to be honest. I said: 'In my own opinion, not very good.' So they had to change the teacher [...].*

The FDWs were aware that their services were going at a bargain and they accepted this as part of their job. As Nelma, another FDW who had tutored the children wryly remarked, her employers had gotten a good deal with her:

> **BL**: Did you tutor the kids?
> *Nag-tutor ka ba sa mga bata?*
> **Nelma**: *Naku day*, it is me! Spelling, homework, Chinese, Hanyu Pinyin from Grade 1 to Grade 4. I've gotten used to it, no extra pay. My employers saved money with me! The Chinese tutor comes twice a week and is paid S$100. I don't get paid for English. But they treat me OK. If they were like Herod, I'd also lose control.
> *Naku day, ako na nga! Spelling, homework, Chinese, 'yung Hanyu Pinyin from the time na Grade 1 to Grade 4. Nakasanayan ko na rin, walang extra pay. Nakatipid nga mga employers ko eh. 'Yung tutor sa Chinese, twice a week pumupunta S$100 ang bayad nila. Ako, sa English, walang bayad. Pero OK naman pakikitungo nila. Kung Herodes sila, aba di magwawala din ako.*

It must be noted that Adora, Connie and Nelma were employed by Singaporeans. The FDWs did not tutor the children when they were employed by expatriates or by Singaporean families who seemed to have a good grasp of standard English.

Apart from tutoring the children, sometimes the FDWs themselves ended up being an English source for their employers. Connie, whose female employer is Taiwanese, told me that she is her employer's walking dictionary:

> **Connie**: It seems to be she's asking me all the time. And right now, she's still asking me a lot of spellings and she calls me 'walking dictionary'. Although, I'm not really that good in spelling but compared to her, maybe that's why she's calling me that. When we're in the car and then she wanted to ask me something and then bbbzzzzzzzz. When I hear that bzzzzzz and then I know that she wanted to ask me something about spelling: 'OK, walking dictionary, this and that.'

The FDWs also portrayed themselves as being 'like secretaries'. In the case of Loida whose employers were Japanese, she and her fellow domestic worker who was also Filipino seemed to take charge of the couple's external communication:

> **Loida**: Their English isn't fluent. [...] we answer all of their calls. Even making an appointment with the dentist, for example. If they're talking to someone in English and they can't understand, they call us.
> *Hindi dire-diretso 'yung English nila. [...] lahat ng calls nila, kami 'yung sasagot. Pati 'yung paggawa ng appointment halimbawa sa dentist. Tapos pag may kausap sila ng English na di nila maintindihan, tinatawag nila kami.*

Glo, on the other hand, portrayed herself as being a secretary for her employer. In this narrative, Glo not only talks about what she does for her employers, she also positions herself and her 'fluency in English' as being appropriate for the 'high-level' positions of her employers:

> **Glo**: My male employer is a vice-president of human resources at Citibank, so it can't be helped that there are many people who call him. And one thing that helped was my fluency in English in the way I talk on the phone to them. They say they feel that they're talking to a secretary in an office. Probably it's the way I would take down the messages; I would ask them what they want. And maybe for them, only secretaries do that and not housekeepers or just anybody. And then when I repeat it to my employer, it's like every word. At some point, he was asked: 'Do you have a secretary at home?'
> *'Yung amo kong lalaki sa Citibank yan vice-president sya ng human resources so di maiiwasan na maraming taong tumatawag sa kanila. And one thing na nakatulong sa pagiging fluent ko sa English is the way I talk sa phone sa kanila. They feel daw na nakikipag-usap sila sa secretary ng opisina. Probably the way I would take down the messages, I would ask them what they want na para bang sa kanila secretary lang gumagawa nun hindi housekeeper or anybody. And then pag inulit sa employer ko it's just like word per se. At some point tinanong pa nga: 'Do you have a secretary at home?'*

Like Glo, Linda, whose employers were Turkish diplomats, told me that her level of fluency in English was one of the reasons why she had been hired. She thought her fluency in English 'matched' the position of her employer.

The value of 'daldal'

Some of the FDWs I interviewed also said to me that it wasn't 'English' as such that got them hired, nor was it the important linguistic resource in their work as domestic workers in Singapore; it was what they could do with English that mattered. Jocel, for example, attributed her being hired by her Indian-Canadian employers to her capacity for 'daldal', or chatting up or making conversation. She said that when they interviewed her, she talked to the child and her emotion work in showing interest in the child was translated into the child expressing a preference for her.

> **Jocel**: During the interview, I talked to the child well. They were choosing between two of us. I went to their house so they could see how I cook, etc. The kid picked me (BL: Why?). She thinks I like kids because I talked to her so much. I asked her: 'What's your name? How old are you? Where do you study?' You know, I chatted her up.
> *During the interview, kausap ko yung bata ng maayos. Dalawa kase kaming pinagpipilian nila. Pumunta ako sa bahay nila para makita nila how I cook, etc. The kid picked me (Bakit daw?). She thinks I like kids because I talked to her so much. I asked her: 'What's your name? How old are you? Where do you study?' Alam mo na, dinaldal ko.*

Glo, who first worked in Kuwait, said that she believed she was hired by her then employer because of her qualities, among them her 'animatedness' and 'patience' in explaining things. Glo's Kuwaiti employer had actually met her face to face in Manila. Glo described him as being in the waiting area of the maid agency she went to. Glo was not even really there to apply as a domestic worker, she was interested but she was mainly there to accompany a friend. She did not know that he was a possible employer. He casually talked to her and her friend in the waiting area and by the end of their conversation, he told the agency – much to Glo's surprise – that he wanted to hire her. When I asked her why she thought she, and not her friend, was selected, she said:

> **Glo**: Maybe what helped is that…One thing that they said about me was that I was animated, I was animated in talking, patient about explaining, maybe I was proficient in English orally and then they said to me, I seem more independent than the other one.
> *Siguro what helped is that…One thing na sinabi nila sa aking was na animated daw ako, animated ako in talking, matiyaga akong mag-explain, siguro proficient din ako sa English orally and then sabi nila sa akin, I seem more independent kaysa sa isa.*

'When we speak to Indonesians, our English is baroque'

Apart from identifying their capacity to do language-based work and their communication skills as qualities that made them more than just maids, the FDWs also embraced a *nationality-based categorization* that was exactly like the categorizations used by maid agencies (see Chapter 4). They constructed the Indonesians as the 'others' to themselves. The observation that FDWs embrace a nationality-based racial categorization to differentiate themselves from other domestic workers is in keeping with the observations that Parreñas (2001) has made of FDWs in Italy and the United States, and Lan (2003) of FDWs in Taiwan.

The FDWs claimed they were 'ahead', i.e. that their 'good English' enabled them to provide better services than their Indonesian counterparts, their nearest competitors in the market of foreign domestic workers in Singapore.

> **Mary**: We are ahead. That's because you only have to teach Filipinas once or twice and they can easily catch up. The Indonesians have a hard time. That's because their English is poor or the English they learned is low-level. I trained an Indonesian who took over my place with my first employer. It was really difficult. I would use actions with English so we'd understand each other.
> *Mas lamang tayo. Kasi ang Pinay, pag tinuruan once or twice, madaling maka-catch up. 'Yung mga Indonesian, nahihirapan. Poor kasi 'yung English nila or mababa lang 'yung English na natutunan nila. Nakapag-training ako ng pumalit sa akin sa first employer ko, Indonesian, mahirap talaga. 'Yung English sinasabayan ko ng action para magkaintindihan kami.*

In highlighting what their 'good English' enables them to do, the FDWs categorize themselves as not being a maid 'who is only for housework' while the Indonesians are the ones who are 'really maids'. This was apparent in my interview with Pearly who claimed that FDWs were 'more accurate' with their work, whereas Indonesians did not even know what a 'simple' English word such as 'ice cube' meant:

> **Pearly**: We are more capable of doing work than the Indonesians. We're more accurate with our work. We also understand things faster. The Indonesians, they don't even know what 'ice cube' means. *We are more capable of doing work than the Indonesians. Mas accurate tayo sa trabaho. Mas madali rin tayong makaintindi. 'Yung Indonesian nga, ni 'ice cube' hindi niya alam eh.*

BL: Ice cube?

Pearly: Yeah, we went once to the house of a sibling of my employer's. They had an Indonesian maid. She was told to get ice cubes. She didn't know. So we had to explain that it's ice in the refrigerator.
Oo, pumunta kami minsan sa bahay ng kapatid ng amo ko. May Indonesian silang maid. Inutusan siyang kumuha ng ice cube. Hindi niya alam. So we had to explain na it's ice in the refrigerator.

BL: So do you think English is important to you?

Pearly: English is important if we are in a foreign country. And even though I'm a maid, at least I'm not a maid who's only for housework. The Indonesians are the ones who are really maids.
English is important if we are in a foreign country. Saka even though I'm a maid at least hindi ako maid talaga na housework lang. 'Yung Indonesian ang maid talaga.

Furthermore, the FDWs cited the Indonesians' 'poor' or 'low level' of English as the reason why they were paid less and why they were being hired by Singaporeans who could not afford Filipinos. The different stereotypes of employers are apparent in the following exchange I had with Fe and Gina:

Fe: When we speak to Indonesians, our English is baroque!
Pag Indonesian kausap namin, baroque English namin no!

Gina: With employers, it's a really big deal if you know how to speak in English. You understand them. You can answer.
Sa employer, talagang napakalaki na marunong kang magsalita ng English, naiintindihan mo sila. Nakakasagot ka.

BL: But there are still those who hire Indonesians.
Pero may kumukuha pa rin sa Indonesian.

Gina: The Chinese but with the 'whites', does anyone want them? None.
Sa Chinese pero sa puti, merong gusto? Wala.

Fe: You don't pay much for Indonesians, 150, very cheap.
Konting bayarin mo sa Indonesian eh, 150 eh very cheap.

Gina: It's now up, 250.
Tinaas eh, 250.

Fe: That's because here, the second level Chinese want Filipinas so that their children would be good in English.
Kasi nga dito, 'yung mga Chinese na second level gusto nila Pinay para 'yung mga anak marunong mag-English.

Gina: That's like my employer, they don't want Indonesians because they don't know how to speak in English.
Katulad ng amo ko, ayaw nila ng Indonesian kasi hindi marunong mag-English.

Fe: They all know Malay but they don't want Indonesians because of English: [switches to Singlish accent] 'reason that's why you must learn because the reason why I hire you is because you can speak English'.
Marunong silang lahat ng Malay pero ayaw Indonesian kasi nga English ang ano: [switches to Singlish accent] *'reason that's why you must learn because the reason why I hire you is because you can speak English'.*

Fe and Gina portrayed the Indonesians as being inferior, not just because of their 'baroque English' but also because of the employers who hired them. Indonesians, they claimed, were not being hired by status employers such as expatriates. They were not even being hired by 'second-level Chinese' who preferred FDWs who could teach their children English. They were being hired by 'Chinese' who could not afford FDWs.

It is important to note that there was another way in which the FDWs used 'good English' to differentiate themselves from the Indonesians. They also portrayed the Indonesians as being more prone to abuse from their employers, as compared to the Filipinos who 'fight' and are 'not afraid to complain':

Jocel: The Indonesians? It's like they're from the village; they look like they're maltreated; they look like the type who'd be maltreated [...]. That's because among the Chinese, when they cannot afford Filipinas because of their salaries, they hire Indonesians because they are cheap. Their salary's only 230 a month and they don't have a day off. Pinay they fight. [...] And generally, Pinays need days off, their salaries are high and they need privacy. Pinays are demanding. They need to rest when they want to rest. They're not afraid to complain or to react because they know how to speak in English. They're too 'class' [...] in the way they dress, eat [...].
'Yung mga Indonesian? Parang taga-village, parang aping-api sa itsura pa lang, and sa ayos, mga tipong minamaltrato [...]. Sa mga Chinese kase, 'yung mga di maka-afford sa sahod ng Pinay, Indonesian ang kinukuha kase mura lang ang Indonesian. 230 a month lang ang sahod saka wala silang day off. 'Yung Pinay kase lalaban. [...] Tapos generally,

> *Pinay kelangan may day off, mataas ang sahod, kelangan may privacy. Demanding ang Pinay. Kelangan mag-rest kung gusto mag-rest. Hindi takot mag-complain or mag-react kase marunong siyang magsalita ng Ingles e. Sobrang class [...] sa pananamit, sa pagkain [...])*

In devaluing the Indonesians, the FDWs replicate and even reinforce existing stereotypes. This highlights the 'bind of agency', that is, while the FDWs may be able to reconstitute the immediate context of their marginalization by mobilizing the symbolic values of 'good English', they are unable to change fundamental structural conditions.

While negative stereotypes of Indonesian domestic workers were prevalent, the FDWs also expressed sympathy and compassion for the Indonesians. FDWs sometimes spoke of how they would help Indonesians by passing food to them or buying phone cards for them, since they were not allowed to have days off. They also told stories of how they would 'scold' Indonesians for letting their employers push them to do dangerous things (e.g. cleaning the windows of high-rise apartments) and how they would teach them how to do these jobs safely. I sometimes had Indonesian students in class, and I once observed Gina sitting down with two of them to explain the ins and outs of maid agencies and how they could get their money back from an agency that did not deliver on its promises. My Indonesian students told me that Gina had accompanied them to the agency. In the university housing community where I lived, the FDWs I knew told me that Chinese employers did not allow their Indonesian maids to go to the playground if they saw FDWs there for fear that the FDWs would 'teach' the Indonesians how to fight back. Crucial to this was teaching the Indonesians 'some English'.

Summary

In this chapter, I have explored how the FDWs' notion of 'good English' is intertwined with their hierarchy of desirable employers and foreign domestic workers, as well as with their sense of empowerment. In terms of a hierarchy of desirable employers, FDWs positioned Singlish-speaking Chinese and English-speaking white expatriate employers as the opposite of each other, with Chinese employers being portrayed negatively as arrogant, strict, unreasonable and distrustful employers and white expatriate employers being stereotyped as progressive, egalitarian, generous and relaxed. In terms of the hierarchy of foreign domestic workers, FDWs reproduced the authoritative regime with Indonesian domestic workers as the 'real' maids who they had to speak to in 'baroque English' and with themselves as 'more than just maids' who, with their English skills, could perform the script of, for example, a secretary. In reproducing such racial and national stereotypes that are indexed by English, FDWs delineate the conditions where their linguistic capital ('good English') may be recognized and used, however temporarily, to subvert power relations. The FDWs' mobilizations of 'good English' are very much situated activities. They seem able to deploy 'good English' vis-à-vis Singlish-speaking employers and Indonesian domestic workers who had limited or no exposure to English before heading to Singapore. They had difficulties generating 'uptake' with expatriate employers and Singaporean employers who were confident about their English. This recuperation of power that, at the same time, reproduces power relations is testament to the bind of agency that FDWs experience in their attempts to make the scripts of servitude assigned to them, their own.

Notes

(1) The FDWs did not differentiate between Singapore Standard English and Singapore Colloquial English (Singlish). They referred to the English spoken in Singapore as Singlish and to the accent as the 'Singaporean accent'. They only differentiate between 'standard' and Singlish when discussing their Singaporean employers' English.
(2) Note that the 'mistake' of the employer is related to pluralization rather than pronunciation.

6 Translating Selves: The Trajectories of Transnational Filipino Domestic Workers

In this chapter, I focus on how Filipino domestic workers (FDWs) talk *about* their use of English in their narratives of their experiences of transnational mobility. My emphasis is on the spatial and temporal trajectories of linguistic capital and, in particular, on how the changing indexicalities of English in this regard signify the space-specific distribution and value of the semiotic resources in the linguistic repertoires of FDWs. As such, I trace how FDWs talk about English in relation to: (1) the Philippines before they migrated; (2) Singapore where they work as domestic workers; (3) the Philippines where they occasionally return to as *balikbayans*;[1] and finally (4) Canada where they project preferred futures as caregivers. These specific time–space configurations invoke particular scripts.

My use of 'trajectories' in this chapter needs to be specified. I use 'trajectories' to capture the spatial and temporal mobility of linguistic resources in an era of globalization. More precisely, what I want to capture is how transnational migrants such as FDWs bring with them the linguistic capital and registers they have acquired, as well as a 'sense' of the values of these linguistic resources, in their transnational journeys; these may change as they travel across space and time and such changes would index shifts in their subject-positions, in their identities. This is because '[t]he sense of the value of one's own linguistic products is a fundamental dimension of the sense of knowing the place which one occupies in the social space' (Bourdieu, 1991: 82).

In this section, I mainly use the 19 in-depth interviews I conducted with FDWs to follow the trajectories of the FDWs' English and trace how they 'translate' their selves, that is, how they negotiate and perform inhabitable identities in view of varying (spatially) and changing (temporally) systems of signification.

English in the Philippines

When I asked the participants about their use of English before they migrated, all of them responded with self-assessments of how 'good' they thought their English was when they were still in the Philippines. Their evaluations ranged from considering their English then to be *'carabao* English' or 'trying hard English' to *'OK na OK* (very OK) English'. When I asked the participants why their evaluations of their English were such, they pointed firstly to their own socioeconomic backgrounds and secondly to their very infrequent use of English in their everyday lives.

As has been pointed out in Chapter 2, proficiency in English in the Philippines is very much a function of economic capital. Apart from socioeconomic status, an urban background and attendance at private schools are also considered to be important determinants of Filipinos' proficiency in standard English. This was reflected in the participants' narratives. Except for Connie, almost all of the participants who had not gone on to post-secondary education laughingly described their English when they were in the Philippines as *'carabao* English'[2] and 'trying hard English'. A number of them blamed this on the inadequacies of their English teachers, as well as their family and work backgrounds where there were little or no opportunities to 'practice English'. Peng, for example, attended a university in Manila for three years before dropping out to support her siblings. She told me that English was 'difficult' for her and she attributed this to her 'inferiority complex' as her parents were 'very poor' and 'irresponsible'. In contrast, those who had college degrees or who had pursued post-secondary education said that English came 'naturally' to them and that they were 'OK' using English. Glo, who had a degree in midwifery, attributed her proficiency in English to her attendance at private schools 'from the start', i.e. from nursery, and to her family's 'professional' background; she described her father's side as being 'medical' and her mother's side as 'a mix of professional also but not really on the medical side'. Edna attributed her *'OK na OK'* English to her father who was a 'government worker'. Jocel said she spoke 'good English' despite the fact that she came from Mindanao, one of the poorest regions in the country, because the Philippine government had made sure that from kindergarten, they learned English. Precy said she was good at English because Igorots prefer to speak in English.

Whether or not they identified themselves as being proficient in English, all of the participants identified English as a school language except for Beth who worked as a reservation officer in a travel agency that catered to Korean tourists. Outside of school and in all of their other domains of language use, they used Filipino (especially if they were in Manila) and/or their respective mother tongues. This infrequent and limited use of English is indicative of their social positions when they lived in the Philippines. Sibayan and Segovia (1984) differentiate between the controlling domains and non-controlling domains of language use. According to them, the use of

English is dominant in the controlling domains of education, professional life, government administration, legislation and business and international relations, while the use of Filipino is prevalent in the non-controlling domains of the home, the neighborhood and middle-level and lower-level business establishments. That the FDWs were not using English frequently, if at all, is an indication that, except for education, they were not part of the 'controlling domains' where the values of linguistic and other forms of capital are being determined and distributed.

However, it must be pointed out that while the FDWs may not have considered themselves to be 'proficient' in English, and while they may not have been part of the controlling domains of Philippine social life, they were certainly part of local linguistic markets where their knowledge of English and/or their proficiency in Filipino and/or their vernacular languages were considered valuable. Cathy, who evaluated her English to be 'trying hard', worked at a day-care center for nine years and she told me how she would teach the young children basic words and songs in English, something the parents of the children (who according to her had difficulties speaking in English) appreciated. Gina, who had worked at various jobs to support herself since she was 15 and who considered her English to be 'carabao English' at best, told me how she was very good at selling things, whether it was hawking wares at a wet market or getting a customer at the fast-food chain she worked for to choose the more expensive meal. She performed these tasks in Filipino.

In contrast to the discourse of the Philippine state and the maid agencies that portray overseas foreign workers (OFWs) in general and FDWs in particular as being uniformly knowledgeable of English, the narratives of the FDWs about their English back in the Philippines reveal a far more heterogeneous picture. Firstly, it seems that the FDWs had different proficiencies in English when they were in the Philippines (as evinced from their self-evaluations). Secondly, it is significant that faced with a question of how they used their English back in the Philippines, all but one of the FDWs constructed narratives around their lack of English, i.e. *carabao* English, and/or their limited use of English, i.e. English as a school language. This signifies that for most of the FDWs, English was not a resource they drew from in order to perform their everyday identities back in the Philippines.

English in Singapore

English became a particularly salient resource in how the FDWs portrayed themselves once they started talking about their experiences as domestic workers in Singapore. This is because with English as the lingua franca between them and their employers, the FDWs found themselves using English far more frequently than they ever did in the Philippines. They were also in a context where their imposed identities as domestic workers were being constructed and performed in English. English, then, became an important instrument with which to negotiate their positions.

'I have lost my English'

All but one of the participants[3] spoke of their initial experiences with English in Singapore in terms of dislocation, of feeling 'out of place'. They attributed their initial experiences of dislocation to Singlish (Singapore Colloquial English), which they variously described as being 'different', 'strange', 'weird', a 'total reversal' of what they thought English was supposed to be and as 'not really English'. Beth, who was a reservation officer at a travel agency in the Philippines and who was used to taking phone messages, found that she could not understand what was being said to her when she had to take down phone messages for her first employer in Singapore:

Beth: My first employer, I do answer the phone. And then sometimes, they make their orders through phone and I cannot get it. I have to keep on 'Pardon, pardon, can you repeat that again' because I cannot understand especially *'yung*, for example, *'yung* 'can you spell it for me', '/hetʃ/, /hetʃ/' 'What?' '/hetʃ/, /hetʃ/'.[4] And then sometimes, somebody will phone and I ask for their fax number and they say 3, 4, 5, /eʔ/, /eʔ/.[5] Oh my God, what does /eʔ/, /eʔ/ mean?! *That's why nagkaroon ako ng inferiority complex nun kasi para bang ako 'yung di marunong mag-English*. [That's why I had an inferiority complex then because it was as if I did not know how to speak in English.]

Beth's displacement is dual. Her sense that she is proficient in English is displaced when she cannot understand what is being said to her. As a result of her not understanding what is being said to her, her competence in answering the phone and giving and taking down information, a skill she would have developed from working in a travel agency in the Philippines, is also displaced.

Beth's experience with Singlish was echoed by many of the participants. Jocel, who described herself as not having a problem with speaking in English in the Philippines, wondered why her Chinese employers did not seem to understand her, and why she could not understand them whenever they spoke to her. She told me that she initially thought her English was wrong. It was not just those who had evaluated themselves as being proficient in English who felt displaced in the linguistic environment of Singapore. Cathy, whose employers were Filipinos, said she felt 'deaf' whenever she was outside the home because she could not understand people when they spoke to her. Adora, Fe and Gina singled out pronunciations of English in Singapore which left them dumbfounded when they first encountered them:

> **Adora**: Like when you buy chicken rice. 'How much is it?' /tʊ/ /tɛntɪ/ [laughter]. Now I understand what does it mean. '/tʊ/ /tɛntɪ/' means 'two twenty'.
> **Fe**: Our pronunciation is different from their pronunciation, isn't it? Like dull, with us it's /dʌl/, with them it's /dɒl/ like a doll.
> **Gina**: Like /æpəl/, /ɛpəl/ [...] /kɑːpɑːk/ [...] /kɑːbɔːd/ [laughs].

Some of the participants also worked for employers who spoke neither Singlish nor 'standard English'. Connie, for example, was first employed by a Chinese family where she had to take care of grandparents who, according to her, did not know a word of English; her employers knew only 'very broken English'. In her first few months in Singapore, she often cried at night, partly out of sheer frustration from not being able to understand her employers.

The participants' sense of dislocation was not only confined to their initial contact with Singlish and the varying proficiencies in English of their employers. A common remark that I heard from the participants as well as my students at the Bayanihan Center was that, in coming to Singapore, they had 'lost' their English. There were three reasons that the FDWs cited for why they felt this way. Firstly, as I described above, they were initially dislocated in the particular linguistic environments they worked in. Secondly, some of the participants felt that they could not produce 'real English' anymore because they had to use only Singlish with their employers in Singapore. Thirdly, while they used English far more frequently in Singapore than they ever did in the Philippines, this use was in a very limited domain. In this way, their sense of dislocation, of having 'lost' their English, was also fundamentally tied to their experience of becoming domestic workers, an imposed identity which all the participants spoke of as a dislocation, citing the de-skilling (*nakakabobo*) nature of the job, and the physical and emotional difficulties of having to be at the beck and call of their employers, 24 hours a day, 7 days a week. This imposed identity was indexed by their feeling of being compelled to understand and use Singlish and by their use of English for the 'limited' purpose of being asked to do something by their employers.

This latter point was brought home to me by Del who, at the time I interviewed her, was working with a French employer who used 'straight' English in communicating with her. I asked her why she still felt that she had lost her English when she was now in a household where Singlish was not spoken. While she was at pains to emphasize that she was learning a lot from her employer, she also told me that the functions of English in her context were very limited:

> **Del**: [T]hey talk to me in English *pero* [but] it's quite different (BL: What do you mean?). I say that different because only they talk to me if they have something to want and they have something to ask me to do, right?

The language journals that four of my students kept illustrate even more the limited functions they used English for. All of these entries were taken from the very first page of their language journals. They had all started writing in their journals on September 19, 2001.

> Monday 17-9-01
> **AM**. My ma'am ask me whats for lunch?
> **PM**. She ask me what available food for dinner? Later she told me that my Sir want porridge for dinner.
> Evening. We talk about what she did in China while waiting for her aircraft to resume flight. She said that she was able to browse and buy in every store selling articles for Chinese Feng Shui. She was able to browse the 10c small stall selling the articles. We also talked about what's happening to the world and this terrorist attack. After dinner, she asked me to prepare and cook the black chicken with herbal for tonic drink.
> [Irene, Singaporean Chinese employer]

> Monday 17.
> At 8:00 am, when my maam came down from upstairs to have breakfast, she asked me to sit with her on the dining table and we discussed about what we are going to cook for our guests on Thursday for lunch.
> [Liza, Singaporean Chinese employer]

> Mon. AM Sept 17 01
> I spoke to my ma'am about our launch, she ask me 'what I want' cos shes going out to buy. And she give me instruction, what Im gonna do? Cos they leaving.

PM
I talked to the elder son when he came back from school. I ask him how he is? And he ask for his snack.
[Anne, Singaporean Chinese employer]

Sept 17
Dear Diary,
Back as usual wake up in the morning at 6:00 am, prepare the lunch box for the boys to school. I made Liz a cup of tea and I wake James and Oliver and get ready for school. This morning Mel, Liz and I sitting on the dining room chair Liz and me organized the food for a week. We got some from the recipe book, magazines and she ask me if I cook the same like in the book and I say yes. When Oliver comes back from school he ask where his mum. I said to him she went out to do her nails. And he ask me again, Yaya could I please have some muffin you made the other day and an icy pole [illegible] pls. thank you yaya. Hes a lovely boy and has lovely manners.
[Joy, British employer]

The entries of Irene, Liza, Anne and Joy demonstrate how the FDWs mainly used English for comprehending their employers' requests and responding to their employers' questions about household-related matters. Irene's conversation with her employer about the latter's trip to China and the 9/11 terrorist attack may be an exception, but the focus of the conversation is still the employer and Irene, arguably, may have been doing the 'emotional labor' (Cameron, 2000b) of listening to and empathizing with her employer. Anne's journal entry demonstrates the limited uptake that FDWs generate in their conversations with their employers and even their employers' children. The son of Anne's employer responds to her question of 'how are you' with a 'request' for his snack to be served. In telling me that they had 'lost' their English, what the FDWs were actually saying was that they had lost their voices.

'You're the one who adjusts, not them, right?'

While loss was one theme in the narratives of the FDWs, 'adjustment' was another. All of the FDWs I interviewed said that they dealt with their linguistic displacement and with being a domestic worker by 'adjusting'. For the FDWs, this meant 'adjusting' to Singlish, developing a linguistic repertoire of Englishes as well as smatterings of Hokkien, Cantonese and any of the other languages their employers may speak, and then calibrating their repertoires to the needs and demands of their employers.

Beth, who could not understand Singlish initially, told me that she eventually got so used to Singlish that when she spoke she could not be distinguished from her Singaporean employer. When she changed employers, she was then able to switch, practically on demand, to the 'English' that her Norwegian employer wanted her to use for answering phone calls.

> **Beth**: Eventually, I get used to Singlish and then when I converse on the phone, it's as if I'm Chinese. My mother once called me and I was the one who heard her on the phone. 'Can I speak to Beth please?' 'Ma, this is me.' 'Is that you? I thought it was your employer!' But when I switched to a Norwegian employer, he asked me if I could change my English because sometimes also I'm answering phone calls [...] so I caught up ... I adjusted. I'm flexible, that's what they say.
> *Eventually I get used to Singlish tapos pag nakikipag-conversation na ako sa phone, para na akong Chinese. Sabi nga ng mother ko tumawag sa akin, one time eh ako 'yung nakarinig sa boses niya. 'Can I speak to Adora please?' 'Ma, ako 'to.' 'Ikaw ba yan? Akala ko employer mo!' Pero nung lumipat ako ng employer sa Norwegian, he asked me kung puwede kong ibahin 'yung English ko because sometimes also I'm answering phone calls [...] so nag catch-up ko ... nag-adjust ako. Flexible ako, sabi nila eh.*

Connie, who worked for a family that had limited English, incorporated Mandarin, Hokkien and 'sign language' into her repertoire so she could communicate with her employers.

> **Connie**: Later on, I was the one who adjusted in their own language, sort of. *Minimix ko 'yung* English with Chinese, Mandarin, Fokkien, whatever. So but we get along with that kind of, you know [makes signs with her hands]. I think it sometimes depends on how you do it and *kung pa'no mo bline-blend* yourself to the family.

With time, some of the participants developed a broad linguistic repertoire for communicating with different employers. Edna, who had worked in Singapore for 15 years and who, at the time of the interview, was a full-time 'part-timer', told me she deployed different Englishes and different communicative strategies for the various employers whose homes she cleaned.

> **Edna**: When I'm talking to a Chinese who can't quite catch up, I really level with her so she would understand me. My work is mostly with Americans, British, Italian, French, my English is different with them. You're the one who adjusts, not them, right?

Pag Intsik ang aking kausap na hindi gaanong maka-catch up talagang I level with her para maintindihan niya ako. 'Yung trabaho ko mostly American, British, Italian, French, iba rin 'yung English ko sa kanila. Ikaw 'yung mag-adjust, hindi sila, di ba?

The FDWs' 'adjustment' in the form of expanding their linguistic repertoires to accommodate their employers is a crucial part of their own script. As Glo remarked, '[i]t's up to you (referring to the domestic worker) so that the two of you would understand each other'. When the FDW is unable to 'adjust' quickly enough, her inability to comprehend and thus to fulfill a request or a command may be interpreted as inefficiency or 'stupidity' and it may cost her, her job. Edna, for example, told me how she learned to 'adjust' after her inability to comprehend a word pronounced by the Singaporean child she was taking care of led to her employers calling the maid agency to demand an explanation for her inability to understand English.

Edna: We say: 'You can have your /bæθ/ now?' With them, it's /beθ/. That's where my *alaga* and I had a misunderstanding, on my first day of work. She had just gotten back from school. [...] She said: 'Auntie, I haven't taken my /beθ/.' [...] I said: 'What?' '/beθ/'. [...] 'I don't understand you.' 'I want to take my /beθ/.' I said: 'I really don't understand you.' She said to me: 'Come I show you.' She took me to the bathroom. 'Oh, you wanna take a /bæθ/!' [...] she said to me, 'No, /beθ/.' When her parents arrived, she told them how come she doesn't understand what I say to her [...]. So, they asked, they called because it was their first time to have a maid, so they called the agency: 'How come ah, she doesn't understand ... like this and like this and like this.' It so happened that a woman from our agency in the Philippines was here and they came over to explain the differences between British and American. [...] That's where I learned adjustment.
Kagaya nga sa atin eh: 'You can have your /bæθ/ now.' Sa kanila eh /beθ/. Yun 'yung di kami nagkaintindihan ng alaga ko noon, first day of work ko. Nanggaling sya ng school. [...] Sabi niya: 'Auntie, I haven't taken my /beθ/.' [...] Sabi ko: 'What?' '/beθ/.' [...] 'I don't understand you.' 'I want to take my /beθ/.' Sabi ko: 'I really don't understand you.' Sabi niya sa akin: 'Come, I show you.' Dinala ako sa banyo. Oh, you wanna take a /bæθ/!' [...] sabi niya sa akin. 'No, /beθ/.' Nung dumating 'yung parents niya, sinabi niya how come she doesn't understand what I say to her [...]. So, tinanong nila, tumawag sila

> kasi first time nilang magkaroon ng maid, so tumawag sila sa agency: 'How come ah she doesn't understand ... like this and like this and like this.' Nagkataon na 'yung babae sa agency namin sa Pilipinas andito so they came over so inexplain niya 'yung differences ng British at saka American. [...] Dun ko naano 'yung adjustment.

The FDWs' narratives of linguistic accommodation can be seen as an index of their subordinate position. Crucially though, while the FDWs acknowledged that they often had 'no choice' but to 'adjust' to their employers, they also highlighted how this flexibility made them the 'better' domestic workers in Singapore, in contrast to the Indonesians who could only understand and respond to 'simple English'. They also emphasized how their ability to 'adjust' was part of the Filipino trait of *pakikisama*, of being able to get along with practically anyone. In this way, the FDWs add to the meanings of their linguistic 'adjustment', calling attention to how this also indexes their being 'better' domestic workers and 'good' Filipinos and, in this way, reproducing the script assigned to them by the Philippine state and maid agencies.

Revising the Script

The FDWs' reframing of their positions and their attempts to have their inhabitable identities recognized is apparent in the forms of address and reference which they preferred and used in their public and hidden scripts of servitude.

'Yung madam/Madonna ko'[6]

Forms of address and reference are important, as they could well be emblematic of the negotiations of power and identity that take place in the everyday interactions between domestic workers and their employers (Weix, 2000). It is necessary to look at forms of address and reference in terms of the signifier and its meaning(s). The signifier and the meaning of a term of address may vary depending on who the audience is.

Scott (1990) elaborates on this notion by referring to a public (onstage) and a hidden (offstage) transcript. The script as introduced and marketed by maid agencies could very well represent the public transcript that is

> [...] to put it crudely, the *self*-portrait of dominant elites as they would have themselves seen. Given the usual power of dominant elites to compel performances from others, the discourse of the public transcript

is a decidedly lopsided discussion. While it is unlikely to be merely a skein of lies and misrepresentations, [...] [i]t is designed to be impressive, to affirm and naturalize the power of dominant elites, and to conceal or euphemize the dirty linen of their rule. (Scott, 1990: 18, emphasis in original)

Co-existing and, in cases of grossly unequal power relations, sharply contrasting with the public transcript is the hidden transcript which 'represents a critique of power spoken behind the back of the dominant' (Scott, 1990: xii). The dominant group is excluded from the audience of the hidden transcript.

In the case of FDWs in Singapore, part of their onstage, public transcript would consist of the forms with which they address their employers and their employers' children in their everyday interactions with them. On the other hand, part of their offstage, hidden transcript consists of the forms with which they refer to their *employers* (Table 6.1) and their *employers' children* (Table 6.2) on their Sundays off, during phone conversations with friends after the employers have left for the day and other similar contexts where the dominant group is not present or, at least, can be prevented from knowing the meaning of a particular word. Let us first turn to the relationship between the domestic worker and her employer and the forms of address and reference used and preferred.

From Table 6.1, one can see that FDWs do observe linguistic deference when they are addressing their Singaporean employers. In this way, they acknowledge the immense social distance between their employer and them, and they maintain the public transcript which requires that a subordinate group verbally (or otherwise) perform acts of deference (referred to by the women I spoke to as 'politeness' and 'respect') toward the dominant group. But while the public transcript looks consistent, the hidden transcript of the domestic workers as gleaned from the forms they used to refer to their employers is much more fractured with occasions where a domestic worker would refer to her female employer as *''yung ma'am ko'* (my ma'am), a reference which could be said to be consistent with the public transcript, even as there are days when the same domestic worker would speak affectionately of her female employer as *'nanay'* and times when she complains about 'Madonna'.

From Table 6.1, two forms of reference must be highlighted: first, forms of reference where the employers are talked about using 'disguised' terms; and second, forms of reference where the employers are spoken about using kinship terms. More than being an indication of how satisfied the domestic workers are with their employer(s) at specific points in time, the forms of reference used by them are also emblematic of the ways by which they

Table 6.1 Forms of address/reference: Domestic workers for employers

Hidden transcript (reference)	Public transcript (address)
Positive	*Positive*
Nanay (mother)	Madam
Tatay (father)	Ma'am
Auntie, Uncle	Sir
'yung ma'am ko/sir ko	
(my ma'am/sir)	
'yung amo ko	
(my 'master')	
Negative	
Madonna	
Prinsesa gudung-gudung	
Dishwasher	
Cory	

negotiate their identities as transnational domestic workers, identities that are very much predicated on their disempowerment.

As a form of resistance, the use of disguised forms such as 'Madonna' is especially interesting for one very soon discovers that in the domestic workers' use of such terms of reference, the signifier has multiple meanings which frequently clash. 'Madonna', for example, could well signify the Roman Catholic Mary or even the pop singer of 'Like a Virgin' fame, but what the domestic worker is actually doing is describing her female employer as being *'madonya'* (from the Spanish *doña*), which traditionally means an older woman from an elite family but which has come to mean someone who expects to be waited on hand and foot. Another example is 'Cory', a female name that to the minds of most Filipinos signifies Corazon Aquino who unseated Ferdinand Marcos' dictatorship through People Power I in 1986. Again, what the domestic worker is doing is describing her employer as being *'kuripot'* (note the similar sound patterns), as someone who is tight-fisted with money. Spontaneously created 'according to personality' (Arlene), these disguised forms of reference enable FDWs to verbally criticize the behavior of their employers in public spaces while ensuring that those not in the know are kept in the dark. By being capable of shifting from 'ma'am' to 'Madonna', FDWs enact a kind of agency over their linguistic use that is in direct opposition to the linguistic deference required by the public transcript and the script of servitude.

But domestic workers cannot be identified entirely as always being in opposition to their employer. The use of kinship terms by the domestic workers, at other times, could be indicative of a desire to obscure their actual relations with their employer through the use of euphemisms. This is more clearly seen in Table 6.2, where the domestic workers most prefer to be referred to as 'friends' or 'companions' or by their first names rather than by their actual occupations, and in Table 6.3, where domestic workers speak of the children they take care of as their own.

When the domestic worker is referred to by her first name or as a 'friend' and 'companion' and refers to her employers and her employers' children as kin, then the identity of the domestic worker also shifts from being a paid domestic laborer to being 'part of the family', a position desired by most of the women I spoke to. For one, becoming part of the family suggests 'a special relationship beyond the simple bond of employment in which the worker will be loved and cared for, entering into a network of rights and obligations' (Anderson, 2000: 121).

What is striking though is that domestic workers seem to negotiate their position in the household, their 'domestic' identity, by, on the one hand, showing deference 'upward', toward their employers, and on the other hand, by asserting themselves symbolically 'downward', vis-à-vis their employer's children. Most, if not all, of the domestic workers did not mind their employers addressing them by their first names, even as they had to respond with 'sir' or 'ma'am'. But most, if not all, of the domestic workers minded their employers' children addressing them using their first names (Table 6.4), citing such behavior as indicative of a lack of respect and/or of parents being remiss in their duties of bringing up their children in a more 'educated' way.

Most of the domestic workers preferred to be called 'Auntie', a Singaporean English term that currently has three meanings summarized as follows: (1) 'the sister of one's mother or father', or an uncle's wife;

Table 6.2 Preferred forms of reference: Employers for domestic workers

Most preferred	Least preferred
(1) First name	(1) Servant
(2) Friend, helper, companion	(2) Maid

Table 6.3 Forms of address/reference: Domestic workers for their employers' children

Hidden transcript (reference)	Public transcript (address)
Alaga ko (my charge)	First name
Anak ko (my child)	Nickname
Baby ko (my baby)	

Table 6.4 Preferred forms of reference: Employers' children for domestic workers

Most preferred	Least preferred
(1) Auntie	(1) First name
(2) Yaya (nanny)	(2) Nickname
(3) Tita, Mama, Kaka	

(2) refers to any female friend of the family who is at least one generation above you, and therefore commands a certain respect in Asian culture; and (3) a term of friendly respectful address to even a total stranger who (i) is female; (ii) is at least one generation older than you; and (iii) has helped you or been friendly to you in some way (Brown, 2000: 22–23).

One can see here that the domestic worker identifies herself, at the very least, as a friend of the family or even a total stranger who has been helpful or friendly to the children of the family. While domestic workers want to teach the children to call them 'Auntie', if and when possible, it seemed that they could only do so if their employers 'allowed' them to. There are cases when the employer herself tells the children to call the domestic worker 'Auntie', as in the case of Aileen, whose employer told the children to call her 'Auntie Aileen' on her very first day with the family, '*pagdating ko sa bahay nila, galing pa lang sa airport*' (as soon as I arrived at their house, fresh from the airport).

But when the employer does not teach the children to call domestic workers 'Auntie', subsequent domestic workers find it difficult to teach the children to change their habits:

Aileen: They called their previous domestic worker by her first name so they also called me by my first name. It isn't nice but if the mother does not teach the child, then nothing, it's difficult to change things.
First name ang tawag sa dating katulong so tinatawag na rin ako ng mga bata sa first name ko. Hindi nga maganda 'yung first name pero pag di tinuruan ng nanay, wala, mahirap palitan.

The employers may, in one way or another, sanction domestic workers who take the initiative to 'train' the children to call them 'Auntie'.

Marian: I told the child I was taking care of: 'Call me Auntie.' S/he said: 'I cannot call you Auntie because you are not my relative, my grandmother said [...]. You don't have any right to kiss me because you are not my relative.' That was so painful to me.

> Sabi ko sa alaga ko: 'Call me Auntie.' Sabi niya: 'I cannot call you Auntie because you are not my relative, my amah say [...]. You don't have any right to kiss me because you're not my relative.' Ang sakit 'nun sa 'kin.

Unlike in the hidden transcript where the agency of domestic workers was more 'elastic', in the public transcript, their agency is met with fierce resistance and they can only marginally cross the line with the cooperation and/or 'permission' of the more powerful group in the dominant transcript. This highlights how, in highly asymmetrical power relationships, it may be very difficult to contest imposed identities, except if such contestations are done backstage.

A register for offstage identities

Table 6.5 details some of the in-group words the FDWs use to refer to their experiences in Singapore. My first batch of students at the Bayanihan Center (in 2001) called my attention to the existence of these in-group codes. I have divided the in-group words into two categories: (a) words used by FDWs to refer to employers and to experiences related to domestic work; and (b) words used to refer to their activities during their days off. A third category was the words the FDWs used to refer to illegal part-time domestic work, sex, prostitution and pregnancy. For ethical reasons, I have chosen not to list them.

I asked the FDWs why many of the words they used to describe their employers and their Sunday activities are in English, instead of being in Filipino or one of their mother tongues. The FDWs pointed out that the use of English allowed them to obscure their opinions and activities (especially in the case of the third category of words) from the 'public' (e.g. employers) without raising suspicion. There is also a playful element to how they resignified the meanings of these words: they told me that it was 'more fun' to twist words in English and that such words had a 'nicer' ring to them. These in-group words also gave them a voice. The FDWs who acted as my informants told me that using English in this context gave them a feeling of exclusivity: while their mother tongues indexed where in the Philippines they were from, this in-group code allowed them to be 'fluent' speakers of English, able to comfortably and speedily deploy English words that were guaranteed to be understood by their friends.

The list of words in Table 6.5 indexes the daily experiences of the FDWs as well as their immediate struggles. The third category of in-group words further reveals just how powerful the public transcript is. The FDWs who told me about these words always highlighted that these were 'secret' words,

Table 6.5 Words used by FDWs to refer to employers and experiences with domestic work (Category A) and activities, etc., on their days off (Category B)

Category A

Academy award	When the domestic worker dares to answer back
Branded	An employer who pretends to be high-class
Buffalo	An employer who gets angry easily
Cory	An employer who is stingy (play on 'kuripot')
Dishwasher	An employer who gossips about his/her maid
Excess	Visitor(s) in the household
High voltage	An employer who screams and shouts at the smallest mistake
Insect	Chinese employers who like to nag
Madonna	A female employer who wants to be served all the time (play of words on 'madonya')
Magic	Certain 'superstitious' measures used to make the employer 'behave' (e.g. spitting on the food)
Music	When an employer scolds everyday (e.g. 'She's like music with wrong time'.)
Operation	To start work
Nanay	A kind female employer
Pastor	An employer who is always scolding the maid ('sermon')
Queen	The female employer
Tatay	A kind male employer
Vacation	When the employers are on holiday because the FDWs consider it as their vacation; cue to invite friends over
Wrong number	When the employer arrives and you're talking on the phone

Category B

Fellowship/party	Gathering of friends
Gulong-Gulong Park	Park beside the Wisma Atria shopping mall on Orchard Road, known as one of the gathering places of FDWs (this space was turned into a shopping complex in 2006)
Jalan-jalan	Going out, walking around (borrowed from Singapore English, see Brown [2000])
Shopping	Seems to be generally used to refer to doing something together; the meaning depends very much on the context in which it is used; if it's used to refer to a couple, it means the couple had a date; if it's used to refer to two friends, it means that they're walking around looking for someone

indicating that the identities these words indexed could only be performed offstage. These in-group words also reveal how multidimensional the identities of FDWs are: they partly reveal how the FDWs feel about their employers, the strategies they adapt in order to 'adjust' and the things they celebrate; they index how, '[a]gainst the grain of overbearing stereotypes, [FDWs] assert their humanity and subjectivity' (Aguilar, 2002: 11).

'Pa-English-English' in the Philippines

The repertoires and, in particular, the Englishes that the FDWs acquired as foreign domestic workers in Singapore took on a different significance when they returned home to the Philippines as *balikbayans*. On her first trip back to the Philippines after four years in Singapore, Glo told me that she 'spouted straight English' at the immigration counter in response to a question from the immigration officer. The immigration officer countered with: 'Don't do that, fellow countryman. You just stepped into a different country and you don't know Tagalog anymore.' (*'Huwag ka naman kabayan. Nakaapak ka lang sa ibang hangin, di ka na marunong mag-Tagalog.'*) The immigration officer's use of *kabayan* and the reminder to use Tagalog were potent reminders to Glo of the different order of indexicality she would now have to orient to in order to be accepted back home.

In this regard, Sibayan and Gonzalez (1996) note that

> Within a certain socioeconomic group, the middle class and the lower middle class, the continuing use of English for everyday conversation and interaction would be considered as a sign of affectation, of putting one over one's peers, of considering oneself better than they are. (Sibayan & Gonzalez, 1996: 144)

The 'snobbishness' that might be associated with them if they used English was recognized by the participants. Connie, for example, who said she often slipped into using English when she went back home because she was so 'used' to it, said that she was aware that people might think she was speaking in English to show off the fact that she came from Singapore:

Connie: I'd feel bad if I'm that way and they might think that just because I'm here, I'm *pa-English-English*. You know how it is back home.
I feel bad pag ganun ako dahil baka iniisip nila na nandito na ako kaya pa-English-English na ako. Alam mo naman na sa atin.

Jo shared a similar experience:

Jo: When I last went home five years ago, I'd sometimes speak in English. I'd say, 'oops, wrong' because people would look at me. They'd stop. With my friends, it's Ilocano and then suddenly, I'd speak in English. They say I've become snobbish. I tell them, if I'm snobbish, then I wouldn't be meeting them.
'Yung huling uwi ko five years ago, minsan napapa-Ingles ako. Sabi ko, 'ay, mali' kasi tinitingnan ako eh. Nahihinto 'yung mga tao. Sa mga kaibigan ko nga, Ilocano kami, tapos bigla na lang mapapa-Ingles ako. Sabi nila sosy na daw ako. Sabi ko, kung sosy na nga ako, di ko na sila pupuntahan.

To prevent themselves from being ostracized for using English, all of the participants closely monitored and censored their language practices when they were back in the Philippines, consciously using their mother tongue in order to deliberately demonstrate their solidarity with their families and communities and to index how they have 'not changed' despite their changed social and economic status. Edna, for example, told me that she deliberately uses Ilocano when she goes home:

Edna: Because I don't want them to say: 'Just because she's gone abroad, she's become a show off, she's *pa-English-English*.'[7] So I really guard myself so they won't say I'm a show off. I make sure that I use Ilocano. So they won't say: 'Why, back then!'
Kasi ayokong sabihin nila: "ba, nakapag-abroad lang 'to, mayabang na, pa-English-English na.' So talagang inano ko 'yung sarili ko na hindi nila sabihin na mayabang ako. Inano ko talaga na Ilocano talaga ako so para hindi nila sabihin na: "ba nung araw!'

In the case of Ilin who had gone home only twice in her 14 years in Singapore, she had to be constantly reminded that she was already back in the Philippines so that she would stop using English. While Ilin portrayed this in a positive light when she was narrating it to me, her story bears traces of how as *balikbayans*, FDWs cannot bring their English with them when they are in the Philippines.

Ilin: My nephew/niece said: "Auntie, say it in Tagalog, we don't understand some of your English."
Sabi ng pamangkin ko: "Tita, Tagalog naman sabihin mo, di namin maintindihan 'yung iba mong English."

BL: Really? You speak in English?
Ay talaga, napapa-English ka?

Ilin: Especially in the airport because it's like I'm used to it being that way. But sometimes, I am surprised.
Lalo na sa airport kase parang nasanay ba ako na ganoon. Pero minsan, nabibigla ako.

BL: What happens to you at the airport?
Anong nangyayari sa iyo sa airport?

Ilin: Once I was told: "Say it in Tagalog." I said: "Sorry." It's because I feel as if I didn't go home there, it's as if I'm still here. That's why my nephews/nieces and siblings say: "You're already here, but you're still speaking in English." Like when they meet me at the airport, I'm speaking in English. They just stare at me. They say: "Auntie, you're already in the Philippines." I'm surprised at that, that I'm talking in English, I don't realize it that I'm already back home. Sometimes my parents also say, "Uy, uy, uy, you just came from Singapore, your language is already different."
Minsan sabi sa akin sa airport: "Tagalugin mo na lang." Sabi ko: "Sorry." Ang feeling ko kasi parang hindi ako umuwi doon, parang andito pa rin ako. Kaya 'yung mga pamangkin ko, mga kapatid ko: "Andito ka na sa 'tin, nag-Eenglish ka pa." Like 'yung pag sasalubong sila sa akin, panay English ko nyan. Napapatanga sila sa akin. Sabi: "Tita, nasa Pilipinas ka na." Parang nabibigla ako na ganun, nagsasalita ako in English, hindi ko alam nandun na pala ako sa atin. Kahit minsan, 'yung parents ko din, sabi nila: "Uy, uy, uy, nanggaling ka lang ng Singapore, iba na ang language mo."

It is interesting to see how the FDWs' use of English as returnees alienates them from their communities, especially when this is contrasted with their earlier narratives of their limited use of English in the Philippines. In this way, the returns of the FDWs are also dislocations. As *balikbayans*, the FDWs have to negotiate their identities yet again. While their changed economic status may be recognized by their communities, as evinced by the many stories I heard from FDWs of their communities asking them for donations for various events and/or of their relatives and neighbors borrowing money from them whenever they returned home, it is a status that they cannot perform with a symbolic resource such as English. There are two possible explanations for this. Firstly, this may be an indication of the durability of unequal structures of symbolic power. FDWs may be economically mobile in their communities back in the Philippines but they are unable to exchange this for the authority that would allow them to use English without being ostracized. Such an authority still seems to be the purview of a few. Secondly, this order of indexicality in local communities may work to prevent *balikbayans* such as the FDWs from distancing themselves from their community, thus helping to ensure that their economic and social capital is distributed more widely. For the FDWs, their *balikbayan* identity involves deliberately not using English and circulating economic resources in their communities so that they can index how they are now economically mobile (because of their having migrated) but still part of the community.

'Lord, help me to English my tongue'

The FDWs' sense of the value of their linguistic capital shifted again when they spoke about their future plans. Many of the FDWs I taught at the Bayanihan Center had explicit plans to go to Canada as caregivers on the Live-in Caregiver Program (LCP) (McKay, 2005 discusses the case of Filipino caregivers in Canada); this was true of the participants as well. In their interviews, Beth, Edna, Loida, Myrna, Nelma, Pearly, Peng and Precy told me that they were making plans to 'go to Canada', i.e. saving money, putting in an application and looking for contacts in Canada who might locate employers for them. LCP applicants were required to be fluent in English and/or French. They were also required to: (1) have the equivalent of a Canadian high-school education, which, in the case of Filipinos, translated to at least two years of college education; and (2) have either caregiver training or equivalent experience. A good number of my students who were very interested in applying could not apply because they only had a high-school education. Among the participants, this was a cause for dismay for Myrna, Nelma and Pearly. Another major hurdle they faced was the interview with the Canadian embassy in Singapore; they were required to go through this interview after a Canadian employer had already expressed an explicit interest in hiring them. After the interview, the Canadian embassy would then decide whether or not to grant them a visa on the LCP track.

The interview with the Canadian embassy was a cause for much anxiety among the FDWs who wanted to apply. My students told me that they feared they would be tongue-tied when they would get there and that their English would fail them. They rightly projected that a different order of indexicality would be at work during the interviews: they would have to speak in 'straight English' and, in contrast to their interviews with Singaporean employers where all they needed to do was to respond with a 'yes' or 'no', they would be asked questions until they 'ran out of answers' (*hanggang sa maubusan ng sagot*). Peng, who had already been interviewed by phone by a prospective Canadian employer, told me that the phone interview had gone well but that the prospect of the interview with the Canadian embassy made her very nervous:

> **Peng**: I get tongue tied [...]. [...] in speaking, I really have a hard time. When I go to the High Comm, I hope that, I pray that 'Lord, help me to English my tongue'. [laughs] (BL: English your tongue?) I hope I can voice out. When my nervousness gets the better of me, it's like, I'm finished.
> *Nabubulol ako [...]. [...] sa pagsalita, talagang nahihirapan ako. Pagdating sa High Comm, I hope na, I pray na 'Lord, help me to English my tongue'. [laughs] (BL: English your tongue?) Sana maka-voice out ako. Pag naunahan kasi ako ng kaba, parang wala na.*

A similar sentiment was shared by Edna and Loida who asked 'in advance' if they could make an appointment with me right before their interviews so they could practice.

For FDWs like Peng, Edna and Loida, who expressed a very strong interest in becoming caregivers in Canada, Canada represented their preferred future and a crucial gatekeeper was linguistic capital – a fluency and comfort in using English as well as familiarity and ease in navigating a different interview genre. Faced with such a different order of indexicality, the FDWs projected – in a similar way to how they recounted their use of English in the Philippines – identities constructed around a sense of inadequacy and a lack of English.

Summary

In this chapter, I looked at the trajectories of the linguistic resources that the FDWs bring with them as they journey between the Philippines and Singapore, and as they project a future as caregivers in Canada. I have shown how the FDWs' sense of the value of their linguistic capital, i.e. English, indexes shifts in their identities as they are positioned and as they position themselves in different spaces with varying orders of indexicality. In looking back at their use of English in the Philippines, the FDWs position themselves as having different proficiencies. When they migrate to Singapore to work as foreign domestic workers, English becomes a salient resource for how they portray their experiences of dislocation and adjustment. When they return to the Philippines as *balikbayans*, their use of English is ostracized and they carefully weave identities through which they can express solidarity with their communities. In projecting a future in Canada, the FDWs' sense of the value of their linguistic capital changes again and they construct identities out of a sense of inadequacy in and lack of English. These shifts are experienced by the FDWs as dislocations that they are only able to partially reconstitute.

Notes

(1) *Balikbayan* is made up of the words 'balik' and 'bayan', which literally mean 'return' and 'country', respectively. Balikbayan refers to an overseas Filipino who returns to the Philippines, either temporarily or permanently.
(2) The *carabao* is a domesticated subspecies of the water buffalo. In the Philippines, they are farm animals, pulling the plow and the cart of farmers. '*Carabao* English' has negative connotations of rural areas, i.e. backward, unrefined, etc.
(3) The exception to this was Glo whose first employer in Singapore was American. An aunt of hers who was already working in Singapore referred her to the employer. Apart from Glo, though, all the other participants had been employed by Singaporeans (who they referred to as 'Chinese') during their first contracts. This pattern is the norm for FDWs and other domestic workers in Singapore.
(4) This refers to how 'h' is spelled out in Singapore.
(5) Meaning 'eight, eight'.
(6) My sources of data for this section on the forms of address and reference were 12 interviews and a straw poll (in my class) that I conducted in 2002. I discuss these sources in Chapter 3.
(7) When someone is described as 'pa-English-English' in the Philippines, this means that the person is using English as a sign of affectation, pretense or distancing.

7 Conclusion

The central question this book has explored is how language is embedded in the labor migration infrastructure that produces transnational Filipino domestic workers (FDWs) and conditions and regulates their mobility. In examining how language is embedded in the labor migration infrastructure, this book contributes to unpacking the role of language in what has been called 'the black box of migration' (Lindquist et al., 2012). I have argued that *scripts* – templates of language practices that indexically link ways of speaking to ways of being and that are differentially convertible to other forms of capital – can serve as starting points for unpacking and understanding the intricate web of practices of different actors at various nodes of the infrastructure of labor migration. I have shown how the regulation of worker mobility in a regime of government-sponsored labor migration has engendered both the multiplication and the multiplicity of scripts as actors at various nodes of the labor migration infrastructure produce particular types of mobile workers, and market and legitimize the linguistic resources of these workers, as well as differentiate and position themselves.

Language and Labor Migration

In tracing the networks of social actors, processes and practices that constitute the infrastructure of government-sponsored labor migration, this book has highlighted the need to understand how language and, in particular, scripts are interwoven into the practice of labor brokering. Labor brokers configure would-be migrants into specific types of mobile, laboring bodies. As has been shown in this book, both state and non-state actors can act as labor brokers who regulate, mediate and produce the supply of and demand for workers in labor markets. This highlights 'the uneasy distinctions between state and market, formal and informal...' (Lindquist et al., 2012: 8); these uneasy distinctions are at the root of the tensions between pride and profit (Duchêne & Heller, 2012b) that animate the scripts produced by the state (Chapters 2 and 3), transnational maid agencies (Chapter 4) and even by the FDWs themselves (Chapter 5). States continue to be 'a powerful organizing force for transnational migration' (Lindquist et al., 2012: 13), perhaps even more so now with the increasing formalization of migration management and the turn to circular labor migration (Castles & Ozkul, 2014; Wickramasekara, 2011; Xiang *et al.*, 2013). As sending countries, states like the Philippines can facilitate and control the labor migration of citizens through, among others, migration requirements and required language training. As receiving countries, states like Singapore specify the entry requirements (including countries of origin) of migrant workers and the migration regimes of receiving countries significantly shape the demand for workers in labor markets and their work conditions. Non-state actors (e.g. privately owned, profit-driven transnational maid agencies) mediate between states and 'local' markets, translating labor quotas into meaningful 'packages' for would-be migrants and 'packaging' migrant workers for specific labor markets. In the case of transnational domestic work, labor brokers form interconnected regimes of control that enable migrant women to be mobile because they are marginal. In such a context, scripts and, for that matter, scripting practices are an essential technology, calibrating the linguistic practices of migrant women to the perceived demands of particular markets, socializing them into their expected (subordinate) roles as domestic workers and signifying them as flexible, self-disciplining, vulnerable and made-to-order laboring bodies.

The notion of scripts emphasizes the structured nature of labor migration, which is not to say that labor migration is not a 'messy' process riddled with gaps, fissures, etc. Labor migration is 'messy', but what the emphasis on scripts and the infrastructure of migration allows is a glimpse at how the mobility of labor hinges on its commodifiability in particular markets.

Language and Transnational Domestic Work

In focusing on *scripts of servitude*, the templates that index the domestic worker and are central to structural and everyday processes of transforming migrant women into particular types of domestic workers, this book has analyzed how transnational FDWs are constructed and produced as 'languaged' workers of the world by themselves, by institutions and in and through social processes. The 'languaging' of domestic work, an occupation that is considered unskilled and that is lowly paid and devalued, is evidence of the increasing centrality of language as both the process and product of work.

The chapters show how language – as discourse, as practice and as a script of servitude – is used as a means of differentiating between and stratifying domestic workers from different countries (Chapters 4 and 5) and different kinds of domestic work (Chapter 5). It is important to emphasize that this differentiation is part of the process by which inequalities are (re)produced, within and across national borders, with particular configurations, particular 'bits and pieces' of language and particular scripts interacting with and being linked to stratified characteristics and configurations of 'person' (nationality, gender, migration status, personal characteristics, appearance, etc.) at various points in the migration trajectory (Chapter 6). This is not to say that 'language' as an identifiable and distinctive system or as a countable entity is no longer relevant. The *idea* of language is still powerful. The Philippine state, transnational maid agencies in Singapore and transnational FDWs all drew, in different ways, from the idea of English as a valuable form of linguistic capital. Without this idea of English, the Philippine state and transnational maid agencies in Singapore would probably not be able to market FDWs at a premium. Without this idea of English, transnational FDWs might have one less tool for temporarily subverting their relations with their employers.

And yet, 'English' alone is insufficient for explaining how transnational FDWs are produced (Chapters 2 through 4) and how FDWs make sense of their experiences (Chapters 5 and 6). In this book, I looked at the specific configurations of language and beliefs about language that constitute scripts of servitude. The recognizability and durability of these scripts of servitude are evidence of historical and structural continuities and enduring structures of inequality that may have taken on new forms in the current era of globalization. Legitimized by language ideologies and enregistered by institutions, scripts of servitude continue to circulate. As has been said earlier, scripts interact with other semiotic economies to produce 'figures of personhood', not just of the one who is performing the script but also of the one for whom the script is performed. In short, the scripts produce – at a particular moment – both the actors and the audience of the performance. The actions of the Philippine state produce not just the workers of the world but also new configurations of the state/nation (Chapter 2). The script of the 'supermaid' does not just enact a figure of the supermaid, it also produces a figure of the employer of the supermaid (Chapter 3). The domestic workers' deployments of 'good English', which are in keeping with how they are portrayed as the English-speaking maids in the script of servitude, produce not just particular positions for themselves, but also racialized hierarchies of employers and other domestic workers (Chapter 5).

This multiplicity and malleability of scripts should not be taken to automatically mean positive change, as '[r]elations of dominance may be maintained precisely through the instabilities of meaning' (Massey, 2005: 174).

Developing Alternative Scripts

My own 'intervention' in the script of servitude was mainly as a volunteer English teacher with the Filipino Overseas Worker in Singapore (FOWS) skills training program at the Bayanihan Centre. When I first started teaching there, the administration told me that the students needed to learn correct spelling, correct grammar and polite ways of dealing with the 'bosses' they would encounter as nursing aides. Fresh from my MA in teaching English to speakers of other languages (TESOL) in the United States, I initially thought about the functions of English in their working lives and on the first day that I was asked to teach, I thought I would teach modals – can, may, could and would – and the use of these in requests after having the students introduce themselves with adjectives they knew. I had so many students and they seemed to have so much fun thinking of adjectives and ways to introduce themselves that in that one hour I never had the chance to go through the modals.

After that experience, and determined to empower my students, I planned my lessons around short readings (in English) that discussed the abuse of domestic workers in Singapore, the experiences of overseas foreign workers (OFWs) in other countries, etc. The students read the texts; I helped them with some vocabulary and then, using some 'comprehension' questions, we discussed their experiences. One morning, about two weeks into the class, during a break, I asked some of my students what they thought of the class. They told me that they looked forward to sharing their experiences and that the lessons were very informative, but when, they asked me, was I going to start teaching English?

This question led me to rethink what English might mean for the FDWs I taught. I realized that, in my teaching, I had been treating English solely as a medium through which my students could access information. While the short readings may have raised awareness about certain important issues, I was not helping my students see how they could turn the medium into an instrument that they could use for their own purposes. My response was to teach them another script, one that some of my students called 'English professionalization'. I called the course 'English for Nursing Aides', but my students preferred to call it 'Medical English'.

And so, I got my hands 'dirty'. Since many of my students wanted to go to Canada to work as caregivers, we studied advertisements for caregivers and I taught them what, in hindsight, could be considered as other scripts – how to write resumes and application letters and how to handle different interview questions. In the context of helping them write their resumes and application letters, I introduced verb tenses and subject-verb agreement as part of the genre, and we talked about their work experiences, the value of the work they did as domestic workers and how this could be presented. For the interviews, we talked about what they should expect from the Canadian High Commission and how they might go about answering questions in an appropriate way. For their mid-terms, the students went through mock interviews with Filipino and expatriate friends of mine who posed as interviewers.

What I did was not without its problems. Viewed from the lens of structure, my students' goals of becoming caregivers in Canada reinforced their script and the existing global division of labor that structures the migration of Third World women into marginalized sectors in First World countries. Likewise, my teaching the students how to write resumes and how to handle 'difficult' interviews may be construed as contributing to the Philippine government's blinkered goal of exporting human resources at great social costs and without really addressing fundamental economic and political problems in the country. Indeed, one Philippine government official who visited my class explicitly encouraged my students to migrate to Canada; she then exhorted them not to forget their families back home who were relying on them. The program I volunteered in shared the same discourses as the Philippine state with regard to the role of language and communication skills in the competitiveness of migrant workers.

But many of my students were convinced that their lives in Canada would be better than in Singapore. Under the Live-in Caregiver Program (LCP), they could apply for permanent residency and eventually citizenship in Canada. As permanent residents, they would be allowed to bring their families. As foreign domestic workers, they had no chance of accessing any of these benefits in Singapore. Looking back, I think my decision of what to teach the FDWs in my classes was a strategic one: it was how I could help my students at that particular juncture in their lives; it was what I could do given how I was positioned in the field (i.e. English teacher, professional Filipino) and especially, given what my students' visions of their preferred futures were.

Preferred Futures

So, did the women I interviewed realize their preferred futures? Did they escape their scripts of servitude? While I lost touch with most of the women I interviewed, three women – a group of friends who first met in my class – kept in touch occasionally through Facebook. I found Beth first and then Edna and Adora friended me (they used pseudonyms on Facebook).

Beth, who had a college degree in tourism and who had gone to Singapore to help her mother pay for her debts back in the Philippines, applied to be an au pair in Sweden. She left for Sweden on an au pair visa in 2008. As part of the au pair requirements, she studied Swedish along with other young women who were also in Sweden as au pairs. She wanted to keep working there and, in fact, worked as a cook on her au pair visa, but she could not secure a work visa. She went back to Singapore in mid-2012 and found work as a senior supervisor at a restaurant. She was no longer on a work permit.

Edna, who had plans to apply as a live-in caregiver in Canada, did not push through with her application for Canada. She stayed on in Singapore and became very active in her Christian church community which has a transnational presence. In November 2014, with economic and social support from her church, she left for missionary work in American Samoa. She now works in a team with an interpreter and another missionary, both of whom are Samoans, and she has returned at least once to Singapore and the Philippines for visits to family and friends before returning to American Samoa to continue her missionary work. In some of her Facebook posts, she talks about starting to understand the language and speaking a few 'syllables'.

Adora, who had said to me in her interview that she did not want to speak Singlish because she would not be 'saying these words forever', went to the United Kingdom with her British employers when they went back 'for good' in late-2008. With the support of her employer, she looked for work that would allow her to live independently. She later found employment as a live-out nanny of the children of another family. In June 2014, she passed, to her relief, one of the requirements for naturalization: the English proficiency test for which she got a 'Grade 5' in spoken English, a result that she was quite proud of. In January 2015, she took the citizenship oath to become a UK citizen. On Facebook, she announced this with a photograph and a comment: 'I finally have my freedom'.

Appendices

Appendix 1: Sample of Bio-Data

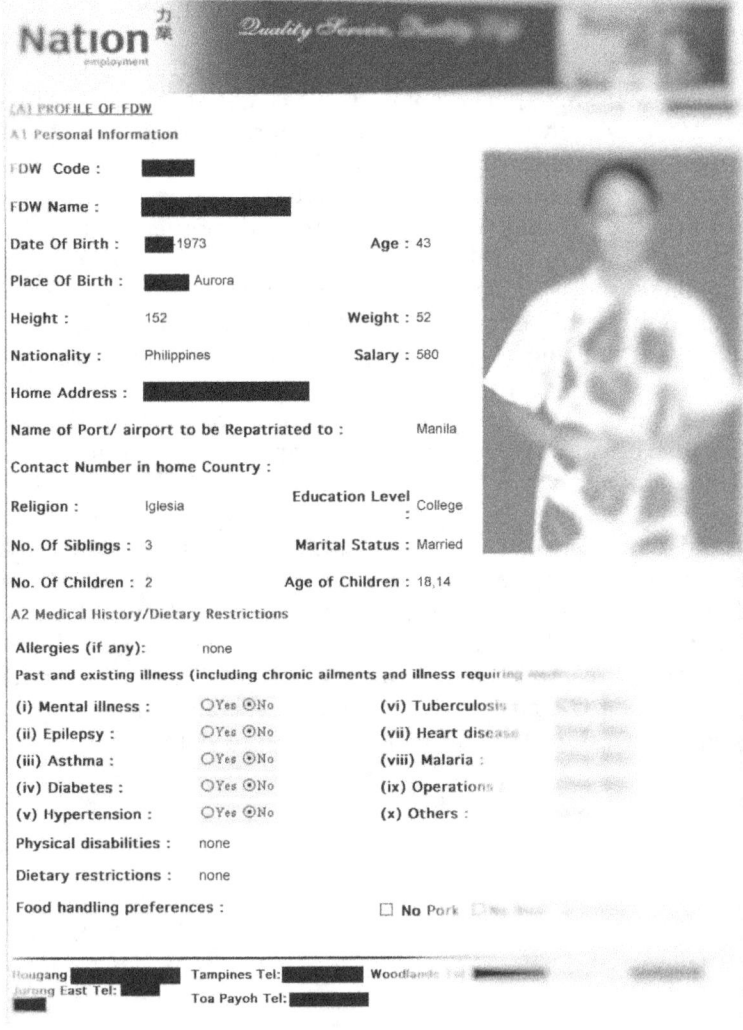

A3 Others

Preference for rest day : 2

Any Other Remarks : other off day to be compensated by employer

(B) Skills of FDW

(B1) Method of Evaluation of Skills

Please indicate the method(s) used to evaluate the FDW's skills (can tick more than one) :

- ☑ Based on FDW's declaration, no evaluation/observation by Singapore EA or overseas training centre/EA
- ☑ Interviewed by Singapore EA
  - ○ Interviewed via Video Conference
  - ○ Interviewed in Person
  - ○ Interviewed via TelePhone/Tele Conference
  - ⦿ Interviewed in Person and aslo made Observation of FDW in the areas of work listed below

No.	Areas Of Work	Willingness	Experience (if yes, state the no. of years)	Assessment / Observation Qualitative Observation of FDW Poor...........Excellent 1 2 3 4 5 N.A.
1.	Care of Infants/Children Pls Specify Age Range: ☑ 0-12mth ☑ 1-5yr ☑ 6-10yr	⦿Yes ○No	⦿Yes ○No No. Of Yrs: 4	○1 ○2 ⦿3 ○4 ○5 ○N.A.
2.	Care of Elderly	⦿Yes ○No	⦿Yes ○No No. Of Yrs: 2	○1 ○2 ⦿3 ○4 ○5 ○N.A.
3.	Care of disabled	⦿Yes ○No	⦿Yes ○No No. Of Yrs: 2	○1 ○2 ⦿3 ○4 ○5 ○N.A.
4.	General Housework	⦿Yes ○No	⦿Yes ○No No. Of Yrs: 7	○1 ○2 ⦿3 ○4 ○5 ○N.A.
5.	Cooking Pls specify cuisines Chinese foods	⦿Yes ○No	⦿Yes ○No No. Of Yrs: 4	○1 ○2 ⦿3 ○4 ○5 ○N.A.
6.	Language abilities (spoken) Please specify English		⦿Yes ○No No. Of Yrs: 7	○1 ○2 ⦿3 ○4 ○5 ○N.A.
7.	Other skills, if any, Please specify none	⦿Yes ○No	⦿Yes ○No No. Of Yrs: 0	○1 ○2 ○3 ○4 ○5 ⦿N.A.

Source: http://www.nation.com.sg, downloaded 10 January 2017.

Appendix 2: General Biographical Profile of Interview Participants at Time of Interview

Name	Age	Marital status	Provinces	'Mother tongue'	Years in Singapore	Employer	P/F*
(1) Adora	33	Single	Davao del Sur	Cebuano	9	British	F
(2) Beth	26	Single	Quirino	Ilocano	2	Swedish	F
(3) Connie	32	Single	Isabela	Ilocano	11	Taiwanese-Danish	F
(4) Cathy	37	Married (3 children)	Leyte	Bisaya	2	Filipino	F
(5) Del	36	Single	Bohol	Boholano	9	Dutch	F
(6) Edna	35	Single	Isabela	Ilocano	15	Part-timer	F
(7) Fe	34	Single	Batangas	Tagalog	12	Singaporean ('Chinese')	F
(8) Gina	32	Married (3 children)	Manila	Tagalog	5	Singaporean ('Chinese')	F
(9) Glo	39	Single	Manila	Tagalog	11	American	F
(10) Ilin	38	Single	Bulacan	Tagalog	14	German	F
(11) Jo	29	Single	Tarlac	Ilocano	7	British-Hong Kong	P
(12) Jocel	26	Single	Davao	Bisaya	5	Canadian	F
(13) Linda	33	Single (1 child)	Bohol	Cebuano	8	Turkish	P
(14) Loida	28	Single	Iloilo	Hiligaynon	6	Japanese	P
(15) Myrna	36	Separated (3 children)	Negros Occidental	Ilonggo	11	American	P
(16) Nelma	29	Single	Samar	Waray	10	Singaporean ('Chinese')	P
(17) Pearly	26	Single	Pangasinan	Ilocano	7	Singaporean ('Chinese')	P
(18) Peng	39	Single	Samar	Bisaya	14	Singaporean ('Chinese')	P
(19) Precy	37	Single	Mt. Province	Ilocano	15	Singaporean ('Chinese')	P

Notes: P: phone interview; F: face-to-face interview.

Appendix 3: Profile of Interview Participants – Education, Previous Work Experience and Reasons for Coming to Singapore

Name	Education	*Previous work experience (before coming to Singapore)*	*Reasons for coming to Singapore*
(1) Adora	One year, BS Education	Domestic worker, assistant at a sari-sari store owned by her employer.	To earn more money as her salary as a domestic worker in the Philippines was too small.
(2) Beth	BS Tourism	Reservation officer at travel agencies in Manila that catered to Koreans (2 years).	To help her mother, a domestic worker in Singapore, pay off her bad loans; to have her own savings before getting married.
(3) Connie	High school	Domestic worker in Manila (4 years); worked in Singapore for 9 years before going back to the Philippines in 1999; was hired by a Danish-Taiwanese couple based in Taipei in 1999; Connie moved with them to Singapore in 2001.	Only girl and the second youngest of seven siblings; to earn her own money because by the time she graduated from high school, the land owned by her parents had been divided among her married brothers and there was nothing left for her.
(4) Cathy	Second year, BS Nursing	Day-care worker (9 years).	To have the money to send her three children to university; her eldest was a first-year nursing student at the time I interviewed her.
(5) Del	High school	Domestic worker in Manila (4 years); service crew at Jollibee, a popular fast-food chain (10 years).	Eighth of nine children; stopped schooling and started working so that her siblings could go to university.
(6) Edna	Agricultural technician (2-year vocational course); 1 year, BS Agriculture	Contractual work with fisheries for less than a year.	To earn her own money and help her parents; wanted to go 'abroad'.

Name	Education	Previous work experience (before coming to Singapore)	Reasons for coming to Singapore
(7) Fe	One year, AB General Science	Worked at the bakery of an aunt; service crew with fast-food chains Minute Burger and Mango Brutus (2 years); factory worker (sewing ballet shoes) for 1 year.	Third of seven children; to help send her siblings to university after their father died.
(8) Gina	Second year, high school	Started work as a messenger for a clinic at 15; factory worker until 1989; service crew for various fast-food chains from 1990–1996.	To earn enough capital to start a business so that her three children can go to university; her husband's and her earnings were not enough for the children to have a 'good education'.
(9) Glo	BS Midwifery (no board)	Contractual work in quality assurance at a factory for a few months while waiting to take the board in midwifery in the Philippines; domestic worker in Kuwait (9 years); went back to the Philippines because of the Gulf War; came to Singapore in 1999.	Decided to 'go for it' after she was 'accidentally' hired to be a domestic worker in Kuwait; wanted to go 'abroad'; could not settle down in the Philippines after she left Kuwait and thought that Singapore would be nearer and safer.
(10) Ilin	High school	Day-care volunteer (2 years), did piecework for a factory.	To earn more money; was encouraged by an older sister who was already working in Singapore.
(11) Jo	High school	Helper at a store in Manila.	Financial difficulties in the family; to earn her own money; was encouraged by an aunt working in Singapore.
(12) Jocel	Third year, BS Social Work	None.	To work; found that coming to Singapore to work as a domestic worker was easier than getting full-time work in the Philippines.
(13) Linda	BS Elementary Education	Sold encyclopedias; worked as a telephone operator and encoder with an electric company.	Family wanted her to stay away from her boyfriend with whom she had a child.

Name	Education	Previous work experience (before coming to Singapore)	Reasons for coming to Singapore
(14) Loida	BS Industrial Technology	None.	To get experience in Singapore before applying to go to Canada; had an aunt in the United States who had promised to help her move there after she makes her way to Canada.
(15) Myrna	High school	Factory worker.	To support her three children as her husband was unemployed, unreliable and unfaithful.
(16) Nelma	High school	Factory worker.	Eldest of five children; started working to help support her siblings' education.
(17) Pearly	High school	Worked in a cottage industry (painting figurines) in Pasig, Metro Manila.	To earn more money; had an aunt working as an FDW who helped her find an employer.
(18) Peng	Third year, BS Business Administration	Salesperson ('salesgirl'), Miranda Bookstore.	Eldest of nine siblings; stopped schooling when her brother started college so she could work and support her siblings as her parents were 'irresponsible'.
(19) Precy	BS Midwifery (no board)	Day-care volunteer.	To find 'good' employment; had a neighbor who was an agent for a recruitment agency.

References

5T Pinoy maids march in Hong Kong vs. new deployment rules. (2007) *Cebu Daily News (Online)*, 15 February. See http://globalnation.inquirer.net/cebudailynews/news/view_article.php?article_id=46222 (accessed 15 February 2007).

Agha, A. (2000) Register. *Journal of Linguistic Anthropology* 9 (1 & 2), 216–219.

Agha, A. (2006) Registers of language. In A. Duranti (ed.) *A Companion to Linguistic Anthropology* (pp. 23–45). Malden, MA: Blackwell Publishing.

Agha, A. (2007) *Language and Social Relations*. Cambridge: Cambridge University Press.

Agha, A. (2011) Large and small scale forms of personhood. *Language and Communication* 31, 171–180.

Aguilar, F.V. (1996) The dialectics of transnational shame and national identity. *Philippine Sociological Review* 44, 101–136.

Aguilar, F.V. (2002) Beyond stereotypes: Human subjectivity in the structuring of global migrations. In F.V. Aguilar (ed.) *Filipinos in Global Migrations: At Home in the World?* (pp. 1–38). Quezon City: Philippine Migration Research Network and Philippine Social Science Council.

Aguilar, F.V. (2014) *Migration Revolution: Philippine Nationhood and Class Relations in a Globalized Age*. Singapore and Kyoto: NUS Press and Kyoto University Press.

Anderson, B. (2000) *Doing the Dirty Work?: The Global Politics of Domestic Labour*. London: Zed Books.

Anderson, B. (2006) Doing the dirty work?: The global politics of domestic labour. In M.K. Zimmerman, J.S. Litt and C.E. Bose (eds) *Global Dimensions of Gender and Care Work* (pp. 226–237). Standford, CA: Stanford University Press.

Arroyo, G.M. (2002) Speech on Migrant Workers' Day, 7 June 2002. See www.ops.gov.ph/ (accessed 15 February 2006).

Asis, M.M.B. (2005) Caring for the world: Filipino domestic workers gone global. In S. Huang, B.S.A. Yeoh and N. Abdul Rahman (eds) *Asian Women as Transnational Domestic Workers* (pp. 21–53). Singapore: Marshall Cavendish.

Bakan, A.B. and Stasiulis, D.K. (1995) Making the match: Domestic placement agencies and the racialization. *Signs: Journal of Women in Culture & Society* 20 (2), 303–335.

Bangko Sentral ng Pilipinas. (2015) *Overseas Filipinos' cash remittances*. See www.bsp.gov.ph/statistics/spei_pub/Table 11.pdf.

Batistella, G. and Asis, M.M.B. (2011) *Protecting Filipino Transnational Domestic Workers: Government Regulations and Their Outcomes*. Makati City, Philippines: Philippine Institute for Development Studies.

Blommaert, J. (2003) Commentary: A sociolinguistics of globalization. *Journal of Sociolinguistics* 7 (4), 607–623.

Blommaert, J. (2005) *Discourse: A Critical Introduction*. New York: Cambridge University Press.

Blommaert, J. (2010) *The Sociolinguistics of Globalization*. Cambridge: Cambridge University Press.

Bourdieu, P. (1986) The forms of capital. In J.G. Richardson (ed.) *Handbook of Theory and Research for the Sociology of Education* (pp. 241–258). New York: Greenwood Press.

Bourdieu, P. (1991) *Language and Symbolic Power* (G. Raymond and M. Adamson, trans). Cambridge, MA: Polity Press.

Brown, A. (2000) *Singapore English in a Nutshell: An Alphabetical Description of its Features*. Singapore: Federal Publications.

Burikova, Z. and Miller, D. (2010) *Au Pair*. Cambridge: Polity Press.

Butler, J. (1990) *Gender Trouble: Feminism and the Subversion of Identity*. London: Routledge.

Butler, J. (1997) *The Psychic Life of Power: Theories in Subjection*. Stanford, CA: Stanford University Press.

Cameron, D. (2000a) *Good to Talk? Living and Working in a Communication Culture*. London/Thousand Oaks, NJ: Sage Publications.

Cameron, D. (2000b) Styling the worker: Gender and the commodification of language in the globalized service economy. *Journal of Sociolinguistics* 4 (3), 323–347.

Cameron, D. (2002) Globalization and the teaching of 'communication skills'. In D. Block and D. Cameron (eds) *Globalization and Language Teaching* (pp. 67–82). London/New York: Routledge.

Canagarajah, A.S. (2005) Dilemmas in planning English/vernacular relations in postcolonial communities. *Journal of Sociolinguistics* 9 (3), 418–447.

Carter, B. and Sealey, A. (2000) Language, structure and agency: What can realist social theory offer to sociolinguistics? *Journal of Sociolinguistics* 4 (1), 3–20.

Castles, S. and Ozkul, D. (2014) Circular migration: Triple win, or a new label for temporary migration? In G. Battistella (ed.) *Global and Asian Perspectives on International Migration* (pp. 27–50). Cham: Springer.

Ceniza Choy, C. (2003) *Empire of Care: Nursing and Migration in Filipino American History*. Durham, NC: Duke University Press.

Cheng, S.J.A. (2006) *Serving the Household and the Nation: Filipina Domestics and the Politics of Identity in Taiwan*. Lanham, MD: Lexington Books.

Churchill, B.R. (2003) Education in the Philippines at the turn of the 20th century: Background for American policy. In C.D. Villareal (ed.) *Back to the Future: Perspectives on the Thomasite Legacy to Philippine Education* (pp. 21–52). Manila: American Studies Association of the Philippines.

Collins, J. and Slembrouck, S. (2005) Multilingualism and diasporic populations: Spatializing practices, institutional processes, and social hierarchies. *Language & Communication* 25 (3), 189–195.

Commission on Filipinos Overseas. (2014) *2013 CFO Compendium of Statistics on National Migration*. Manila: Commission on Filipinos Overseas.

Constable, N. (1997) *Maid to Order in Hong Kong: Stories of Filipina Workers*. Ithaca, NY: Cornell University Press.

Constable, N. (2002) Filipino workers in Hong Kong homes: Household rules and relations. In B. Ehrenreich and A.R. Hochschild (eds) *Global Woman: Nannies, Maids and Sex Workers in the New Economy* (pp. 115–141). New York: Metropolitan Books.

Constantino, R. (2002) The miseducation of the Filipino. In A.V. Shaw and L.H. Francia (eds) *Vestiges of War: The Philippine-American War and the Aftermath of an Imperial Dream 1899–1999* (pp. 177–192). New York: New York University Press.

Cox, R. (ed.) (2015) *Au Pairs' Lives in Global Contexts: Sisters or Servants*. Houndmills: Palgrave Macmillan.

Dalangin-Fernandez, L. (2006) Arroyo: Philippines to send 'super maids' abroad soon, 3 August. See http://globalnation.inquirer.net/news/news/view_article.php?article_id=13304 (accessed 15 February 2007).

Dean, M. (2010) *Governmentality: Power and Rule in Modern Society*. Los Angeles, CA: Sage.

Deboneville, J. (2014) Les écoles du care aux Philippines: Le devenir travailleuse domestique au prisme de l'altérité. *Revue Tiers Monde* 217, 61–78.

Department of Labor and Employment (DOLE) (2005) Remittances of OFWs contribute 9.2 percent to country's GNP. See www.dole.gov.ph/news.

Department of Labor and Employment (DOLE) (2007, 12 February) Gov't debunks issues concocted by vested interest groups vs. standards to prevent abuses on HSWs. See www.dole.gov.ph/news.

Dicarlo, L. (2003, May 22) The Philippines fights for US business. *Forbes*.

Divita, D. (2013) Language ideologies across time. *Critical Discourse Studies* 11 (2), 194–210.

Duchêne, A. and Heller, M. (2012a) Multilingualism and the new economy. In M. Martin-Jones, A. Blackledge and A. Creese (eds) *Routledge Handbook of Multilingualism* (pp. 369–383). London/New York: Routledge.

Duchêne, A. and Heller, M. (eds) (2012b) *Language in Late Capitalism: Pride and Profit*. New York/Abingdon: Routledge.

Duchêne, A., Moyer, M. and Roberts, C. (2013) Introduction: Recasting institutions and work in multilingual and transnational spaces. In A. Duchêne, M. Moyer and C. Roberts (eds) *Language, Migration and Social Inequalities: A Critical Sociolinguistic Perspective on Instiutions and Work* (pp. 1–24). Bristol/Buffalo/Toronto: Multilingual Matters.

Ehrenreich, B. and Hochschild, A.R. (eds) (2002) *Global Woman: Nannies, Maids, and Sex Workers in the New Economy*. New York: Metropolitan Books.

England, K. and Stiell, B. (1997) 'They think you're as stupid as your English is': Constructing foreign domestic workers in Toronto. *Environment & Planning A* 29 (2), 195–215.

Extra, G., Spotti, M. and Van Avermaet, P. (eds) (2009) *Language Testing, Migration and Citizenship: Cross National Perspectives*. London/New York: Continuum.

Fernandez, B. and de Regt, M. (eds) (2014) *Migrant Domestic Workers in the Middle East: The Home and the World*. Houndmills: Palgrave Macmillan.

Fielding, H. (2013) *Bridget Jones: Mad about the Boy*. London: Jonathan Cape.

Filipinos' English skills on the decline (2003) *Manila Times*, 23 October. See www.manilatimes.net/national/2003/oct/23/top_stories/20031023top3.html (accessed 24 October 2003).

Foucault, M. (1991) Governmentality. In G. Burchell, C. Gordon and P. Miller (eds) *The Foucault Effect: Studies in Governmentality* (pp. 87–104). Chicago, IL: University of Chicago Press.

Foucault, M. (1997) Technologies of the self. In P. Rabinow (ed.) *Ethics: Subjectivity and Self* (pp. 223–252). New York: New Press.

Fujita-Rony, D.B. (2003) *American Workers, Colonial Power: Philippine Seattle and the Transpacific West, 1919–1941*. Berkeley, CA/London: University of California Press.

Gal, S. (2006) Migration, minorities and multilingualism: Language ideologies in Europe. In C. Mar-Molinero and P. Stevenson (eds) *Language Ideologies, Policies and Practices: Language and the Future of Europe* (pp. 13–27). Houndmills: Palgrave Macmillan.

Giddens, A. (1986) *Central Problems in Social Theory: Action, Structure and Contradiction in Social Analysis*. Berkeley, CA: University of California Press.

Glenn, E.N. (1992) From servitude to service work: Historical continuities in the racial division of paid reproductive labor. *Signs* 18 (1), 1–43.

GMA News (2014) Over 300 Pinoy nurses, caregivers to undergo Japanese language training, 13 November. See www.gmanetwork.com/news/story/387869/pinoyabroad/news/over-300-pinoy-nurses-caregivers-to-undergo-japanese-language-training.

Goffman, E. (1959) *The Presentation of Self in Everyday Life*. New York: Doubleday.
Gonzalez, A. (1980) *Language and Nationalism: The Philippine Experience Thus Far*. Quezon City: Ateneo de Manila University Press.
Gonzalez, A. (1985) The legacy of American higher education in the Philippines: An assessment. In P.G. Altbach (ed.) *An ASEAN-American Dialogue: The Relevance of American Higher Education in Southeast Asia* (pp. 91–110). Singapore: Regional Institute of Higher Education and Development.
Gonzalez, A. (1988) *The Role of English and its Maintenance in the Philippines: The Transcript, Consensus, and Papers of the Solidarity Seminar on Language and Development*. Manila: Solidaridad Publishing House.
Gonzalez, A. (1998a) The language planning situation in the Philippines. *Journal of Multilingual and Multicultural Development* 19 (5/6), 481–525.
Gonzalez, A. (2004) The social dimensions of Philippine English. *World Englishes* 23 (1), 7–16.
Gonzalez, J.L. (1998b) *Philippine Labour Migration: Critical Dimensions of Public Policy*. Singapore: Institute of Southeast Asian Studies.
Guevarra, A.R. (2003) Manufacturing the 'ideal' workforce: The transnational labor brokering of nurses and domestic workers from the Philippines. Doctoral dissertation, University of California at San Francisco, San Francisco.
Guevarra, A.R. (2010) *Marketing Dreams, Manufacturing Heroes: The Transnational Labor Brokering of Filipino Workers*. New Brunswick, NJ/London: Rutgers University Press.
Guevarra, A.R. (2014) Supermaids: The racial branding of global Filipino care labour. In B. Anderson and I. Shutes (eds) *Migration and Care Labour: Theory, Policy and Politics* (pp. 130–150). Houndmills: Palgrave Macmillan.
Gunigundo, M. (2010) House Bill 162. See http://mlephil.wordpress.com/2010/09/04/h-b-no-162-gunigundo-multilingual-education-bill/.
Hall, K. (1995) Lip service on the fantasy lines. In K. Hall and M. Bucholtz (eds) *Gender Articulated: Language and the Socially Constructed Self* (pp. 183–216). New York: Routledge.
Haskins, V.K. (2012) *Matrons and Maids: Regulating Indian Domestic Service in Tucson 1914–1934*. Tucson, AZ: The University of Arizona Press.
Haskins, V.K. and Lowrie, C. (eds) (2015) *Colonization and Domestic Service: Historical and Contemporary Perspectives*. New York: Routledge.
Hau, C.S. and Tinio, V.L. (2003) Language policy and ethnic relations in the Philippines. In M.E. Brown and S. Ganguly (eds) *Fighting Words: Language Policy and Ethnic Relations in Asia* (pp. 319–349). Cambridge, MA: The MIT Press.
Heller, M. (2002) Globalization and the commodification of bilingualism in Canada. In D. Cameron and D. Block (eds) *Globalization and Language Teaching* (pp. 47–64). London and New York: Routledge.
Heller, M. (2010) Language as resource in the globalized new economy. In N. Coupland (ed.) *The Handbook of Language and Globalization* (pp. 349–365). Malden, MA: Wiley-Blackwell.
Heller, M. and Duchêne, A. (2012) Pride and profit: Changing discourses of language, capital and nation-state. In A. Duchêne and M. Heller (eds) *Language in Late Capitalism: Pride and Profit* (pp. 1–21). New York/Abingdon: Routledge.
Higman, B.W. (2015) An historical perspective: Colonial continuities in the global geography of domestic service. In V.K. Haskins and C. Lowrie (eds) *Colonization and Domestic Service: Historical and Contemporary Perspectives* (pp. 19–40). New York: Routledge.

Hochschild, A.R. (2012) *The Managed Heart: Commercialization of Human Feeling* (3rd edn). Berkeley/Los Angeles/London: University of California Press.

Hogan-Brun, G., Mar-Molinero, C. and Stevenson, P. (eds) (2009) *Discourses on Language and Integration: Critical Perspectives on Language Testing Regimes in Europe*. Amsterdam: John Benjamins.

Huang, S. and Yeoh, B.S.A. (1998) Maids and ma'ams in Singapore: Constructing gender and nationality in the transnationalization of paid domestic work. *Geography Research Forum* 18, 21–48.

Huang, S., Yeoh, B.S.A. and Abdul Rahman, N. (eds) (2005) *Asian Women as Transnational Domestic Workers*. Singapore: Marshall Cavendish.

Hymes, D.H. (1974) *Foundations in Sociolinguistics: An Ethnographic Approach*. Philadelphia, PA: University of Pennsylvania Press.

International Labour Organization (2010) *Decent Work for Domestic Workers*. Geneva: International Labour Organization.

International Labour Organization (2011) *Global and Regional Estimates on Domestic Workers*. Geneva: International Labour Organization.

International Organization for Migration (2013) *Country Migration Report: The Philippines 2013*. Makati City/Quezon City: International Organization for Migration and Scalabrini Migration Center.

Jaymalin, M. (2014) Foreign language: Next hot job skill. *The Philippine Star*, 10 March. See www.philstar.com/headlines/2014/03/10/1299131/foreign-language-next-hot-job-skill.

Jenkins, R. (2002) *Pierre Bourdieu* (2nd edn). London and New York: Routledge.

Koven, M. (2004) Transnational perspectives on sociolinguistic capital among Luso-descendants in France and Portugal. *American Ethnologist* 31 (2), 270–290.

Lan, P.C. (2003) 'They have more money but I speak better English!' Transnational encounters between Filipina domestics and Taiwanese employers. *Identities* 10 (2), 133–161.

Lan, P.C. (2006) *Global Cinderellas: Migrant Domestics and Newly Rich Employers in Taiwan*. Durham, NC/London: Duke University Press.

Leidner, R. (1993) *Fast Food, Fast Talk*. Berkeley/Los Angeles/London: University of California Press.

Lindquist, J., Xiang, B. and Yeoh, B.S.A. (2012) Opening the black box of migration: Brokers, the organization of transnational mobility and the changing political economy in Asia. *Pacific Affairs* 85 (1), 7–19.

Lippi-Green, R. (1997) *English with an Accent: Language, Ideology, and Discrimination in the United States*. London: Routledge.

Lorente, B.P. and Tupas, T.R.F. (2002) Demythologizing English as an economic asset: The case of Filipina domestic workers in Singapore. *The Ateneo Center for English Language Teaching (ACELT) Journal* 6 (2), 20–32.

Lutz, H. (2002) At your service madam: The globalization of domestic service. *Feminist Review*, 70, 89–104.

Mabalon, D.B. (2013) *Little Manila is in the Heart: The Making of the Filipina/o American Community in Stockton, California*. Durham, NC/London: Duke University Press.

Makoni, S. and Pennycook, A. (2007) Disinventing and reconstituting languages. In S. Makoni and A. Pennycook (eds) *Disinventing and Reconstituting Languages* (pp. 1–41). Clevedon: Multilingual Matters.

Marcelo, P. (2007) Labor execs stick to skills as OFW protector. *OFW Journalism Consortium Website, Inc.* See www.ofwjournalism.net/previousweb/vol6no5&6/prevstories6505.php (accessed 19 January 2010).

Massey, D. (2005) *For Space*. Los Angeles, CA: Sage.

McDowell, L. (2009) *Working Bodies: Interactive Service Employment and Workplace Identities*. Malden, MA/Oxford/Chichester: Wiley-Blackwell.

McKay, D. (2005) Success stories? Filipina migrant workers in Canada. In S. Huang, B. S.A. Yeoh and N. Abdul Rahman (eds) *Asian Women as Transnational Domestic Workers* (pp. 305–340). Singapore: Marshall Cavendish.

Meier, S. and Lorente, B.P. (2014) Making 'new speakers': Preparing Philippine nurses for work in Germany and Switzerland. Paper presented at the Second International Symposium on New Speakers in a Multilingual Europe, Barcelona, Spain.

Menard-Warwick, J. (2009) *Gendered Identities and Immigrant Language Learning*. Bristol: Multilingual Matters.

Ministry of Manpower (2014, September 25) Foreign workforce numbers See www.mom.gov.sg/statistics-publications/others/statistics/Pages/ForeignWorkforceNumbers.aspx.

Mirchandani, K. (2004) Practices of global capital: Gaps, cracks and ironies in transnational call centres in India. *Global Networks* 4 (4), 355–373.

More rallies vs hiring policy for Pinoy DH. (2007) See www.gmanews.tv/story/27059/More-rallies-vs-hiring-policy-for-Pinoy-DH.

Neuman, W.L. (2000) *Social Research Methods: Qualitative and Quantitative Approaches* (4th edn). Boston, MA: Allyn and Bacon.

OFW Tribune (2012) Skills enhancement training to standardize OWWA-PDOS training, language instruction. See https://ofwtribune.wordpress.com/category/comprehensive-pre-departure-education-program-cpdep/.

Oishi, N. (2005) *Women in Motion: Globalization, State Policies and Labor Migration in Asia*. Stanford, CA: Stanford University Press.

Ong, A. (2006) *Neoliberalism as Exception: Mutations in Citizenship and Sovereignty*. Durham, NC/London: Duke University Press.

Otis, E. (2012) *Markets and Bodies: Women, Service Work, and the Making of Inequality in China*. Stanford, CA: Stanford University Press.

Overseas Workers Welfare Administration (2007) OWWA Performance Highlights. See www.owwa.gov.ph/.

Overseas Workers Welfare Administration (2008) OWWA Performance Highlights. See www.owwa.gov.ph/.

Overseas Workers Welfare Administration (2009) Language training and culture familiarization program. See http://owwa.gov.ph/article/articleview/238/1/19/ (accessed 15 September 2009).

Pakir, A. (1999) Connecting with English in the context of internationalisation. *TESOL Quarterly* 33 (1), 103–113.

Park, J.S.Y. (2014) Figures of personhood. Paper presented at the AAAL Annual Meeting, Portland, OR.

Park, J.S.Y. and Wee, L. (2012) *Markets of English: Linguistic Capital and Language Policy in a Globalizing World*. New York/Abingdon: Routledge.

Parreñas, R.S. (2000) Migrant Filipina domestic workers and the international division of reproductive labor. *Gender and Society* 14 (4), 560–580.

Parreñas, R.S. (2001) *Servants of Globalization: Women, Migration, and Domestic Work*. Stanford, CA: Stanford University Press.

Paul, A.M. (2011) The 'other' looks back: Racial distancing and racial alignment in migrant domestic workers' stereotypes about white and Chinese employers. *Ethnic and Racial Studies* 34 (6), 1068–1087.
Pennycook, A. (1998) *English and the Discourses of Colonialism*. London: Routledge.
Pennycook, A. (2010) *Language as Local Practice*. London/New York: Routledge.
Pennycook, A. (2012) *Language and Mobility: Unexpected Places*. Bristol: Multilingual Matters.
Philippine Overseas Employment Administration (2006a) Annual Report 2005. See www.poea.gov.ph.
Philippine Overseas Employment Administration (2006b, 12 December) Filipino workers: Moving the world today. See www.poea.gov.ph/about/moving.html (accessed 18 February 2007).
Philippine Overseas Employment Administration (2010) *Overseas Employment Statistics*. See www.poea.gov.ph/stats/2010_Stats.pdf (accessed 16 March 2015).
Philippine Overseas Employment Administration (2014) *2010–2014 Overseas Employment Statistics*. See www.poea.gov.ph/.
Piller, I. (2001) Naturalization language testing and its basis in ideologies of national identity and citizenship. *The International Journal of Bilingualism* 5 (3), 259–277.
Piller, I. and Pavlenko, A. (2009) Globalization, multilingualism, and gender: Looking into the future. In L. Wei and V. Cook (eds) *Contemporary Applied Linguistics* (Vol. 2, pp. 10–27). London: Continuum.
Piller, I. and Lising, L. (2014) Language, employment and settlement: Temporary meat workers in Australia. *Multilingua* 33 (1–2), 35–59.
Pratt, G. (1997) Stereotypes and ambivalence: The construction of domestic workers in Vancouver, British Columbia. *Gender, Place & Culture: A Journal of Feminist Geography* 4 (2), 159–177.
Pratt, M.L. (1991) Arts of the contact zone. *Profession* 91, 33–40.
Rahman, N.A. (2003) Negotiating power: A case study of Indonesian foreign domestic workers (FDWs) in Singapore. PhD thesis, Curtin University of Technology. See http://adt.curtin.edu.au/theses/available/adt-WCU20040119.111646/.
Rahman, N.A., Yeoh, B.S.A. and Huang, S. (2005) Dignity overdue: Transnational domestic workers in Singapore. In S. Huang, B.S.A. Yeoh and N.A. Rahman (eds) *Asian Women as Transnational Domestic Workers* (pp. 233–261). Singapore: Marshall Cavendish.
Rampton, B. (1995) *Crossing: Language and Ethnicity among Adolescents*. London: Longman.
Rampton, B. (1999) Styling the Other: Introduction. *Journal of Sociolinguistics* 3 (4), 421–427.
Ray, R. (2009) *Cultures of Servitude: Modernity, Domesticity and Class in India*. Stanford, CA: Stanford University Press.
Republic of the Philippines (1995) *Migrant Workers and Overseas Filipinos Act of 1995*. See http://www.poea.gov.ph/laws&rules/files/Migrant%20Workers%20Act%20of%20 1995%20(RA%208042).html (accessed 8 June 2017)
Rodriguez, R.M. (2010) *Migrants for Export: How the Philippine State Brokers Labor to the World*. Minneapolis, MN/London: University of Minnesota Press.
Rodriguez, R.M. and Schwenken, H. (2013) Becoming a migrant at home: Subjectivation and processes in migrant-sending countries prior to departure *Population, Space and Place* 19, 375–388.
Rosario, B.R. (2005) Bill on English as medium in schools endorsed. *Manila Bulletin*, 27 September.

RP gets serious on outsourcing biz (2003) See www.mctimes.net/2003/New/news_20030226 (accessed 26 February 2003).
RP workforce losing edge in English (2004) *Philippine Daily Inquirer*, 3 May. See http://money.inq7.net/features/view_features.php?yyy=2004&mon=05&dd+03&file=4 (accessed 30 May 2004).
Salonga, A.O. (2010) Language and situated agency: An exploration of the dominant linguistic and communication practices in the Philippine offshore call centers. Doctoral dissertation, National University of Singapore, Singapore.
Sassen, S. (1988) *The Mobility of Labor and Capital: A Study in International Investment and Labor Flow*. Cambridge/New York: Cambridge University Press.
Scarcella, R. and Brunak, J. (1981) On speaking politely in a second language. *International Journal of the Sociology of Language* 27, 59–75.
Schwartz, A. (2006) The teaching and culture of household Spanish: Understanding racist reproduction in 'domestic' discourse. *Critical Discourse Studies* 3 (2), 107–121.
Scott, J.C. (1990) *Domination and the Arts of Resistance: Hidden Transcripts*. New Haven, CT: Yale University Press.
Searcey, D., Porter, E. and Gebeloff, R. (2015) Health care opens stable career path, taken mainly by women, February 22. *The New York Times*.
Seargeant, P. (2009) *The Idea of English in Japan: Ideology and the Evolution of a Global Language*. Bristol: Multilingual Matters.
Sibayan, B.P. and Segovia, L.Z. (1984) *Language, Identity and Socioeconomic Development*. Singapore: SEAMEO Regional Language Centre.
Sibayan, B.P. and Gonzalez, A.B. (1996) Post-imperial English in the Philippines. In J.A. Fishman, A.W. Conrad and A. Rubal-Lopez (eds) *Post-imperial English: Status Change in Former British and American Colonies, 1940–1990* (pp. 139–172). Berlin: Mouton de Gruyter.
Simpson, M. (2010) *My Hollywood*. New York: Alfred A. Knopf.
Slade, C. and Mollering, M. (eds) (2010) *From Migrant to Citizen: Testing Language, Testing Culture*. Houndmills: Palgrave Macmillan.
Sunni, M. (2014, November 20) Correspondence.
Superpay for supermaids. (2007) *The Manila Times*, 25 January, p. A4.
Syjuco, A.B. (2007, July 31) Inauguration of the TESDA Language Skills Institute. See www.titoboboy.com/speech01.html (accessed 12 December 2009).
Tadiar, N. (1997) Domestic bodies of the Philippines. *SOUJOURN* 12, 153–191.
Takaki, R.T. (1998) *Strangers from a Different Shore: A History of Asian Americans* (Updated and revised edn). Boston, MA: Little Brown.
Tan, A. (2015) Hiring maids becoming more costly with tighter regulation. *The Straits Times*, January 19. See www.straitstimes.com/news/singapore/more-singapore-stories/story/hiring-maids-becoming-more-costly-tighter-regulations-20.
Technical Education and Skills Development Authority (2007) Crossing the language divide. See www.tesda.gov.ph/page.asp?rootID=9&sID=224&pID=9 (accessed 12 December 2009).
Technical Education and Skills Development Authority (2014, March 9) Foreign language next hot job skill. See www.tesda.gov.ph/News/Details/384.
Terry, W.C. (2014) The perfect worker: Discursive makings of Filipinos in the workplace hierarchy of the globalized cruise industry. *Social and Cultural Geography* 15 (1), 73–93.

The Asian Parent Singapore (2014) Which country should you hire your maid from? See http://sg.theasianparent.com/which-country-should-you-hire-your-maid-from/.

The Economist (2006, November 25) Migrants' remittances (p. 114).

Thompson, J.B. (1991) Editor's introduction. In J.B. Thompson (ed.) *Language and Symbolic Power* (pp. 1–31). Cambridge, MA: Harvard University Press.

Toh, S.H. and Floresca-Cawagas, V. (2003) Globalization and the Philippines' education system. In K.H. Mok and A.R. Welch (eds) *Globalization and Educational Restructuring in the Asia Pacific Region* (pp. 189–231). Houndmills: Palgrave Macmillan.

Tollefson, J.W. (1991) *Planning Language, Planning Inequality: Language Policy in the Community*. London: Longman.

Transient Workers Count Too (2011) Fact sheet: Foreign domestic workers in Singapore (basic statistics). http://twc2.org.sg/2011/11/16/fact-sheet-foreign-domestic-workers-in-singapore-basic-statistics/ (accessed 8 June 2017).

Tupas, R. (2014) The politics of 'p' and 'f': A linguistic history of nation-building in the Philippines. *Journal of Multilingual and Multicultural Development* 36 (6), 587–597.

Tupas, T.R.F. (2001a) Linguistic imperialism in the Philippines: Reflections of an English language teacher of Filipino overseas workers. *The Asia-Pacific Researcher* 10 (1), 1–40.

Tupas, T.R.F. (2001b) The study of English and the problem of consciousness in the Philippines. Doctoral dissertation, National University of Singapore, Singapore.

Tupas, T.R.F. (2003) History, language planners, and strategies of forgetting. *Language Problems & Language Planning* 27 (1), 1–25.

Tupas, T.R.F. (2004a) Anatomies of linguistic commodification: The case of English in the Philippines vis-à-vis other languages in the multilingual marketplace. Paper presented at the Singapore Association of Applied Linguistics Symposium on 'The Mother Tongue Issue in Multilingual Communities', Singapore.

Tupas, T.R.F. (2004b) Back to class: The medium of instruction debate in the Philippines. Paper presented at the Language, Nation and Development in Southeast Asia Roundtable, Singapore.

Tupas, T.R.F. (2007) Go back to class: The medium of instruction debate in the Philippines. In L.H. Guan and L. Suryadinata (eds) *Language, Nation and Development in Southeast Asia Roundtable* (pp. 17–38). Singapore: Institute of Southeast Asian Studies.

Tupas, T.R.F. (2009) Language as a problem of development: Ideological debates and comprehensive education in the Philippines. *AILA Review* 22, 23–35.

Tupas, T.R.F. and Lorente, B.P. (2014) A 'new' politics of language in the Philippines: Bilingual education and the challenge of the mother tongues. In P. Sercombe and T.R.F. Tupas (eds) *Language, Education and Nation-Building: Assimilation and Shift in Southeast Asia* (pp. 165–180). Basingstoke/New York: Palgrave-MacMillan.

Tyner, J.A. (1999) The web-based recruitment of female foreign domestic workers in Asia. *Singapore Journal of Tropical Geography* 20 (2), 193–209.

Tyner, J.A. (2000) Migrant labour and the politics of scale: Gendering the Philippine state. *Asia Pacific Viewpoint* 41 (2), 131–154.

Tyner, J.A. (2004) *Made in the Philippines: Gendered Discourses and the Making of Migrants*. London: RoutledgeCurzon.

Urciuoli, B. (1995) Language and borders. *Annual Review of Anthropology* 24, 525–546.

Urciuoli, B. (1996) *Exposing Prejudice: Puerto Rican Experiences of Language, Race, and Class*. Boulder, CO: Westview Press.

Urciuoli, B. (2008) Skills and selves in the new workplace. *American Ethnologist* 35 (2), 211–228.

Urciuoli, B. and LaDousa, C. (2013) Language management/labor. *Annual Review of Anthropology* 42, 175–190.

US firms shifting call center operations to RP. (2003) See www.inq7.net (accessed 17 April 2003).

Uutiset (2012, October 16) Filipino nurses prepare to work in Finland. See http://yle.fi/uutiset/filipino_nurses_prepare_to_work_in_finland/6336793.

Vertovec, S. (2001) Transnationalism and identity. *Journal of Ethnic and Migration Studies* 27 (4), 573–582.

Vertovec, S. (2009) *Trasnationalism*. London and New York: Routledge.

Weix, G.G. (2000) Inside the home and outside the family: The domestic estrangement of Javanese servants. In K.M. Adams and S. Dickey (eds) *Home and Hegemony: Domestic Service and Identity Politics in South and Southeast Asia* (pp. 137–156). Ann Arbor, MI: University of Michigan Press.

Wickramasekara, P. (2011) *Circular Migration: A Triple Win or Dead End?* Geneva: International Labour Office.

Wong, D. (1996) Foreign domestic workers in Singapore. In G. Battistella and A. Paganoni (eds) *Asian Women in Migration* (pp. 87–108). Quezon City: Scalabrini Migration Center.

Woolard, K.A. and Schieffelin, B.B. (1994) Language ideology. *Annual Review of Anthropology* 23 (1), 55–82.

Xiang, B. (2005) The fixed and the fluid. Paper presented at the Migration Cluster Seminar, Asia Research Institute, National University of Singapore, 27 July.

Xiang, B. (2013a) Multi-scalar ethnography: An approach for critical engagement with migration and social change. *Ethnography* 14 (3), 282–299.

Xiang, B. (2013b) Return and reordering of transnational mobility in Asia. In X. Biao, B. S.A. Yeoh and M. Toyota (eds) *Return: Nationalizing Trasnational Mobility in Asia* (pp. 1–20). Durham, NC/London: Duke University Press.

Xiang, B. and Lindquist, J. (2014) Migration infrastructure. *International Migration Review* 48 (1), 122–148.

Xiang, B., Yeoh, B.S.A. and Toyota, M. (eds) (2013) *Return: Nationalizing Transnational Mobility in Asia*. Durham, NC/London: Duke University Press.

Yeoh, B.S.A. and Huang, S. (1998a) Maids and ma'ams in Singapore: Constructing gender and nationality in the transnationalization of paid domestic work. *Geography Research Forum* 18, 21–48.

Yeoh, B.S.A. and Huang, S. (1998b) Negotiating public space: Strategies and styles of migrant female domestic workers in Singapore. *Urban Studies* 35 (3), 583–602.

Yeoh, B.S.A. and Huang, S. (1999) Singapore women and foreign domestic workers: Negotiating domestic work and motherhood. In J.H. Momsen (ed.) *Gender, Migration, and Domestic Service* (pp. 277–300). London: Routledge.

Yeoh, B.S.A., Huang, S. and Gonzalez, J. (1999) Migrant female domestic workers: Debating the economic, social and political impacts in Singapore. *International Migration Review* 33 (1), 114–136.

Index

Page numbers followed by n refer to notes with their number.

abuse 14–15, 55–6, 67, 95n4, 123
accents 79–80, 100–4
adherence of skills 76–7, 79, 81
adjustment (language) 132–5
Adora (interviewee) 19, 153, 156, 157
    employers 105, 113, 118
    English language 99, 117
    Singlish 102–3, 130
    video performance 87–8
advertisements, maid agencies 69–73
agency 13, 105, 125
Aileen (interviewee) 139
America *see* United States
American English 97, 100–1, 134
Anna (interviewee) 96
aptitude (language learning) 40–1
Aquino, Corazon 137
Aquino III, Benigno 30
Arabic language 49, 53, 59
Arabic Language and Culture Training 53–4, 63
Arroyo, Gloria Macapagal 27, 30, 47, 56–7
au pairs 15, 153
authenticity 8, 97, 101, 103–4
authority 11, 144–5

Bahasa Indonesia language 77
balikbayans 126, 142–5, 147n1
Bangladeshi domestic workers 16
behaviour, styling 80–2, 89–94
Beth (interviewee) 19–20, 145, 152–3, 156, 157
    employers 105–6, 113
    English language 98, 127
    Singlish 100, 102, 129, 133
    video performance 87–8
Bilingual education policies (BEPs) 43–4

bi-lingualism 41, 72, 79
bio-data 66, 73, 82, 84, 154–5

call centers 7–8, 48, 92
Canada 7, 15, 37, 78–80, 151–2
    Live-in Caregiver Program 79, 145–6, 152
Cantonese 53, 59, 63, 132–3
capital 10
    linguistic capital 5, 10, 49, 76–80, 109, 125, 126, 145–7, 150
    social capital 10, 145
carabao English 99, 127, 128, 147n2
care work 2, 14, 37, 39, 79, 145–6, 151–2
Caribbean domestic workers 79
Cathy (interviewee) 19, 20, 21, 128, 130, 156, 157
centering institutions 11–12, 22, 67–8, 73, 76, 79, 80
Certificate for Household Service (NC II) 57–8, 60–1
children 110, 112
    childcare 78–9, 80, 115
    forms of address 138–9
    language tuition 76, 108–9, 115–18, 128
Chinese employers (Singaporean) 96–7, 104–13, 124, 130
circular migration 6, 35–7, 149
coaching for roles 80–94, 149
    see also training programs
colonial period 31–2, 42–3
commodification 14
    bi-lingualism 79
    Filipino workers 28, 69, 149
Commonwealth Act 570 (1940) 43
communication 107–13, 120

barriers to 110–12
workplace communication skills 27, 49–50, 60–2
competency standards 49–50, 60–5
competitive position 40, 48, 50, 52, 58
Comprehensive Pre-Departure Education Program (CPDEP) 53–4, 59
Connie (interviewee) 21, 130, 156, 157
   English language 117–18, 127, 142
Contemplacion, Flor 55–6
context-specific resources 76–80
control 105–6, 107
controlling domains 127–8
cultural capital 10
cultural training 53–4, 62–4

daldal 120
Del (interviewee) 98, 106, 116, 131, 156, 157
de-sexualization 81
Detsie (video script) 83–4, 86
direct hire workers 66, 87
directive language 64
disciplining 89
   self-discipline 64, 149
discourses
   adherence 76–7, 79–80
   of English advantage 79–80
   Philippine state 128
disguised terms 136–7
dislocations 129–30, 144–5, 147
DOLE Labor Opportunities Program (DOLOP) 34
domestic workers 5–6, 14, 56
   hierarchy 74–7, 116–25
   ideal 76, 78, 79–80
   language skills 101
   as products 69, 73–7, 149
   as social indexes 14
   see also Filipino Domestic Workers (FDW)

economic capital 10
economic status 144–5
Edna (interviewee) 19–20, 145–6, 153, 156, 157
   employers 113–14
   English language 127, 133–5, 143

educational system (Philippines) 42–9, 52, 98, 145
   interviewees' educational background 19–20, 157–9
emotional labor 7, 14, 114, 132
employers 92, 102, 138
   expats 71, 96–7, 102, 105, 109, 113–19, 124–5, 133
   forms of address 113–14, 136–8, 140–1
   hierarchy 96–7, 104–16, 124, 150
   language skills 96–7, 108–13, 115–16
   Singaporean Chinese 104–13, 124
   Taiwanese employers 118
employment agencies 3, 35, 58, 66–73
employment conditions 17–18, 29, 105–8, 113–15
   pay 3, 15, 57, 58, 66–7, 74, 94–5n2
Employment Permit System Test of Proficiency in Korean (EPS-TOPIK) 51
empowerment 56, 123–4, 137
English-knowing multilingualism 41, 72
English language
   accents 79–80
   adherence of other skills 76
   adjustment 132–5
   American English 97, 100–1, 134
   carabao English 99, 127, 128, 147n2
   'good' English 97–104, 109, 117, 124
   as lingua franca 3, 102, 129
   loss of English 129–32
   market segmentation 28, 73–7
   medium of instruction (MOI) 42, 44
   OK na OK (very OK) English 127
   in Philippines 42–4, 46, 126–8, 142–7
   proficiency 15, 98–9, 100–1, 103–4, 126–32
   puro Ingles 97–9
   in recruitment process 3–4, 81–9
   semiotic resources 97
   skill stereotypes 74–7, 78
   standard variety 115, 127
   status 43, 77, 97–104, 150
   straight English 109, 142, 145–6
   training 21–2, 27, 46–52, 53
   see also Singlish
equality 4, 113–19, 136
ethics of domestic workers 64
European domestic workers 78–80

examination system 45–6
expat employers 71, 102, 105, 113–15, 118, 124–5, 133
  language skills 96–7, 109, 115–16
export-oriented industrialization (EOI) 29, 32, 45, 46

Fe (interviewee) 107–8, 156, 158
  English language 98, 103, 122–3, 130
females
  domestic workers 5–6, 13–14
  feminization of migrant labor 2, 14, 15–16, 19–20, 38–9, 55, 59
Filipino Domestic Workers (FDW) 19–21, 38–9
  conditioning 71–2, 129
  in-group words 140–2
  ideal 28, 41, 72–3, 76, 78
  language skills 40–2, 101, 148–9
  ostracism 103–4, 143–5
  pre-departure training 51, 53–4, 59
  protection 55–6
  roles 16, 57, 76, 78–9, 105, 119, 153
  status 3, 74–7, 78–80, 116–25
  training 60–5, 150
  see also domestic workers; Overseas Filipino Workers (OFWs)
Filipino language 43–5, 44, 127–8
Filipino Overseas Workers in Singapore (FOWS) program 21–2, 96, 151
Finland 51
first-timers 67, 70–1, 82
formalization of scripts 65
forms of address 81, 84, 86, 91–2, 135–40
forms of reference 141–2
freelancers 67
French language 79

Gancayo Commission 55–6
German language 51, 79
Gina (interviewee) 21, 90, 93, 124, 156, 158
  English language 98, 103, 112, 122–3, 128, 130
Glo (interviewee) 20, 107, 109, 120, 147n3, 156, 158
  English language 115–16, 119, 127, 134, 142
  Singlish 102

globalization 4, 8, 19–20, 68
  labor markets 2, 11–12, 13–14, 45, 47–8, 52, 126, 150
'good' English 97–104, 109, 117, 124

Hawaiian Sugar Planters' Association (HSPA) 32
Hebrew 53, 59, 63
hidden transcripts 135–7, 140–2
hierarchy
  domestic workers 74–7, 116–25
  employers 96–7, 104–16, 124, 150
Hokkien language 132–3
Hong Kong 2, 14, 29, 37, 53, 104, 111
household service workers *see* Filipino Domestic Workers (FDW)
housekeepers 16, 57, 76, 78, 79

identity 126
  imposed 129, 131
  negotiation of 137, 144, 146
Ilin (interviewee) 143–4, 156, 158
Ilocano language 143
Immigration Nursing Relief Act (1989), United States 50
indexicality
  English language 9–10, 16, 77, 81, 94, 103, 125–6, 145–6
  institutions 11–12, 73
Indian domestic workers 16
Indonesian domestic workers 15, 16, 50, 74–7, 116
  language skills 78, 101, 121–4, 135
  pay 3, 94–5n2
in-group words 140–2
interactive service work 6–7
internalization 7–8
interviews 120
  Canadian Embassy 145–6
  video performances 1–2, 3–4, 66, 81–9
Italian language 27, 53, 59, 63
Italy 37, 121

Japanese language 49, 51
Jo (interviewee) 100, 104, 111, 143, 156, 158
Jocel (interviewee) 20, 21, 120, 123–4, 156, 158
  English language 117, 127, 129–30

Singlish 99–100, 111
jokes 96, 111–12

kinship terms 136–40
Korean language 27, 49, 51

labor brokerage 27–30, 40–2, 67–77, 148
labor markets, globalization 2, 11–12, 13–14, 45, 47–8, 52, 126, 150
labor migration *see* migration
language skills 40–2, 52, 149
Language Skills Institute (LSI) 27, 40, 49
language training 51, 53–4, 59
Linda (interviewee) 106–7, 109, 156, 158
linguistic accommodation 132–5
linguistic behaviour, styling 80–2
linguistic capital 5, 10, 49, 150
    power relationships 109, 125
    shifts in 76–80, 126, 145–7
linguistic deference 63–5, 81–2, 86, 88–9, 91–3, 136
linguistic economy 4–5, 8, 77, 79, 110
linguistic repertoires 9–10, 126, 132–3, 142
    maid agencies 80–2
linguistic Taylorism 7–8
linguistic templates 6–11
Live-in Caregiver Program, Canada 79, 145–6, 152
Loida (interviewee) 20, 145–6, 156, 159
    English language 101, 110–11, 119

Madonna 136–7
maid agencies 6, 66, 87
    advertisements 69–73
    positioning domestic workers 73–7, 78–9
    styling domestic workers 80–94
maids *see* domestic workers
Mandarin 27, 49, 53, 59, 63, 133
Marcos, Ferdinand 29, 46, 137
Marian (interviewee) 139–40
Marivic (interviewee) 114–15
marketing 69–73
    Filipino workers 28, 34, 40, 54, 56–7, 150
    positioning 73–7, 80–2
markets
    demand-driven 69
    segmentation by language skills 73–7, 94

Mary (interviewee) 121
media of instruction (MOI) 42–3, 44, 48–9
mediating institutions 12, 67–73, 80
methodology 21–3
Middle East 5, 14
    Filipino migrants 2, 33, 45, 53, 111
Migrant Workers and Overseas Filipinos Act (RA 8042, 1995) 34, 56
migration 13, 29, 68
    circular migration 6, 35–7, 149
    feminization of migrant labor 2, 14, 15–16, 19–20, 38–9, 55
    infrastructure 4, 11–21, 42–52, 148–9
    patterns 35–9
    from Philippines 30–9
    see also Overseas Filipino Workers (OFWs)
Ministry of Manpower (MOM) 66
mobility 6, 126, 148–9
    linguistic capital 77–8
Mother-Tongue Based Multilingual Education (MTBMLE) 49
multinational companies 41
Myanmar domestic workers 16, 74–5, 95n2
Myrna (interviewee) 1–2, 21, 111, 112, 145, 156, 159

nannies 76, 78, 79, 153
National College Entrance Examination (NCEE) 45–6
national language (Philippines) 43–5
NC II Certificate for Household Service 57–8, 60–1
negotiation
    identity 137, 144, 146
    position on the household 138–9
Nelma (interviewee) 83, 99, 101, 108–9, 118, 145, 156, 159
Nepalese domestic workers 16
niched indexical order 81–2
norms, establishment of 72
nurses 32, 39, 50, 51

office work 105, 119
offstage transcripts 135–7, 140–2
oil workers 39
OK na OK (very OK) English 127
onstage transcripts 135–7, 140–2

ostracism 103–4, 143–5
Overseas Filipino Workers (OFWs) 27, 45
  annual deployment 35–9, 59
  destinations 29–30, 37–9
    Filipino Overseas Workers in Singapore (FOWS) program 21–2, 96, 151
  gender 2, 14, 15–16, 38–9, 55, 59
  linguistic capital 14, 49
  occupations 31–2, 37–9
  skills training program 53–5
  see also Filipino Domestic Workers (FDW); migration
Overseas Workers Welfare Administration (OWWA) 22, 34–5, 53–4, 60
  language and culture training 57–8

Pakistani domestic workers 16, 50
part-timers 67
pay 32, 58, 94–5n2
  deductions 66–7
  effect of skills 3, 15, 57, 74
Pearly (interviewee) 83, 106, 145, 156, 159
  English language 110, 121–2
Peng (interviewee) 20, 21, 104, 145–6, 156, 159
  English language 116, 127
performance
  scripts 93, 150
  video performance 1–2, 66, 80–9
personal qualities 69, 80
  video performance 82–9
  see also stereotypes
personhood 4, 6, 9
Philippine Overseas Employment Administration (POEA) 22, 34–5, 54, 56, 57–8, 60
Philippine state 6, 45, 55–9, 67, 150
  labor brokerage 27–30, 40–2
Philippines
  attitudes to labor migration 47, 55
  economy 29, 30, 32–3, 46
  educational system 19–20, 42–9, 52, 98, 145
  English language in 42–4, 126–8, 142–7
  labor migration 30–9
  languages in use 42–9
  recruitment agencies 68

physical appearance 3, 83, 88
Pilar (video script) 85–6
Pilipino language 43
Pinoy Workers of the World (Pinoy WOW) 27
politeness formulae 84, 86, 91–2, 136
power relationships 63–5, 136, 144
  linguistic capital 109, 125
Precy (interviewee) 19, 83, 127, 145, 156, 159
pre-departure training 51, 53–4, 59
pronunciation 79–80, 100–4
protection of domestic workers 55–6
public transcripts 135–7, 140–2
puro Ingles 97–9

Qatar 29, 37, 53
qualifications, household service workers 57–8

receiving countries 2, 5, 15, 37, 50–1, 68
  Asia 14, 29, 53, 104, 111, 121
  Europe 121, 153
  Middle East 29, 33, 39, 45, 53, 111
  North America 29, 30, 32, 39, 50, 78–80, 145–6, 151–2
  see also Singapore
recruitment
  agencies 3, 58, 66–7
  processes 1–2, 3–4, 66–7
Reform Package for Household Service Workers 38, 54, 56–7
register 9–10, 63–4, 126, 140–2
regulations 6–7, 35, 56, 59–61, 148
  maid agencies 81, 88, 90–1
  Singapore 17–18
rehiring 35–9
relocalization of scripts 8–9, 12
remittances 28, 30, 33
repertoires
  linguistic 9–10, 126, 132–3, 142
  maid agency practices 80–2
Republic Act 8042 (1995) 56
residence rights 79
roles
  coaching for 80–94, 149
  variations 57, 76, 78–9, 105, 119, 153
Russian language 27

sailors 31
Saudi Arabia 2, 29, 37, 39, 53
school system (Philippines) 42–9, 52, 98, 145
scripts 97
  alternative 151–2
  Arabic Language and Culture Training 54
  for employment 63–5
  multiplication 8, 65, 148
  multiplicity 8–9, 148, 150
  of servitude 5, 13, 105, 125, 135, 149, 150, 152
  revision by workers 97, 105, 135–42
  scripted interactions 7–8, 87–8, 92–3
  templates 3, 4–5
  value 10–11
  video performances 3, 82–94
self 6, 9, 13, 126
  presentation of 4
  self-discipline 64, 149
semiotic economies 76–7, 79–80, 150
semiotic instruments 3, 80–2
sending countries 2, 35, 50, 68
  Philippines 45, 52, 149
service guarantee 69, 84, 85, 86
servitude 5
  displaying 88–93
  forms of address 135–40
  performance 82–94
  socialization 64, 149
  styling 80–2
  temporary reversal 112, 150
Singapore 2, 6, 53, 76
  English language in 99–103, 118–25
  Filipino Domestic Workers (FDW) 16–17, 19–21, 29, 37, 73–7
  Flor Contemplacion case 55–6
  Foreign Maid Scheme 17
  maid agencies 68–77
  regulations 17–18, 149
  Singaporean employers 71, 96–7, 102, 104–13, 118, 124, 130
  societal changes 14, 16–17
  transnational domestic work 14–15, 16–21
  see also receiving countries

Singlish
  attitudes towards 96–7, 99–103, 111, 124–5
  experience of 98, 108, 110, 129–31, 132–3
  see also English language
Sinhalese language 77
social capital 10, 145
socialization 89–94, 94, 149
space-specific resources 76–80
Spanish colonial period 31
Spanish language 27, 42, 49
speech styles 86
Sri Lankan domestic workers 3, 50, 75–7, 94n2
state, functions of 11–12
status 127
  domestic workers 3, 74–7, 116–25
  employers 96–7, 104–16, 150
  English language 43, 77, 97–104, 150
stereotypes
  gendered 68
  nationality-based 15, 68, 74–7, 78–80, 104, 121–4
straight English 109, 142, 145–6
styling 80–2, 89–94
subjectivity 13
subservience
  displaying 88–93
  forms of address 135–40
  performance 82–94
  socialization 64, 149
  styling 80–2
  temporary reversal 112, 150
Supermaid program 56–65, 150
Syjuco, Augusto Boboy 27, 40
symbolic capital 4, 10–11

Tagalog language 43–4, 142, 143
Taglish 98
Taiwan 14, 15, 53, 111, 121
  Filipino migrants 37
Tamil language 77
Taylorism, linguistic 7–8
Technical Education and Skills Development Authority (TESDA) 27, 34–5, 49
  NC II Certificate for Household Service 57–8, 60–1

templates 3, 4–5, 6–11, 149
Thai domestic workers 16
Tina (interviewee) 91–2
training programs 56–7, 60–5
    language 27, 63–5
    pre-departure training 51, 53–4, 59
    see also coaching for roles
trajectories 19–21, 126, 128–35, 142–7, 152–3
transcripts 135–7, 140–2
transfer maids 67, 70–1, 82
transnational domestic work 13–21, 148–50
transnational labor brokers 12, 67–77
transnational workers 41
Triple Win Project 51
trying hard English, English language 99, 127, 128, 147n2

unemployment 32–3, 47

United Arab Emirates 2, 29, 37, 53
United States 121
    colonial period 31–2, 42–3
    Filipino migrants 29, 30, 32, 39, 50
    US Exchange Visitor Program (EVP) 32
    see also American English

video performance 1–2, 66, 81–9
visas 50, 145, 153
voice 132, 140–2
vulnerability 55–6

Western Europe 2
women *see* females
work permits 51, 67, 69
working conditions 17–18, 29, 105–8, 113–15
    pay 3, 15, 57, 58, 66–7, 74, 94–5n2
workplace communication skills 27, 49–50, 60–2

For Product Safety Concerns and Information please contact our EU Authorised Representative:

Easy Access System Europe

Mustamäe tee 50

10621 Tallinn

Estonia

gpsr.requests@easproject.com